# A DARK ROOM IN GLITTER BALL CITY

# A DARK ROOM IN GLITTER BALL CITY

## MURDER, SECRETS, AND SCANDAL IN OLD LOUISVILLE

## DAVID DOMINÉ

PEGASUS BOOKS
NEW YORK  LONDON

A DARK ROOM IN GLITTER BALL CITY

Pegasus Crime is an imprint of
Pegasus Books, Ltd.
148 West 37th Street, 13th Floor
New York, NY 10018

Copyright © 2021 by David Dominé

First Pegasus Books cloth edition October 2021

Interior design by Timothy Shaner, NightandDayDesign.biz

ISBN: 978-1-64313-863-3

10 9 8 7 6 5 4 3 2

Printed in the United States of America
Distributed by Simon & Schuster
www.pegasusbooks.com

*For Louisville . . .*

# CONTENTS

## PART THREE

# A
# DARK
# ROOM
## IN
# GLITTER
# BALL
# CITY

# PROLOGUE

OUT ON Fourth Street, the asphalt shimmered under the light patter of rain. A crow cawed from its perch atop an ornate Flemish gable, then raised its wings and hopped into the air. Soaring across the grassy median and walkways of Fountain Court, it alighted seconds later on the steep parapet of the Victorian house on the other side. It shook out its wings and crowed again, unbothered by the drizzle.

"You see how big that crow is?" Ramon raised his hand and pointed.

"It's loud, that's for sure." I looked down at the mound of *Courier-Journals* that had collected at the front door. I was too lazy to reach down and pick one up, so I toed the pile with my shoe, scattering the newspapers to better see what had made the front page in the last week or two. Or three. There had to be at least two dozen newspapers on the porch.

"You'd think the real estate agent would have cleared those away by now." Ramon walked over to a window and peered inside. "Nothing says break and enter like a pile of newspapers outside the front door."

I studied one of the headlines near my feet. Local activists were alleging media bias in the coverage of Nakhia Williams, a transgender woman murdered by a group of men outside her Louisville apartment, and that the police had conducted a very lackluster investigation into the death. Another front page reported that police arrested three local teenagers for plotting to kill a fellow student over the weekend.

A soft crackle of lightning flashed through silver-gray clouds hugging the distant treetops. Seconds later, a thunderclap rumbled. Across the road, a disheveled man stumbled down the sidewalk, an overstuffed garbage bag slung over his shoulder. He mumbled unintelligibly, but several identifiable curse words managed to punctuate the air. Ramon turned away from the window and stood at the edge of the porch, where rainwater dripped from the soffit. "It's really starting to look like a dump in there." He shook his head and exhaled loudly as the man continued his rantings. "I don't know why you'd want to move back to Old Louisville anyway."

"What are you talking about? You suggested we come and look at this house in the first place, not me."

Ramon crossed his arms, his gaze shifting again to the crow across the street. It shrieked and flew back to the rounded gable on the other side of the walking court. "I know how much you love Old Louisville," he grumbled.

"I'm fine with living in the Highlands. Definitely much quieter than Old Louisville."

"You were happier down here, though. When we had the house on Third."

I was happy in that house, but the ballooning mortgage had become too much to handle in the end. And now we were talking about buying a home twice the size. Over nine thousand square feet.

"They're not asking all that much for this place." He sidled up to me, using his foot to push one of the newspapers back onto the pile. A photo of David Camm, a local state trooper accused of murdering his wife and two children, took up most of the front page. He was preparing for a third trial after the reversal of his second conviction.

"Well, let's take one last look since we're here," I said.

Just then, the real estate agent rushed up the walkway, collapsing her umbrella under the cover of the porch. "Sorry I'm so late," she said. "Police had the two blocks north of Oak Street cordoned off. I heard they found a dead body in an alley dumpster."

Ramon rolled his eyes and muttered. "Old Louisville."

The agent jiggled a handful of keys and pushed open the front door. "Sorry, did you say something?"

"No, no, he didn't." I cut in front of Ramon and followed her through the leaded-glass doors.

The lights were off, and I paused to let my eyes adjust to the darkness. Despite the gloom, the foyer glowed. The parquet floors, the wooden moldings, the walnut wainscoting and elegant fireplace mantel, the elaborately carved newels and balusters—they all gleamed with the silver sheen of storm clouds sifting through stained-glass windows.

The agent hit a switch and a light bulb flashed, dull and yellow. She walked to a card table and folding chair in the corner and set down a clipboard. "Since you've been here already, I'll just let you wander around on your own while I do some paperwork. You can actually go inside the carriage house now." She removed a pen from the front pocket of her blazer and began scribbling. "Let me know if you need anything."

"Thanks." I turned to go up the stairs but stopped. "Say, I've heard lots of stories about this place. What do you know about the previous owner? The elderly lady who lived here." When the woman didn't look up from her clipboard, I raised my voice. "Excuse me. The old nurse who had this house since the '60s—whatever happened to her?"

Still, the real estate agent acted as if she hadn't heard.

Ramon walked over and tapped the tabletop. "So, what about the old lady who lived here before? The nurse?"

Without looking up, the agent stopped writing and cleared her throat. "Oh, she was old. She, um . . . died. She died." The scribbling resumed.

"Oh, okay. Thanks." I turned away and exchanged glances with Ramon.

He went up the grand staircase. "That was weird."

"I know." I followed.

We entered the hallway on the second floor and poked our heads into sparsely furnished bedrooms, where peeling wallpaper and ceilings with water stains and cracked plaster greeted us. Dull brass numbers on the heavy wooden doors hinted at the days when the old mansion had served as a rooming house. The spaces on the third floor appeared to be in need of even more attention. A broken windowpane let cool air stream into one room and in another a huge jagged fissure worked its way across the wall. As we descended the back stairs, Ramon shook his head and chuckled. "Looks even worse than it did last month. Hobo central."

"Let's check out the back and the carriage house," I said. "Then we can go."

The kitchen looked a fright, as we already knew, with crumbling plaster ceilings and peeling wallpaper. Linoleum floors buckled with water damage. A cracked window over an old porcelain sink afforded a glimpse of the unkempt backyard. Next to the rear door hung a framed lithograph of a regal-looking gentleman from the late 1800s, probably from one of the old city newspapers. Before stepping outside, I paused to read the caption underneath: "Richard Robinson, a most honored and respected resident of the city. His unfaltering honesty, his kindly purposes, his recognition of the good in others, his broad sympathy and unbounded charity—these endeared him to all with whom he came in contact."

"Who's that?" Ramon peered over my shoulder.

"The original owner, maybe? A dry goods merchant."

"I'm sure he'd love seeing what the house looks like today."

"Whatever." I playfully pushed Ramon out the back door, and we stopped in the middle of an overgrown garden. The drizzle had turned into a fine mist, but angry storm clouds still roiled overhead. Weeds grew atop piles of dirt. Near the entrance to the carriage house stood a mound of rotting timber that I assumed had come from the interior. A grimy disco ball, still sparkly in patches, crowned the top of the heap.

Across the back alley soared the roof of the Samuel Culbertson Mansion. It faced Third Street, the old Millionaires Row of Louisville, which a historian once described as: "a genteel area at the edge of a burgeoning city, reflecting the tastes and extravagances of the late Victorian era. The residents worked hard to live up to the magnificence of their houses which were furnished as lavishly as social position required and wealth allowed."

The glazed orange-brick exterior of the mansion shimmered under a thin film of precipitation. When I moved to Louisville in 1993, I had spent my first few years in an apartment there; now it operated as a bed and breakfast. Samuel Culbertson, president of Churchill Downs, called the fifty-two-room Renaissance Revival construction home from

1897 to 1948. Credited with first draping a garland of red roses over the champion of the Kentucky Derby in 1932, Culbertson had sons who achieved fame in books written by local author Annie Fellows Johnston. The eponymous first volume would become famous when Shirley Temple tap-danced in the silver screen version with Bojangles, the Black butler: *The Little Colonel.*

"Hey." Ramon stooped to examine a soggy cardboard box next to the pile of boards. "Come look at this."

Books and magazines spilled out. On one cover, an angry, ruler-wielding nun was spanking a bare-bottomed woman bent over her knee. "Good lord." I reached down and flipped several pages. "Old porno magazines. All nuns, and all women."

"Yuck. Not even the good kind of porn."

"Oh my god." I stood up quickly and looked back at the house.

"What?"

"Remember that night we saw all the nuns on the front porch?" I widened my eyes. "This is the place!"

"Wait. That was this house?"

"Yes, I remember now; it happened right across from the entrance to Fountain Court."

On a balmy summer evening several years before, our friend Skippy had come over for dinner and we had taken the dogs for a walk after. As we strolled down the 1400 block of Fourth Street, a strange sight awaited: a group of ancient nuns, perhaps a dozen of them, all in identical black and white habits, lined the porch of a large, red-brick house. Stone-faced and silent, they stared out at the street, as if they had been arranged for a group photograph. But there wasn't a photographer in sight.

"Another reason why this house gives off such a strange vibe." Ramon laughed. "You don't want to live in an old building associated with nuns, do you?"

"But I love nuns. They add character to a neighborhood."

"The nuns in this box don't add the kind of character we're looking for." He rose and brushed off the front of his pants. "I wonder if there's such a thing as hobo porn."

"Let's see if there's any in the carriage house." Against a wall rested another cardboard box chock-full of erotic, sister-centric paperbacks and magazines. From the cover designs, they appeared to be from the '50s and '60s. Next to that box rested another containing old copies of the *Courier-Journal*. One front page ran a story about the history of the Scripps National Spelling Bee, which traced its origins to Louisville in 1925.

Ramon shook his head. "No hobos."

"Who knew there was so much pulp fiction about nuns?" I said. "I wonder if it belonged to the old nurse or one of her tenants. She had all kinds in here."

Ramon didn't answer. Instead, he folded his arms across his chest as he took in the interior. Although someone had made a valiant attempt at making the coach house presentable, it still looked terrible. Boards covered most of the windows, and holes in the walls and ceiling revealed an assortment of wooden beams. Another disco ball sat in a far corner.

"Someone sure loved glitter balls," I said.

Ramon remained silent.

"So, what do you think?"

"It needs a lot of work, but if you want to, let's do it." He uncrossed his arms, ambled to the door, and looked out. "But, if we move back, you need to learn how to say no every once in a while. You let people take advantage of you. All the committees and boards you're on. People traipsing through the house for the holiday tours. Being tour guide and all the money going to everyone but you." He looked over his shoulder at me. "Writing a cookbook for free for the neighborhood even though they managed to come up with fifteen thousand dollars for the photographer."

"Blah, blah, blah." I nudged him over the threshold and into the backyard. A loud squawk tore the air, and we looked up. An inky black bird had perched atop a gutter, where it peered down at us. Just then my cellphone chittered. I looked down to see a text from my brother.

"Who's that?"

"My brother. Paul. Probably looking for money again."

"He's the biggest hobo of all." Ramon shook his head as we continued to the back of the house. Then he pointed. "That's not the same crow, is it?"

"I don't know. They're supposed to be really smart. Maybe it's following us."

"So, what do you want to do?"

"Let's check out the basement before we go. Maybe we can get in through the side door. There's something creepy about it, dungeon-like. Did you see that one room full of junk, the one with the dirt floor and the shelves? It looks like an old wine cellar." I headed back to the house. "I'd love to have a wine cellar."

"That's not what I meant. Do you want the place or not?

"I don't know. It's up to you."

"We better decide fast," said Ramon, hurrying to catch up. "The agent said there's a guy moving back from Chicago who's coming to look at it in a few minutes and he's serious. Wants to turn it into a bed and breakfast. And I don't think she's just making it up."

I stopped and gazed up. "I don't know." Hugging myself for warmth, I studied the back of the enormous house. "I kind of like where we are now." Thunder clapped overhead and the soft patter of raindrops followed.

I looked at Ramon.

"You decide, hobo," he said.

# PART ONE

# I

## GET YOUR CASH TODAY

LITTLE JOHN'S, near Churchill Downs Racetrack, attracted tourists from all over the world. In a presidential tone and tailored suit, the diminutive Filipino pawnbroker explained that gold was selling at "an awesome" fifteen hundred dollars an ounce, "but not for long." Now was the time to sell your unwanted jewelry, he insisted.

In the breakfast room, I popped the last bite of toasted onion bagel into my mouth before grabbing the remote. Behind Little John, a cop, a construction worker, a cowboy, and a Native American clumsily danced and sang to the melody of the disco classic "Y.M.C.A." by the Village People. "We're going to Little John's today / To take our jewelry in and get our cash today / You will get a good deal / And you get paid for real / So bring it to Little John!" The train-wreck appeal of the commercial's bad singing and acting had earned its originator cult status.

I started to turn off the TV and return to my writing when a local newsflash broke onto the screen. A reporter stood in front of a huge, somewhat run-down brick house, where yellow crime scene tape cordoned off the front yard. Behind her, a pair of policemen hulked at the front door. Two men in hazmat suits jostled a blue-gray rubber storage bin down the walkway and into a waiting vehicle at the curb. Curious passersby looked on from the other side of the lawn as an early morning June breeze rustled the leaves on a nearby sycamore. The wind picked up and drowned out the reporter's words for a moment, but then it died down, and her voice rose. "An LMPD spokesperson said they discovered the body early this morning in what appeared to be a wine cellar of this dilapidated mansion in Old Louisville." She turned to point at the façade of the building.

Old Louisville. The preservation district with hundreds of Victorian mansions just south of the downtown area, the neighborhood where Ramon and I had lived until a few years before. I stared at the screen, and something slowly dawned on me: This was the house we had considered buying. The house with the wine cellar. 1435 South Fourth Street.

The Richard Robinson place with its impressive parquet floors and a dozen bedrooms sat across from the entrance to one of Louisville's famed walking courts, the pedestrian-only thoroughfares designed to add a bit of London flair when planners laid out the neighborhood. We had lived right around the corner, on Third Street. The seller didn't want all that much for the mansion, but it needed so much work. Rotting wood dangled from the eaves and cornices. The wreck of a carriage house and the bombed-out kitchen presented a challenge I welcomed, but in the end, we decided to stay in Louisville's Highlands neighborhood. It took just ten minutes to walk from my front door to my students at Bellarmine University, after all.

As far as I knew, the house had remained unoccupied, abandoned, but the reporter made it clear the mansion indeed had residents. Authorities had taken a couple into custody and charged the two men with murder.

Things had started the previous night, when police arrived at the residence after a 911 call about a domestic disturbance. One man had been arrested, and the police quickly heard grumblings about a body buried in the basement. The other had been taken in for questioning after police dug a rubber storage bin out of the dirt floor and sent its gruesome contents to the coroner. What had started out as an apparent lovers' quarrel had quickly and unexpectedly led to the discovery of a homicide.

The reporter interviewed a neighbor, who, shaking her head, looked uneasily over her shoulder at the looming house. "I always knew there was something weird about this place," she confided in a low tone. "It always gave off creepy vibes."

Creepy, for sure. Unsettling stories abounded about the old house. Whether or not they could be substantiated was another thing. People claimed early occupants had died under mysterious circumstances and a drug addict had attacked and killed someone in the house. A blind tiger had attracted crowds during the Roaring Twenties, and in the '70s a secret society used to meet in the house. Rumors claimed a sadistic doctor once practiced there and that for a time, when the house sat abandoned, a satanic cult had carried out rituals in the cellar of the mansion.

A chill worked its way up my spine. I wondered if strange rites had played out in the same part of the basement where they had unearthed the body on the news, in that little dark room.

From my experience as a researcher and writer of true-crime and paranormal stories, I knew claims involving satanic cults usually proved to be exaggerated, if not altogether false: satanic panic. True or not, I understood how such stories could arise from that basement. Cellars of old houses were inherently frightening, but the basement at the old Richard Robinson place fell in a category all its own. When I had walked through it two years before, a feeling of oppression pervaded the dimly lit interiors and seeped from the bare stone and brick walls. The layout was dizzying, even disconcerting. Instead of one large open space, the underground chambers of the mansion comprised a confusing warren of smallish rooms. That particular basement would have been an ideal location to film a horror flick.

On another local channel, the screen cut to the mugshots of two guys. Both looked to be in their thirties. The one on the left had spiky brown hair, narrow eyes, and prominent ears. A caption identified the clean-shaven individual as Jeffrey Mundt. Stubble and the hint of a soul patch covered the other's chin, and his hairline receded at the temples. He looked away from the camera and wore something of a scowl. White block letters on a blue background identified him as Joseph Banis. Staring at the images, I listened as the newswoman said their names and revealed them as the two men arrested by police earlier that morning. Slowly, a flicker of recognition registered somewhere, and I squinted to better see their faces. I must have seen them in the neighborhood. Or did I know them from somewhere else?

On the coffee table, my cellphone started to vibrate. Ramon, calling from work.

"Are you watching the news?" he said.

"The house in Old Louisville? The one on Fourth Street?"

"I'm so glad we didn't buy it." He snorted softly. "And you saw who they arrested, right?"

"I just saw their names now. Mundt and Banis. Do we know them? They look so familiar."

"Seriously?" Ramon stifled a laugh. "You don't recognize them? You're such a hobo."

"I do, but I'm not sure from where."

"The one was the bartender at Q. The other was his boyfriend, the really stuck-up one who moved back here from Chicago. Remember?"

My breath caught in my throat. "That's right." It all came back to me.

At the club everyone called Joseph Banis *Joey*. The so-called bad boy from a wealthy family. He had drug problems and had been to prison numerous times. Usually, when we saw him behind the bar fixing drinks, he wore only a pair of ratty jeans held up by a silver-studded belt. Temporary tattoos and colorful, phosphorescent body paint often adorned his sinewy upper torso. Bright pinks, yellows, and greens. One evening he had sported a stunning blue mohawk. Everyone called his boyfriend Jeff or Jase but we had never had any direct interaction with him.

Except for that rainy morning when Jeffrey Mundt arrived for his appointment with the real estate agent at 1435 South Fourth Street. Rushing up the front steps, he had brushed by without so much as a nod of the head as we returned to the sidewalk out front.

He had bought the old Robinson place after all.

The only other time we had seen him came one morning while waiting for a table at a popular St. Matthews breakfast place, where he stood ahead of us in the line. "Top o' the morning to you," he'd cry out whenever he saw anybody who warranted greeting. "God, what a cheeseball," I had muttered under my breath.

"They know the name of the body yet?" Ramon asked.

"I don't think so. They believe it might have been drug-related."

"Hmm. Just what Old Louisville needs. Another dead body. Glad we stayed in the Highlands."

"Nobody gets a break down there." I walked into the kitchen for another bagel.

Many viewed Old Louisville as the redheaded stepchild of the city. Although people moved in from all over to restore once-neglected mansions and charming Victorian cottages, some still considered it a bad part of town. Thirty or forty years before, that might have been a valid claim. But since the 1970s, when residents fought to have the forty-some square blocks immediately south of the downtown area declared a historic preservation district, the neighborhood had seen an upswing. Nationwide, architects and historians acclaimed the impressive collection of antique homes; nonetheless, old-timers viewed Old Louisville as a Bohemian, if somewhat seedy, enclave where students mixed with upwardly mobile gay couples, intellectuals, and those looking to escape the cookie-cutter life of suburbia.

Every time they took a step forward, they took two steps back in Old Louisville. Despite the grandeur and opulence found in the core of the neighborhood, where old-growth trees shaded stunning sections of Millionaires Row and gas lamps evoked Victorian charm on secluded St. James Court, residents still had to exercise caution on certain blocks after dark.

Ramon and I knew this firsthand: the six-bedroom 1890s house we restored sat near the infamous corner of Fourth and Oak. Or, as the locals called it, *Fourth and Crazy*. And we were well acquainted with the prostitutes, drug dealers, and panhandlers who helped cast Old Louisville in an unfavorable light. Every now and then, the news reported a random shooting, stabbing, or mugging, and this didn't help either.

Now, they had found a body in a basement.

"You know, that storage bin wasn't very big," said Ramon. "They must have chopped him up to fit inside."

"Gross." Another shudder crept up my spine. "Do they know it was a *he*?"

"That's what they're saying. Gotta run. Bye."

I switched to another local station. Two reporters at a sleek desk discussed the "body in the basement" and the Old Louisville mansion. A large monitor showed a straight-on shot of the imposing brick residence, then switched to a split screen with the faces of the suspects. I studied the images. The photo of Mundt appeared to be the same as the one shown on the previous channel, but Banis looked different. This time, he stared straight at the camera, but sculpted eyebrows added to the severity of his gaze. He was clean-shaven, save for a thin strip of beard that ran from below his lower lip down across his chin. Despite the circumstances, both looked relatively normal. Granted, Joseph Banis had that hard edge, but Jeffrey Mundt appeared to be your run-of-the-mill thirtysomething-year-old.

What between them had led to a body in the basement? An accident? Or something darker? Questions swam in my head, but I reminded myself the only thing known for certain was that they had found a corpse in the basement of the house at 1435 South Fourth Street. And that Jeffrey Mundt and Joseph Banis sat in jail.

I continued to stare at the images, a slight pang niggling in my stomach.

Someone rang the doorbell just then. Skippy, our friend stopping by to pick up a basket of books and bourbon for a silent auction at that weekend's Pride celebration, waltzed through the front door. He'd already seen the news.

"It doesn't surprise me in the least," Skippy said. "That guy Joey is crazy as a loon. I told you what happened the last time I was at Q, didn't I?"

"No, what happened?"

"I went to close out my tab at the end of the night, and it was like sixty dollars total on my credit card. When I checked my account the next day, there was another three-hundred-dollar charge on that card. When I called the club to complain, Joey cussed me out and said it was my fault."

"Well, I don't think he's going to be running credit cards any time soon."

"Let's hope not," said Skippy. "Have you heard anything about who's in the tub? I heard that it was a three-way gone wrong. Supposedly it was a trick of theirs and things got out of hand. Rough sex."

"Ah, I'd say so. Very rough." We walked into the kitchen and I poured myself a cup of coffee. "Want some?"

"Nah. I still have to pick up a ton of donations. Need to run."

"OK, see you this weekend at Pride. I'm sure the fact that there's a gay murder will give lots of ammunition to the Bible-thumpers."

"Yeah, I heard the nutjobs from Westboro Baptist Church are supposed to show up. Here it is 2010 and they're still living in the dark ages." Skippy changed his tone then. "So, is this a story you're interested in?"

"You mean for my next book?"

Skippy scoffed. "You've got a gay murder, beautiful but spooky Victorian mansions, and lots of eccentrics. Then there's all the neighborhood drama and infighting. Old money and nouveau riche. Hustlers and prostitutes. Drag queens and cross-dressers up the wazoo. It's like a movie waiting to happen. And there's something about that house."

"Maybe."

Many of my books strove to capture the weird and wonderful that made people either love or hate Old Louisville, and the case unfolding now seemed to have it all. But this project would entail new territory. Sitting through trials. Getting on people's nerves for dredging up painful memories and exposing the soft underbelly that always gets exposed when writing about real-life individuals. People still living and people who were dead. Things I had never done before. I'm sure I had gotten on people's nerves in the past, but this would be different. I wasn't convinced I had what it took to write this kind of book.

"Say, have you found me a bottle of Pappy twenty-three-year-old yet?" I said. Skippy worked at Brown-Forman, the huge wine and spirit distributing company based in Louisville.

"Hold your horses. I'm working on it. See you later." After Skippy left, I finished my coffee. In the breakfast room, I returned my attention to the television. Bright morning sun filled the backyard. The newsflash had ended and when I searched on the other local channels, their coverage had finished as well. Before I turned off the TV, I heard the familiar strain of a Village People song. The cheesy Little John's commercial was starting up again.

## 2

# PROUD NEIGHBORHOOD

**TWO DAYS** later, a friend held a Pride-related fundraiser on South
Third Street, the old Millionaires Row of Louisville. On the way there,
I stopped on Fourth Street. A squad car sat halfway down the block
from 1435, but whether the police had business related to the house
was unclear. Yellow crime scene tape cordoned off much of the porch
and the front door, next to which rested two stacked cardboard boxes.
Evidence? More nun porn?

My phone started ringing, and when I answered, a cheery voice
greeted me.

"Hi, Frances. How've you been?"

"Oh, darlin', keeping okay for an old woman. How about you?"
She laughed without giving me a chance to answer. "Have you been
keeping up with that murder in Old Louisville? My goodness, that's
right around the corner from the mansion where my husband's parents
used to live, isn't it?"

"Yes, it—"

"Did you know those two young men or that poor man they dug
out of the floor? What a scandal! No one's going to want to live in that
house, are they now, darlin'?"

"Well—"

"That's just two blocks down from the Woman's Club! Goodness gracious, I'm sure they're all in a tizzy over there. And my
Antiques Club? That's all they can talk about! Lord, half of them

go to Dr. Banis to get their facelifts." Frances paused for a breath of air, and I could envision her clutching the chunky pedant that always hung from a chain at her throat. "Say, has Lucie Blodgett been in touch yet? She's writing another article and wanted some information. Hey, how's about we do lunch soon?"

"That sounds good, Frances," I said. "I'll be needing to pick your brain about Louisville society anyway, and you know every—"

"Oh, darlin', I don't know if I know everybody in Louisville society, but I know what they *say* about everybody in Louisville society!" Frances crowed with delight and cut me off before I could say anything. "And don't forget you're taking me to the next Fillies Ball!"

"Alright. I won't." Started in 1958, the Fillies Ball was one of the most anticipated events on the Louisville social calendar. Part coronation gala for the queen of the Kentucky Derby, part fundraiser, it kicked off the two weeks of celebration leading up to the famous Run for the Roses on the first Saturday in May.

Frances suddenly lowered her voice. "You know I was one of the founders, right?"

"Yes, I know. And that as a Filly you're obligated to further the fame of the Commonwealth of Kentucky and always bet at least two dollars on any filly entered in the Derby."

"That's right. Well, I must go and watch my program. It's coming on now. Call when you want to do lunch and we can gossip and talk about all kinds of useless stuff. I'll tell Lucie Blodgett and Louise Cecil to join us."

I hung up and a ginger-haired man emerged from around the side of the house, followed by a taller man. Both wore suits and held manila folders. Without a word, they sauntered to the sidewalk, turned, and headed in the opposite direction of the patrol vehicle. Detectives or insurance adjusters? Someone from the bank or a crime lab?

Neighbors said there had been a steady flow of people in and out of the house since the discovery of the body, so who knew? I stared at the peeling paint on the porch and imagined the interior of the house. Surely, the elegant mantelpiece and the intricate carvings on the grand staircase still gleamed, but the façade appeared sad and forlorn, a physical manifestation of the tragic events that had played out within its walls.

I started the car. At the corner of Fourth and Crazy, I spied a familiar face at the bus stop. Mark Anthony Mulligan, a folk artist known for his exuberant colored-marker streetscapes inspired by riding public transit through different parts of the city, sat there and beamed. A beloved fixture in the Highlands neighborhood, he also frequented Old Louisville and the nearby homeless shelters. Wherever he found himself, a steady stream of passersby honked or yelled their greetings at him, to which he would joyously wave in return.

That day at the bus stop, true to form, Mark Anthony chatted happily with a female motorist idling at the traffic light. However, the corpulent Black man didn't have on a stitch of clothing.

I quickly pulled over in front of the stone church on the corner and exited the car. Odd sights were not altogether uncommon here, but people usually kept most of their clothes on. In the 1970s, locals had dubbed the corner "Fourth and Fellini" because at any given moment you might come across an array of colorful characters straight out of the famous Italian director's films, but it was just "Fourth and Crazy" now.

"Mark Anthony!" I called out, in what I hoped wasn't a too-loud voice. "You need me to get you something to wear?"

Seeing me approach, he widened his eyes and smiled. "Whassup?" Then he started waving frantically.

"Not much. How are you? Need something to put on?"

"Nah, I'm fine." He turned his head and directed his waves at a laughing pickup truck passenger who had called out his name.

Just then a squad car pulled up and bleeped its siren. An officer emerged with an Army-issue woolen blanket and draped it over Mark Anthony while the other squawked something into a walkie-talkie. Eyes still wide and beaming, the large man kept waving at passing cars and smiling. The policemen scratched their heads and paced around.

"See you later, Mark Anthony." I was already late for the party, so I started back for my car.

A voice at my back ordered me to stop, and I turned to see a female officer emerge from a car that had just pulled up. "What's your business here?" she demanded.

"Ah, I saw Mark Anthony Mulligan sitting here totally naked so I stopped to see if I could get him some clothes."

"Oh, really. You got any ID on you?"

I looked around me. On the opposite corner, two trans sex workers were quickly moving in the other direction. Ten yards away, three men had passed out on the lawn of the church. One of them had his zipper wide open. I stared at the policewoman.

The officer held out her hand impatiently.

"My wallet is in my car." I gestured at the nearby vehicle.

The patrol woman rolled her eyes. "You carry your identification on you at all times. You should know better than that."


Dale and Bill hosted the event in the opulent Gilmer Speed Mansion. Built in 1899, the brick-and-stone residence had Beaux-Arts details and an impressive grand stairway with a lower landing big enough for the twenty-member choir that usually serenaded guests at their famous Christmas parties. The first occupant came from the Speeds, one of Kentucky's early great families, whose 1815 hemp plantation, Farmington, counted as one of the most visited historic homes in the city. Known as Abraham Lincoln's "most intimate friend," Joshua Fry Speed had a visit from the future president there in 1841. Departing Kentucky on a steamboat three weeks later, Lincoln witnessed a sight that would haunt him for years to come, slaves auctioned downriver at the waterfront. Just a couple of miles from Old Louisville. In a letter to Speed's half-sister Mary, Lincoln wrote: "They were chained six and six together. A small iron clevis was around the left wrist of each . . . So that the Negroes were strung together precisely like so many fish on a trot-line." Years later, Lincoln remarked that the scene had never stopped tormenting him.

The Speeds of Third Street had a reputation for lavish entertaining and wonderful parties, but it all came to an end in the 1920s, when Gilmer contracted gangrene after stubbing his toe during a London business trip and died. Lettie, his wife, moved out. After, the house served as headquarters for the American Red Cross for many years— till Dale and Bill moved in and started reclaiming its former glory.

The evening of the party, the house sparkled with polished chandeliers and enormous candelabra, a clear indication that the two gentlemen did their best to keep the tradition of lavish hospitality alive. A flute of champagne in hand, Dale greeted guests at the front door, a huge construction of wood and beveled glass framed under a portico and sharp gable supported by columns and pilasters. Beyond him, the large entry hall thrummed with lively chatter and a colorful assortment of guests. In the doorway to the parlor, two drag queens, one in an emerald ball gown and the other in a pink poodle skirt and white blouse, entertained a coterie of onlookers. A mane of white hair swept back from his forehead, Dale smiled and reached out a hand as I approached. "Well, good to see you," he said. "But didn't I see you just last week?"

I laughed. "I guess you did."

A few days before, I had spent the day with director Baz Luhrmann, who had traveled to Louisville to scout out potential locations for the new *Great Gatsby* movie. He and an assistant had come to the hometown of Daisy Buchanan to get a better sense of the life she would have led and the places she would have known in preparation for filming—and they asked to get inside some of the more impressive homes.

Dale and Bill immediately came to mind, so the tour included a stop at the Gilmer Speed residence. While Dale regaled them with mint juleps and tales of Gilded Age Louisville, Bill, a former teacher, talked about F. Scott Fitzgerald's stay in Louisville, when the famous Seelbach Hotel downtown kicked him out for drunkenness and poor behavior. As a soldier, Fitzgerald quartered at Louisville's Camp Zachary Taylor for a brief time in 1918. According to local lore, this period inspired him to write the book that would make him most famous.

"I can't wait to see the movie," Dale said. "I hope they use some footage from Old Louisville."

Behind him, one of the drag queens cut up and sent the crowd into gales of laughter.

Suddenly the curve of Dale's smile straightened to a line and he lowered his voice. "And isn't terrible about what happened in that house on Fourth Street?" He shook his head.

"It's a shame." I accepted a flute of champagne from a passing waiter and tipped it in Dale's direction.

Just then, a woman with a frizzy head of auburn hair emerged from behind Dale. "Yeah, it's really sad," she said. "More ammunition for the East End housewives. Fuck 'em. Let 'em stay out in their

McMansions." Debra Richards, a local preservationist and longtime resident of Old Louisville, never minced words.

"Yes, such bad timing." Dale frowned. "Just what the neighborhood needed. And it really put a damper on the Pride festivities." His glass clinked against mine, and a shoulder shrugged. "It's all anyone is talking about in there." He looked over his shoulder and returned the greeting when a tall man in a seersucker suit raised his glass in salute.

"Hey, you guys hear about the big church on the corner? They're trying to build a new shelter on the other side of Oak Street, and the neighborhood's going to fight them." Debra snagged a finger sandwich from a waiter stationed against the wall and took a bite.

"Not again." I rolled my eyes. "How many social service agencies and soup kitchens does this neighborhood already have?"

"There's a dozen clustered around Oak Street alone," she said. "And the churches involved are always terrible. Congregations are the worst custodians of historic properties. Nimbyism at its finest." Debra spotted a familiar face and ran off to say hello. "Catch you later!"

I took the opportunity to excuse myself and join the festivities inside. "Thanks again for hosting, Dale."

"Make sure you try the pimento cheese finger sandwiches," he said. "I used the recipe from your last cookbook."

I wended my way through the crowd and into the dining room, where an enormous table groaned with silver platters of crudités, assorted cheeses and fruits, country ham biscuits, and pork tenderloin. A gigantic punch bowl stood at the center, and a sideboard held crystal dishes heaped with bourbon balls, petit fours, lemon tartlets, and chocolate fudge. I grabbed one of the pimento cheese sandwiches and nodded my approval after the first bite. Before I could finish, the tall man in the seersucker suit approached me, a book held out. I had seen him in the neighborhood, but we had never actually met.

"You're an author. Have you seen this book?" He brandished a copy of a coffee-table-type volume entitled *Edwardian Men*.

I had actually attended the recent book launch. An artistic montage of male nudes photographed in an Old Louisville mansion, the book featured a collection of seductively posed models standing at fireplace mantels, draped over davenports, looking pensively through windows gauzed with lace—all in sepia.

"I'm in this, you know," he said. "Let me show you."

But the two drag queens walked up and elbowed him to the side. "Honey," drawled the one in the poodle skirt, "how's about we do a book called *Edwardian Drag Queens*? Wouldn't that be a hoot?"

"Oh, yes," purred the one in the emerald gown. "I'd love to be photographed spread-eagle on the bench in front of that old pump organ over there. Now that would sell some books."

"What do you think, Mr. Author?"

I fumbled for a response, but the drag queen in green raced on. "Did you hear we're finally getting another gay bar along Bardstown Road? It's about time. Next to Old Louisville, the Highlands is the gayest part of the city, so it's only fitting."

"I hope they get some strippers better than the ones I saw last night," cooed the one in the poodle skirt.

"Oh, girl. What happened to the days when strippers were muscly and smooth and shiny all over?" She reached into a sequined hand-bag that matched the emerald hue of the gown and withdrew a silver compact.

"They've been lowering their standards. Guess it's getting harder to get guys to take their clothes off."

She paused to check her makeup in the mirror of the compact. "The batch last night all looked like lumberjacks! Wolfman Jack much?" She took out a tube of lipstick and touched up the red around her mouth. "I swear one of them was part werewolf."

"Girl, I know what you mean!" chortled the other. "If I want to see Grizzly Adams showing off his poontang, I'll go up to Montreal for the Black and Blue Festival."

"Oh, Can-a-da!"

They abruptly stopped their back-and-forth and returned their attention to me. "Why are you so quiet, Mr. Author?" The one in pink snatched the compact from her friend and checked her teeth for lipstick smudges.

"Yes, cat got your tongue?"

"Well—"

"For someone who writes so much, you sure don't talk a lot, do you?"

"I—"

"Girl, you don't want to gab, you just stand there and listen then. I got a ton of stories. You can write a whole book about the messes drag queens get themselves into." While she spoke, she raised the sequined purse over the platinum blond wig on her head for emphasis; I took the opportunity to finish the pimento cheese sandwich on my plate.

"Yes." The one in pink winked at me. "Like that mess from the Connection who lost all her money at the track yesterday. No names mentioned."

"Girl, can you believe it? She had to pawn her gold and diamonds at Little John's to pay for it all." The drag queen in green seized the compact, snapped it shut, and returned it to her purse. "You know"—she leaned in for a conspiratorial whisper—"she knew those two freaks who buried that guy in the wine cellar. Spent a lot of time in that creepy old mansion."

"Oh, I've been in the house myself, that little room in that musty dusty basement," said the one in pink. "Didn't really know Jeff too well, but Joey? Talk about a psycho mess. That's one bad hombre."

"Girl. He's not right in the head. He'd chase people out of the club, yelling and screaming if they didn't tip him enough."

"Did you know them, Mr. Author?" A hand in a pink glove tapped my forearm.

"Well, not—"

"Hey, did you hear who they found in the tub?" Her friend's voice rose with excitement. "An ex of mine is a detective in Lexington, and I was talking to him last night." She lifted a hand to her mouth for a dramatic stage whisper—"But don't tell his wife about that"—and then coyly brushed back a strand of hair from her temple. "He said it was that guy we met last year at the Christmas party. Jamie, the one who did hair in Lexington. You know, the one who got us our party favors that night." She turned and looked at me. "Girl, I love me some *par-ty fa-vors.*"

The poodle-skirted drag queen widened her eyes. "Little Jamie? No way!"

"That's what Tony said."

My ears pricked at the mention of the victim's supposed identity, and I shifted to reporter mode. "So, the last name of—"

"Jamie's last name?" said the one in pink. "I don't know if I ever knew it. Did you?" She swatted her friend on the shoulder.

"Don't know. He was just *Little Jamie.*"

"Ha, kind of like Little John, the pawnbroker. He's teeny tiny-tiny. Have you ever seen him?" With her six-inch heels, the drag queen in the poodle skirt had to be at least seven feet tall, so Little John must have seemed exceptionally small to her.

"Girl, I haven't had to hock the family jewels yet, thank the lord."

"Guuurrrlllll, I'm telling you."

They both lifted their flutes and daintily sipped champagne, and I tried to seize the moment. "So, how old was—"

The tall man with the book edged in. "You know, this really is a lovely tome." His back to the drag queens, he fanned the pages and held up an image for inspection: A brooding young man lounged on an ottoman in front of a peer mirror.

"Beyotch, let me see that book you're so obsessed about." Gazing over the man's shoulder, the green drag queen plucked the book up before pushing him aside. She smoothed a hand across the page and studied the image.

"Girl, look at those eyebrows! And that chiseled face," said her cohort. "Looks like Victor Mature, don't you think?"

"He does! Kind of like in *Samson and Delilah.*"

"You know he was from Louisville, don't you? My mamaw used to get her knives sharpened by his father. They lived over by Shelby Park."

Victor Mature was born in 1913, the son of an Italian-speaking father, just a mile away from Old Louisville. He had discipline issues at St. X High School, and at the Kentucky Military Institute, fellow student Jim Backus—who would achieve fame as Mr. Magoo and Thurston Howell III on *Gilligan's Island*—reported that "Vic and I weren't very successful cadets . . . We were always in trouble." As a teen, Mature operated the elevator at the famed Brown Hotel on Fourth Street, and he would eventually drop out of school to pursue entrepreneurial interests. By seventeen, he owned his own restaurant, but in 1935 he moved to California to "do something different."

At six-foot-two, the two-hundred-pound Mature had a muscular physique, a deep voice, and wavy dark hair that framed a handsome face with brooding eyes, an aquiline nose, and sensuous lips. In 1939, he landed his first role, and twenty thousand fans wrote the studio demanding more parts for him. The following year, Mature returned to Louisville's Loew's Theater for the world premiere of *One Million B.C.*, the role that would solidify his reputation as the original Hollywood "hunk."

According to *Courier-Journal* reporter Roger Fristoe, one of Mature's fellow cast members in the Broadway musical *Lady in the Dark* coined the term when she exclaimed, "My God, girls, what a beautiful hunk of man! And he's got a voice that goes through you like a pound of cocaine!"

A wounded look on his face, the tall man reached for his book. "Do you mind?"

"Not at all, honey. Have your little book back." The drag queen in pink pushed it into his hands and patted his shoulder.

Her friend grabbed his arm, turned him ninety degrees, and then urged him in the direction of a nearby cluster of guests. "Buh-bye," she drawled.

"So, Mr. Author, you need to know anything else about crossdressers or bodies in basements?"

"Girl, have you tasted these bourbon balls? These are *Happy Balls*, the best balls around!" The one in green snagged a handful of candies from a waiter and popped one into her friend's mouth. She squealed her delight, and, as they chattered back and forth, I made my exit and headed for the bar at the back of the house. I had a headache.

I knew the bartender, as he had worked several parties at our former house on Third Street. A full-time EMT, he did bartending gigs on the side. "Hey," he said, as I approached the grand piano where the bar had been set up. "How've you been? Ready for a mint julep?"

"Of course. You make the best ones in town."

The smile on his face grew broader, sending a large furrow across his forehead. "Comin' right up." He muddled mint in a silver cup, added crushed ice, and topped it off with syrup and a generous slosh of Old Forester. By the time he handed it to me, an icy film of condensation had formed on the sides.

I took a sip and raised my eyebrows in approval. "So, any gossip from the neighborhood?"

"Me? Why would you think I'd have any gossip?" He nonchalantly handed over another drink to someone who had sidled up next to me. The tall man in the seersucker suit, still clutching his book.

Before he could engage me in conversation, I moved closer to the bartender. "Because you're my inside guy, I guess. You always seem to be there for the drug overdoses and neighborhood shootings."

He chuckled and scooped ice into another silver cup. "Usually it's just the old ladies who've fallen and can't get up."

"You know anything about the two guys around the corner who buried their friend in the basement?"

He jerked his gaze up and shot me a serious look. "I was on duty that day, but I didn't go into the cellar till after everything was cleared out. Got the scoop, though." He popped a sprig of fresh mint into a cocktail and handed it to another guest. "Well, at least what scoop I could get. A lot of shit went down in that house, from what I hear."

"So, what happened?" I set down my drink. "Did they really chop the poor guy up like everyone is saying?"

"Naw, that's all a bunch of hype," he said. "Most likely because the plastic storage bin was on the small side, people assumed that they cut him up to fit inside. His name was Jamie Carroll."

"Well, that's good. Cold comfort, though."

"Yeah, but they hog-tied him pretty good. Kind of folded him up so he'd fit. Had to break his knees first, though."

My face screwed up at the unpleasant image. Had Jamie Carroll died that way? Or did they tie him up afterward? I found myself hoping for the latter. "But why did they kill him?"

"That's the thing everyone's not sure about. Drugs? Money?" He shook his head. "It seems like all three were in bed together, so there was probably something kinky going on."

"Did someone say *kinky*?" Smiling hopefully, the man in the seersucker suit scuttled in our direction.

But the two drag queens stepped out of the crowd and elbowed him to the side. "Kinky?" whispered the one in the emerald ball gown. Her eyes twinkled with excitement. "I got kinky, if you want *kinky*."

I drained the last of my mint julep. "Ah—"

"Yes," drawled her pink sidekick, "we can hook you up if that's what you're looking for." She glanced over her shoulder at the man in the suit and then redirected her gaze at me. "There's a *club* or two you might be interested in down here in Old Louisville."

"Yes, *special* clubs," hummed her friend.

"Oh, I like special clubs." The seersucker man tried to worm his way between the two drag queens.

The bartender stopped what he was doing and stared, his eyes darting my way for an explanation. I shrugged and hoped my upturned palms would signal that I was as baffled as he was.

"Honey, I am sure you do," said the pink drag queen, "but we're not talking to you right now." She nudged him away and gave me a coy smile.

"Well, I need to be heading out." I waved to the bartender. "Talk to you soon."

"Yeah," he said. "See you."

I exited the room, but the two drag queens followed, chittering at me the whole time; Mr. Seersucker trailed behind, no doubt hoping for juicy morsels of conversation. By the time I thanked Dale and Bill and exited the front door, I knew much more about Old Louisville's underground sex party scene than I wanted.

They shadowed me down the front walk and to my car. In the few seconds of dialogue afforded me, I promised to stay in touch. They dramatically threw kisses as I got behind the wheel and started the engine. On the sidewalk, a man walking his poodles scowled.

It was a beautiful day, the neighborhood basking in soft sunlight and the gentle green of fresh summer leaves, so instead of driving home right away, I decided to park and take a stroll. I meandered through Central Park and found myself on Ormsby Avenue. Down the block sat the enormous Florence Irvin House, a rambling brick Victorian Gothic with dull green trim and Egyptian sunbursts that looked down from under large gables as I walked by. The fifty-seven-year-old Irvin, a wealthy widow of a steamboat captain and distraught over the recent death of her only son, scandalized the city in 1897 when she married William Botto, a New Orleans ne'er-do-well—and thirty-four years her junior. She died several years later, and the court battle over the legality of her will titillated the city.

I had just turned to head back to the car when I heard a soft whishing at my back, like someone's pants legs chafing as they quickly walked. I craned my head to see who had come up behind me, but before I knew it, I felt something cold and metallic pressed into the small of my back.

"Raise your hands and turn around slowly," commanded a deep voice.

# 3

## A DARK ROOM

SUDDENLY SHAKING, I slowly turned around. First, I saw the barrel of the gun pointed at me; then I beheld the officer brandishing her badge at me and the squad car parked several yards away. That's when I realized it was the same female officer I had just seen several hours before.

"Let me see your ID," she ordered, lowering the gun just slightly.

"I don't have it with me," I stammered. "It's in my car. What's going on?"

"And where's your car?"

"A couple of blocks down on Third."

"You have to have an ID on you at all times."

As I opened my mouth to protest, the officer suddenly whipped out a pair of handcuffs with her free hand and before I knew it, she had me up against the police vehicle with my wrists locked together. "Are you serio—?"

"You should know better." She barked something into her radio and then glared at me. "And don't move."

Trembling, I wracked my brain, trying to figure out what I had done. Would they throw me in jail? My stomach suddenly dropped. Oh no. Was the family "curse" finally catching up with me?

As far as I could tell, I was the only one in my immediate family who hadn't been arrested yet, including my own mother. With an impressive litany of charges including DUIs, drug possession, shoplifting, and disturbing the peace, my three younger brothers had solidified their reputations as perpetual juvenile delinquents early on. My father, known to be quite a hellion in his younger days, had a number of run-ins with the police. And in the 1970s, when streaking was all the rage, my mother ended up handcuffed in the back of a squad car one moonlit summer night after she and a friend attempted to run naked along a very short stretch of beach at Lake Wazeecha. It was after midnight and we were the only ones camping in that part of the park, yet somehow, my mother managed to run into the only Wisconsin Rapids police officer on duty. Charges weren't filed—I'm sure the officer was more amused than anything—but she was arrested and taken into custody, nonetheless.

"What's your name and address?" she demanded from the driver's seat. I told her, and in the crackled conversation that ensued with the dispatcher, I heard the words "suspect already in custody" from the other end.

The patrolwoman exited the vehicle and undid the cuffs. "You matched the description of someone we were looking for, but it appears they already nailed the perp several blocks from here. You're free to go." Without another word, she hopped behind the wheel and sped off.

I heaved a sigh of relief, but my ears burned with humiliation and indignation. I made my way back to the car, furious at being too rattled to have taken down the officer's squad car or badge number. The only thing I really remembered was how much she looked like a friend of mine by the name of Janet.

That night, all the local television news stations had updates on the murder and arrests. Reports indicated that the killing and cover-up resulted from a warped lovers' triangle, which local writer and attorney Thomas McAdam and others in the press had dubbed "the pink triangle murder." One station reported that one of the accused killers' families had retained a high-profile defense attorney who had gained notoriety for the murder acquittal of a corrections officer accused of stomping on an inmate's head.

Authorities revealed that the victim, James Carroll, was thirty-seven years old and came from the eastern part of the state. He had lived and worked for a while in Lexington, where he ran a hair salon. By all accounts, he had a checkered past and some knew him as a ruthless drug dealer. He often went long periods of time without speaking to his family, so nobody had reported him missing. His body had lain, buried, in the dank cellar for at least six months.

The court set the pretrial for the end of the summer, with the possibility of the prosecution seeking the death penalty. Although much of the furor surrounding the killing had subsided across the city, the details of the case still consumed Old Louisvillians and many wondered about the fate of the house. Who would want to buy a home where such a grisly murder had taken place? Few would have the money or desire to restore it to its former grandeur. Some thought it better to bulldoze the whole place. Most didn't seriously consider the notion of razing the house, however. The residence had structural solidity, and local preservationists such as Debra Richards would never consent to its destruction. Divided and difficult as residents of Old Louisville might be, they could be counted on to come together and fight to save an old house. For the time being, though, 1435 South Fourth Street sat abandoned.

As I lay in bed that night, I ticked off the reasons why I shouldn't write about the Jamie Carroll murder. I feared I lacked the gumption for such a project. I didn't know what angle to take. I would surely offend people, and the book would take years to write.

Downstairs, the grandmother clock chimed three in the morning, and thoughts of spooky old houses with creepy cellars and makeshift graves kept me wide awake.

Before any final decisions were made, I wanted to do two things: first, sit in on the pretrial; second, go back to the Richard Robinson place on Fourth Street and see where Jamie Carroll had been buried. I wanted to see the basement, let the house speak to me.

Outside, an owl released a reverberant *hoo-hoo* in the branches of the towering ashwood trees. It called again, followed by an airy echo from another bird high in a distant tree.

I decided I could either lie in the cool darkness of my bedroom, doing nothing except tossing and turning, or I could be a responsible adult and make better use of my time by driving to Old Louisville and breaking into the cool darkness of the basement at 1435 South Fourth Street.

Muttering, I pulled on some clothes. "Well, there's no time like the present." Then I crept down to the front door.

"Where are you going, hobo?" Rubbing sleep from his eyes, Ramon creaked his way down the stairs and stopped mid-landing to give me a *What-are-you-crazy?* look. "It's three o'clock in the morning."

"I won't be gone long. Just going down to Old Louisville to check out the Murder House."

He stared blankly, then shook his head. "I can't believe I live with a writer." He turned around and started creaking his way back up.

Outside a light breeze picked up, sliding a bank of clouds over a fat sliver of moon. As I hopped into the car, the hooting birds made their moody presence known again. My phone chirruped and I discovered a text from a friend in Old Louisville, Margie. *You're being a night owl, aren't you? Blessed be.* Margie had the uncanny ability to always know what I was doing, at all hours of the day.

I texted back. *Stop that. You're freaking me out.*

The phone lit up with her reply. *Come and see me some time.*

As I backed out of the driveway, an owl swooped down and scooped up a small creature from the front yard before soaring to a treetop to inspect its catch.

Only two other vehicles passed as I maneuvered along Eastern Parkway, one of the city's tree-lined boulevards designed by famed father of American landscape architecture Frederick Law Olmsted. In Old Louisville, Fourth Street appeared darker than usual because many of the streetlights on the 1400 block had gone out.

I parked across the street and then found an enormous elm that afforded a hidden vantage spot.

An old-fashioned gas lamp near the sidewalk cast the crumbling porch of the old Robinson place in a yellow pallor, but complete darkness enveloped the rest of the house. The residence to the left and the large brick apartment block to the right were devoid of light as well. After a glance over my shoulder, I hustled up the walkway and paused at the front steps. Crime scene tape still sealed the front door, and a bit of color on the tattered welcome mat caught my eye. Someone had left a bunch of bright pink roses, tied together with a yellow ribbon. A prayer candle, the kind that looked like a tall drinking glass with colorful saints and Virgin Marys splashed across the front, leaned against the front door. I studied the improvised altar for a moment, and, before anybody could see me, I darted around to the side of the house, where a rickety-looking metal scaffold rose to the third floor.

Framed by a bottom portion of scaffolding, another door beckoned, its flaking white paint strangely iridescent in the darkness. Caution tape had run across this entrance as well; however, somebody had torn through the yellow and black plastic, and tatters fluttered in a light breeze. The wooden door stood ajar, no doubt forced open by thrill-seekers or curious neighbors, and relief washed over me when I realized my job of gaining entry to the cellar had been made all the easier. Still, I hesitated before going inside. What if somebody else was already down there? Could the cops still be around?

I took a breath to calm my nerves. Grit and sand beneath my feet, I eased myself through without having to push the door any wider. On the landing, I pulled out a small flashlight and used it to get my bearings. One side had a flight of stairs that went up into the main part of the house; the other had steps leading down.

After a pause, I started for the basement; then I reconsidered and decided to check out the upper rooms first. How had it changed in the last two years? I adored exploring old houses, even in the middle of the night without electricity and even if a recent murder had been committed there. My hand followed the handrail up to a narrow opening with a partially closed door. I slithered through and came to stand in the foyer, where a dim stream of light shone through the leaded glass in the front window and cast a distorted rectangle onto the parquet floor. Although mud and dirt had been tracked here and there, patches of hardwood still gleamed. The darkness only served to make the front hall even more imposing than the last time I had seen it.

Emerging from beneath the coffered and paneled grand staircase, I studied the intricate carvings of the banister and the sculpted legs on the newel posts anchored to the bottom landing. Four steps led up to the landing, and then another short flight proceeded to a larger platform framed with an impressive arrangement of leaded-glass windows on the left. From that landing, the stairs doubled back and ascended in a straight shot to the next level.

Within ten minutes I had reconnoitered the second and third floors, the flashlight beam guiding me from room to room. Some stood empty; others had a random piece of furniture or a couple of boxes stacked against the wall. The space that aroused my curiosity most was the front left corner room on the second floor. Room number six. According to the police report from the week before, Joey had threatened to kill Jeffrey and Jeffrey had barricaded himself in this room. Why did Joey want to kill him? Nobody had explained this yet. The 911 dispatcher only reported that Jeffrey claimed his boyfriend was trying to break through the wooden door with a hammer so he could come inside and murder him.

Sure enough, when I examined the wood of the door, I made out scrapes and clear indentations that fit the flat head of a hammer. There was also a very small hole with clean, neat edges. From a bullet?

From what I had read, things began to get interesting after the officers arrested Joey and took him into custody. One of the two residents of 1435 South Street brought up the body in the basement—but who and why remained a mystery. After police dug the body out of the old wine cellar, they arrested Jeffrey as well and charged both with murder. Each had accused the other of committing the murder.

I pushed the door open and, inside, the beam of light picked up traces of the black powder used when dusting for fingerprints. Outside, a dog howled. Despite the summer heat, a chill pervaded the space. Had Jamie Carroll met his end in this room? On a far wall, a dark stain shimmered next to a carved fireplace mantel. An ugly drape dangled limply, only partially covering the window.

I turned and made for the bottom floor via the servants' stairs. Though sparsely furnished, the living room, dining room, and a large study had beautiful floors, moldings, and wainscoting. Sconces decorated several walls, and marble surrounds with hand-carved griffins accented mantelshelves on the fireplaces.

The kitchen, on the other hand, had only several battered cupboards left as reminders of what the space had been intended for. Through a streaked window, I saw the dilapidated carriage house across the overgrown backyard, cast in the eerie glow of the streetlamp in the alley. Suddenly, the halcyon glow of the bulb intensified and then came an electric pop as it flashed and burned out.

I looked at my watch; already a half hour had passed. I followed the hallway back to the foyer and entered the narrow flight of stairs that snaked under the grand staircase. Before descending, I paused; the flashlight illuminated something I hadn't noticed on the way up. In a cloakroom, two old and battered canes hung from a shelf. Perhaps carved of oak or hickory, one had a simple design while the other sported a gentle corkscrew shape on the shaft. Was one for Joey and one for Jeffrey? Jeffrey would have used the fancier one. I imagined him wielding the walking stick as he tottered through the breakfast joint where I had seen him chirping "top of the morning!" to all within earshot.

I resisted the urge to pinch the walking sticks and took the steps. At the side entrance landing where I had entered initially, I halted. A cool early morning breeze channeled through the still half-opened door. My ears perked up. Had I just heard something move in the cellar? I listened for a minute or two, heart pounding in my chest, but no sounds followed, except for the rustle of leaves outside. After another minute, I directed the flashlight at the narrow flight of stairs and down I went.

Sandy footprints tracked across the filthy concrete floor and clumps of mud popped up here and there. Shadows danced in the rafters as I shone the beam around the small space at the bottom of the steps. The light scraped across the doorway of one of the adjacent rooms, briefly illuminating the white rectangular shape of some appliance in the far corner. I shuffled into the room, looked around, and then slunk through another doorway. Jamie's body had been found in the front corner room on the right, so, after passing through several more spaces, I turned right and headed to the part of the house facing Fourth Street. The closer I came to Jamie Carroll's makeshift grave, the more intense my sense of unease became. My heart pounded with a steady thump-thump-thump, but it almost gave out when a soft noise caught my ear.

It could have been the sound of the side door being opened or closed. Or maybe a footstep gliding along the grit of the cellar floor.

I doused the light. My ears strained, but I heard nothing else, save for the racing of my heart as I wedged myself into a corner and waited.

A minute passed, then two more. Only silence followed, so I turned the light back on and tried to breathe. Without a sound, I inched toward the front of the house.

I passed through a large room with cement block walls and a mound of what appeared to be refuse on one side. When I stepped into the next room, the poured concrete floors gave way to hard-packed soil. Only a few rooms had dirt floors in the basement, and they discovered Jamie in one of them. A momentary once-over with the flashlight revealed no signs of the burial pit in this room, so I illuminated the doorway on the opposite side and went that way.

Two solid walls with small windows at the top revealed the space I entered next as a corner room. It had a hard-packed dirt floor. A marked shift in the tone of white paint indicated the outline of a large piece of furniture, maybe a wardrobe or massive peer mirror, that had once rested against a wall. Cobwebs dangled from several hooks embedded in the rafters. Old wooden shelves looked like they once held bottles of wine. Something sparkled in a far corner when my light hit it, but I kept the beam moving until it illuminated a neat, gaping hole in the shape of a rectangle off-center from the middle of the room. Next to the pit, a huge mound of dirt rested on a stained tarpaulin.

I released a gasp that echoed off the walls. My heart pounding again, I took a single step forward. The grave where Joey and Jeffrey had buried Jamie Carroll. Immediately, the room took on a dark and oppressive air, and, once more, I willed my feet forward.

Standing at its edge, I looked down into a rectangle of blackness. Trembling, my hand directed the light beam to the bottom of the hole, scoured the corners. It had to be five or six feet deep. Hard to fathom. Just a week ago, it had been covered over, and only those who had a hand in it knew the secret of Jamie's demise and internment. Now, the entire city was privy to the dark mysteries at play in the house in Old Louisville.

But had the mansion given up all its secrets? A cold shudder tickled its way across my shoulders, and my nose picked up on a faint odor. The musty, dirty smell so typical of basements. But I got a whiff of something else. The distant stench of rot and decay? No, I had to be psyching myself out. But I closed my eyes and inhaled. It reeked of death, sickly sweet and light in the air.

There was a change, and my nostrils flared. It smelled more like smoke now. Cigarette smoke.

And a man's menacing voice jolted me out of my reverie.

"Fancy meeting you here."

# 4

## WHORES IN HOT PANTS

I SHRIEKED and spun around. The flashlight slipped from my hands and bounced across the hard-packed ground, the beam of yellow light throwing frantic, shimmering shadows as it rolled toward the corner with the sparkly object. My left foot scraped the edge of the pit as I struggled to maintain my balance, and my body began toppling backward into the hole.

But I steadied myself at the last second and lurched forward to land on my knees. I scurried forward and retrieved my source of light. Before I shone the beam in the direction of the voice, I could make out a dim figure in the shadows, one that held a cigarette to his lips. Or her lips? Scuttling back to the relative safety of the nearest wall, I managed to bathe the form in light. I saw a dress. A red satin party gown trimmed in black velvet and cinched at the waist with a shiny leather belt. And a mink stole and string of pearls. All topped off with a matching beret.

"Well, whores in hot pants! I didn't mean to scare you," said the person. "What are you doing here?"

"What the hell—?"

"Don't be afraid, doll. It's only me." A husky laugh ensued.

"Do I know you?" I stammered, getting to my feet. Fortunately, it didn't appear this individual planned on killing me, so I started to regain my composure.

"Sure you do. But it's been years since we talked last." A hand with rings on each finger lifted a long black cigarette holder and took a luxurious drag. Red embers flared to orange at the tip. That's when recognition set in.

"Candy?" I leaned forward. "Is that you?"

"Sure is, doll. How've you been?"

I sighed. "Not too bad, but you scared the bejesus out of me."

"That's what you get for creepin' around basements of abandoned houses where murders were committed."

"What about you then?" Chuckling, I brushed dirt off my knees and took a step closer.

"Oh, I'm gettin' cheap thrills, that's all, honey." Candy took another drag on her cigarette. A small purse with Art Deco patterns hung from a shoulder.

I had met Candy some ten years before, on a moonlit night in Fort George, a tiny overlooked park with a family burial plot on Floyd Street. I was doing research for my very first book, when Ramon and I had the house on Third Street. Candy had sat on a bench in the shadows, smoking a cigarette from a long black holder like this one, and after some small talk he introduced himself as Randy, the name he went by when not in female attire.

Randy lived with his wife in one of the nearby bungalows and after "that banshee" went to bed, he often borrowed her clothes and strolled about the neighborhood. At those times, he liked to be addressed as Candy. As I studied her, I realized Candy wore similar garb the time we first met. If memory served, she had on the exact same ensemble.

Candy's eyes narrowed to suspicious slits. "I know what you're thinking," she said. "That this is the same outfit I was wearing when we met in Fort George?"

"I had wondered about that. It is a very nice outfit."

"Thanks, but I do wear more than just red and black party gowns." She reached down with her free hand and ruffled the black velvet trim at the hem. "I think I've worn this getup only four or five times, so it's just coincidence I have it on again. My wife bought it right after we got married."

"Well, it is a great dress, and it's good seeing you again, but you scared me to death." I directed the light beam into an adjacent space that looked like a utility room. "Was that you I heard before?"

"Probably."

Candy exhaled a long stream of smoke and smiled. "Heard you creepin' around up there and tried to stay still as a church mouse down here, but once or twice I bumped into things on accident. That happens when you stand around in the pitch dark."

"Don't you have a flashlight?"

"Naw, I know this basement pretty well and I can usually get around without any help. Knock into a wall every now and then, but, for the most part, I know the layout down here. Been here every night since they dug up that tub with the body in it." Candy pointed the cigarette holder in the direction of the grave, then raised it to her lips.

"You have? Doing what?"

"Just hangin' out. Watching people, mostly."

"What people?" I said.

"Oh, tons of them," said Candy. "Of course, you and I haven't been the only ones sneaking down here. There was a couple here right before you came."

"I figured as much when I saw the caution tape had been ripped away and the side door was half-opened."

"Yeah, a lot of demented people get off on places like this. The first night, it was impossible because the police were still hanging around and shit, but by the second night it was pretty easy to get inside."

I shuffled my feet and directed the beam of light to the pit behind me. "I must be demented then."

"No, you're doing this for research, aren't you?" Candy laughed. "Probably gonna write a book about it, right?"

"I have been thinking about it."

"That's okay then. And I live in the neighborhood, so I have a vested interest in knowing what's happening to this old place. But all these other people? What a bunch of freaks."

"Why? What's been going on?"

"Whores in hot pants!" said Candy. "This is one sick fucking neighborhood, let me tell you." A chuckle rumbled at the back of her throat as she sucked greedily on the cigarette. "All these old houses and so many people living in close quarters, decade after decade. It attracts the freakazoids."

"Hmmm."

"Yeah, take the two right before you arrived." Candy took a step in my direction and peered into the hole behind me. "She was a bimbo, wearing daisy dukes that only covered half her ass, and before you knew it, they were making out, totally unaware that I was watching from the shadows of the next room. Nobody bothers going there once they've found this spot." A twinkle filled her eyes. "Yeah, he had the tramp bent over the edge here and she was crying 'Yes, daddy, do me, do me, and then bury me in this hole,' just like a horny, sex-starved harpy."

"What the hell."

"Whores in hot pants. You should have heard her wailing and moaning: 'Fuck me dead, daddy. Fuck me dead!' I'm surprised the whole damn neighborhood didn't hear them and call the police."

Candy stepped away from the pit and looked up into the rafters while blowing out a long puff of smoke. "I guess I'm not surprised, given the history of this place." She turned to me, hip thrust forward and one elbow propped in the other hand in a Bette Davis stance while languidly smoking the cigarette. "And I don't mean the spooky shit. I'm talking about the sex club that used to be here."

"What?"

"Yeah, it was only for a year or two, back when this place was practically empty. A friend had a room upstairs and the landlord let him use a couple rooms down here. She was clueless, though, getting old. Never came down here. You could go downtown to Latex or come here, if you had the password for the side door. Fun times."

"Uh . . . okay. I guess that was in the '70s?"

The sparkle returned to her eyes, and Candy walked over to the corner and pointed up. "There was a sling hanging over here. You can still see the holes where they had the chains bolted in." She closed her eyes and hugged herself. "I remember one night they had me hangin' upside down and trussed up like a sow, takin' turns like I was the biggest slut on the planet."

I coughed nervously. Definitely a racier version of the Candy I had met ten years earlier. I also realized she must have been older than I initially had pegged her for. Late sixties or early seventies? If Randy was borrowing his wife's wrinkle cream as well, it had paid off.

"Yeah, with all the shit that went on down here, it's not surprising that those two psychos living here would absorb some of the kinky vibes. But we never killed anybody, so I don't know where that came from. It was all pretty innocent." She turned and pointed to the next corner. "That must be one of the disco balls."

I swung my light in that direction, finally recognizing the object half-buried in the dust. A number of the mirrors still shimmered and they sent silver squares dancing over the walls.

Candy harrumphed. "Or mirror ball. Or glitter ball—whatever you prefer to call it."

"I prefer glitter ball myself."

"You ever hear a company here in Louisville made most of the world's disco balls back in the day?"

"Yes, I've heard that before. Louisville—Glitter Ball City."

Candy killed her cigarette with one long drag. Then she extracted the filter and ground it under the heel of a shiny leather pump. "Poor guy. Nobody deserves to be treated like that. Buried in a tub, like he was a piece of trash. Nobody to mourn for him." Candy returned to the edge of the grave and peered down. "I don't care if he was a drug dealer or had a criminal past. He had hopes and this neighborhood killed him. Old Louisville is a fair but fickle mistress."

She reached into the sparkly handbag and took out a flat silver case. She opened it, lifted out a new cigarette, and placed it in the end of the black lacquered holder. "At least you'll have some interesting stuff to write about."

"Speaking of which, I'm writing a kind of memoir about the house I used to have on Third Street, and you'll be making a cameo appearance because of that night I met you at Fort George and the story you told me about the voodoo that supposedly used to go on there."

In the process of lighting her new cigarette, Candy quickly lowered the lighter and beamed. "Really? I'm going to be in one of your books?"

"If you don't mind."

"Not at all." She lifted the lighter again. Suddenly, her eyes narrowed and a line of worry worked its way across her forehead. "But you won't use my real name, will you?"

"Whatever you'd like."

"Well, leave out the last name then. And concentrate on the Candy part of my persona."

"That shouldn't be a problem. Especially because I only know you as Candy. You never told me your last name."

"That's right." She smiled and christened her new cigarette with a luxurious drag. "I'm an enigma."

I took a step in the direction of the hole and peered down again. In the recesses of my stomach, something dark and heavy twinged.

"You know, I've been keepin' my eye on you. Got all your books and enjoyed 'em."

"Thanks, that's good to know."

"Really looking forward to this one." She extended an arm in a sweep of the room. After a noisy exhalation and a cough, her expression changed to one more serious. "But you're gonna piss people off, you know that, don't you?"

I shrugged half-heartedly. "I suspect so. Hopefully, it won't be too many."

"Whenever you write the truth, people get angry. Especially when you're revealing the seedy side of something. People are too concerned with appearances. Like that guy with the poodles a few doors down." Candy reached a toe forward and brushed the edge of the pit with the tip of her shoe. A loose clump of soil broke free and fell into the hole. "He was standing out front the other night, complaining to the neighbors about the 'reprobates' who lived here. All high and mighty. And his own kid a damn heroin junkie."

I nodded.

"You've got your work cut out for you. Old Louisville is something else, especially some of those bitches and backstabbers over on the neighborhood council." She sucked on her cigarette, discarded the butt, and ground out the orange embers with the toe of a deep-red leather pump. "You going to the trials? I probably will." Candy's mood changed again and her face brightened. "Hey! There's a secret S&M club that meets over on Sixth Street, in case you're interested. I can tell you the password to get in."

I had no intention of visiting a secret sex club, but then I wondered if it might be prudent to know the password, just in case. Who knew? Maybe it would come in handy, for research purposes. If nothing else, I wanted to satisfy my curiosity about what kinds of passwords were getting people into sex clubs nowadays. "Ah. So, what is the password?"

Candy opened her cigarette case and extracted another smoke. "Whores in hot pants."

# 5

## FAMILY SECRETS

I DIDN'T see Candy at the pretrial hearing in August. At least, I don't think I did. Maybe Randy hadn't been able to sneak anything out of his wife's closet and came dressed as his male self. A sparse crowd milled around in the hallway outside the courtroom, but I glanced at the few men, trying to recognize any signs of Candy in their features. If Randy was in attendance, he didn't greet me or acknowledge my presence in any way.

Near the elevators stood several reporters from the local news. I went to chat with the ones I knew, but none of them had anything to report, and they were anxious to see what would be revealed in the pretrial.

An elevator opened with a loud *ding*, and three men in suits stepped out. Taken aback at first, one of them nudged the others and pointed at the courtroom door. "That must be the hearing for those two freaks in Old Louisville. You know, the ones who buried their *special friend* in the basement."

One of them laughed. The other, a silver badge clipped to his belt, shook his head and scowled. "Goddamn faggots. I hope they fry them all." The men shuffled down the hallway and disappeared through the door to an adjacent waiting area. I winced, a rush of heat flooding my cheeks.

A minute later, a bailiff emerged and unlocked the door, allowing access to the courtroom. Only a couple of people entered and sat down, however. I settled onto a bench near the door as the attorneys filed down the aisle and took seats at their respective tables. As I looked around, a low hum seemed to pervade the room, perhaps coming from the stark ceiling lights.

Across the aisle sat a well-dressed woman, a pained look on her face. Her profile seemed familiar, and I as I studied it, it dawned on me where the similarities came from. Joey Banis. Was this the accused killer's mother?

A sick ache caused my stomach to cramp, and I recalled a different time and place. The late 1980s, during my year abroad at the University of Bielefeld in Germany.

Despite the excitement of living in Europe, I hated it. Northern Germans seemed an unfriendly lot, something, I realized later, had more to do with me than them. I missed my friends and pined for a secret love in Mexico. I hadn't come out of the closet and was more than slightly neurotic. Constantly gray skies and drizzly weather added to the depression.

Rain poured down one afternoon as I rushed home from classes. On the kitchen table, two letters waited for me, both from friends back home. The thinner of the two bore a brief message scrawled across a mostly empty white page: "Your brother did something really bad. If you don't know yet, let me know and I'll give you the details. Katie." My heart lurched.

I knew instinctively which brother she meant. Paul, the oldest of my three younger brothers, was always getting into trouble. God, what had he done now? My hands started to tremble as I seized the other envelope, stuffed with clippings from our hometown newspaper. My best friend Pat had sent them, along with an unceremonious message scribbled across a half-sheet of yellow legal paper: "Your brother is in trouble again."

My eyes darted from headline to headline, landing on words and phrases such as "inebriated," "drug-fueled night," and "lengthy prison sentence." Slowly, I unfolded the articles and flattened them on the wooden tabletop.

The last one comprised the entire front page of the newspaper back home, and a grainy photo took up the top half. As my eyes studied the black-and-white images, a face leaped out at me. Paul. He was handcuffed and being led into a packed courtroom. His head hung, but the camera had flashed at the very moment he had gazed up, revealing his eyes and memorializing his expression.

I knew that face: he always wore that look when he did something wrong—and got caught.

My hands still trembling, I took a deep breath before arranging the clippings in chronological order. A quarter hour later, I had read everything.

I collapsed on the sofa, my stomach in knots. Although the details were confusing, the gist was clear. My brother and two friends had been out one night, partying. Drunk and high, they left the bar in two vehicles in the early morning hours. Alone, my brother followed in the second vehicle on the backroads. Somehow, in the course of a very short period of time, the first vehicle had broken down and ended up facing the other way on the shoulder. His two friends were standing in front of the truck, looking under the hood, when my brother's car sped up and collided with them. They were crushed.

Miraculously, both had survived, but just barely. They said the guy might never walk again. The girl had both legs amputated. Paul was already in prison.

The whole thing had been going on for weeks and my hometown was in an uproar. And I was just finding out about it.

I picked up the phone. When my mother answered, she sounded like her normal self.

"Mom, Paul is in *prison!* Why didn't you let me know?"

A brief silence ensued, but then she spoke in a softer tone. "I didn't want to spoil things for you over there."

"Didn't you think I'd find out eventually? Katie and Pat sent me letters with all the gory details." I exhaled loudly. "I shouldn't be the last one to know stuff like this."

Again, silence. When my mother didn't want to talk, she didn't talk.

"What happened?" I finally said. "I don't even understand how the accident occurred. It doesn't make sense."

There came a soft sigh from the other end. "Your younger brother was in the vehicle that ran into—"

"Mother, he drove the car! He maimed people! Some are saying he did it on purpose!" I resisted the urge to hang up on her. "Stop always making excuses for him."

"At least he didn't kill anyone," she said stubbornly, if without conviction. "He carried that girl in his arms for almost a mile before they found help."

The sick knot in my stomach turned over at the thought of my brother stumbling along a dark country road, struggling with the mangled and bloody mess in his arms.

From the other end echoed the barest hint of a sniffle.

I lowered my voice. "I can't believe you didn't tell me about this."

Silence.

I put down the phone. For the next week I couldn't eat a thing.

My mother moved out of state several months later. Angry stares and whispered comments followed her wherever she went. Anonymous phone calls and threatening letters made her life miserable. She never returned to our hometown in Wisconsin. Dysfunctional as it was, our family was never the same afterward.

I wrote my brother a letter or two, but I never visited him in prison.

I looked around the courtroom and tried to imagine who had ties to these defendants. Did they get threatening calls and accusatory glares for matters over which they had little or no control? Did they have a supportive network of family and friends? What must be going through their heads as they sat there and wondered about the fates of their loved ones?

Delving into the background of these defendants would rub salt in an open wound.

My spine stiffened.

The door opened with a loud creak, and in walked a reporter from one of the local channels. She waved at me and directed her cameraman to a far corner. Just then Sheriff Michael Brown, the bailiff, emerged through a side entrance; a minute later, Banis and Mundt entered.

Joey wore the typical orange prison jumpsuit over a white long-sleeved T-shirt. His hairline receded dramatically, and what hair was left had been buzzed back to a thin layer around the sides. With his glasses and beaten-down demeanor, he cut an entirely unrecognizable figure to those who remembered his days as a painted and tatted party boy. Jeffrey was similarly attired, but in drab gray. His hair had been buzzed as well, and although it receded at the temples, he didn't appear to be balding to the same extent as his former lover. His complexion sallow, Jeffrey looked up as the bailiff led him to the table with the attorneys; the angle of his chin hinted at an attempt to maintain a degree of dignity.

Both had aged considerably in the period of just a few months, but time behind bars will do that to a person. The first time I saw Paul after his release, I almost gasped. My younger brother looked twenty years older.

I heard a sharp intake of breath. An elderly couple sat behind me. Smartly dressed, they had snowy white hair and stoic expressions. Nonetheless, a momentary crack showed in the lady's façade and she raised a hand to cover her mouth. Jeffrey's mother and father? I couldn't discern any resemblance between either of them and the man who now sat before the judge, but it had to be Mundt's parents.

I felt my innards twisting into knots again. A heavy feeling pressed my chest from the inside out.

I looked around the courtroom, watched the attorneys settle in and examine their files as the bailiff retreated and the judge called the room to order. Now, more than ever, I realized what an outsider I was. A voyeur. Intruding on another's tragedy, and not just Jamie Carroll's. That of Jeffrey Mundt and Joey Banis as well.

Again, I gazed at the older couple, saw the weariness in their eyes. I sighed, long and slow. I got up and bolted for the exit.

I would find out what happened on the evening news.

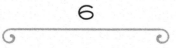

# 6

## THE PLOT THICKENS

A LARGE Black man in sunglasses and an ill-fitting blue and red unitard bounded into the scene, coming to stand in front of a shop counter where a stogie-chomping pawnbroker prepared to fleece an unwitting customer. The words *Super Gold Man* emblazoned across his chest, the would-be superhero started singing: "I'm Super Gold Man / The fairest in the land / I'm taking you to Lit-tle John's." Then he grabbed the customer by the arm and leaped into the air, a gold lamé cape fluttering lamely behind. Soaring through clouds in front of the Louisville skyline, he continued his off-key ditty: "Broke from the smash / He pays you cash / So bring it in and get your cash today!" At least, it sounded like that. Not only did Super Gold Man not know how to sing, he didn't enunciate very well either.

I groaned. This one was even worse than the Y.M.C.A. commercial. But I remained glued to the screen, waiting till Little John appeared in person and proudly announced: "I'm Little John. Don't mail it in. Bring it in! And get your cash today!" Standing next to Super Gold Man, John Tan appeared to be about half his size.

I flipped the channel, looking for the most recent local coverage of the Jamie Carroll case. Instead, I landed on CBS News, which reported that forty-seven-year-old Stanley Neace, enraged over how his wife cooked his eggs, shot and killed her, his stepdaughter, and three witnesses with a shotgun in Jackson, Kentucky, before killing himself over the weekend. I shook my head and switched the channel again. I caught the tail end of a story about an art exhibit featuring work by

Mark Anthony Mulligan, who stood next to a colorful rendering of a Mobile gas station sign and waved.

Finally, I found what I was looking for on WDRB, the local Fox affiliate. "Details of a love triangle involving sex, drugs, and a body buried in a basement . . . emerged this week as prosecutors submitted evidence in a Louisville murder case," reported Bennett Haeberle. "During a hearing Friday, Circuit Judge Mitch Perry denied a bond reduction for Joseph Banis. Banis and his former lover, Jeffrey Mundt, face several charges in connection with the death of James Carroll. Prosecutors say the two men were involved in a drug-induced sexual encounter with Carroll and then killed him and robbed him of his drug money."

As images flashed across the screen, the reporter provided a brief rundown of what had led to the discovery of the body and then announced that at the pretrial, prosecutors had submitted more than five hours of police interviews, as well as crime scene photos taken in the basement of the home on South Fourth Street. "Carroll's body was found shot, stabbed, and buried in a plastic container," he said, going on to quote Louisville Metro Police Detective Barry Wilkerson. "Apparently this individual was involved sexually in a relationship. They had made some sort of plan to rob him of narcotics. And during that robbery, that's when the murder was committed and they decided to bury the body . . ."

Up to that point, nothing new had been revealed, but it confirmed rumors that drugs had been a major factor. Just then the screen cut from a photo of the basement to the reporter. "Now, Fox 41 News has obtained new evidence in connection with the case—including video of police interrogations of Mundt and Banis," he said. "In interviews with police, the two suspects point the finger at each other." The shot cut to an interrogation room with Banis on one side of a table and a detective on the other. "On police video, Banis says, 'Before I knew it, Jase stabbed Jamie. There was blood flying, there was a lot of yelling.' But Mundt says under interrogation, 'This is not a relationship. This is him using me to try to do something.' Both men are still facing several charges related to the murder of Carroll. Banis's bond is currently set at $1 million. His attorney wants a judge to reduce it, arguing he is not a flight risk and could live with his parents."

That the two turned on each other didn't surprise me, but Jeffrey's claim that Joey used him "to try to do something" brought me up short.

What did he mean? I scratched my head and—assuming the report was ending—prepared to flip the channel again.

But the reporter continued. "This isn't the first time the pair have been in trouble with the law. In April, they were arrested in Chicago at the Hyatt Regency hotel after they were allegedly found with roughly fifty-five thousand dollars in counterfeit money, a suspected date rape drug, several handguns, and fake IDs."

I blinked. Counterfeit money? Fake IDs? No big surprise about the pistols or drugs, but phony cash and identifications?

Joseph Banis and Jeffrey Mundt had suddenly become much more interesting.

I hurried to the Magic Library and fired up the laptop to search for details. The Magic Library, as I called it, was where I did much of my writing. When we looked at the 1940s limestone house in Louisville's Highlands neighborhood, the large room behind a hidden door next to the living room fireplace had cinched the deal. We decided against the huge Richard Robinson house on Fourth Street and moved in. I lined the shelves with books, strung brightly colored lights from the ceiling, and in came my favorite travel souvenirs and beat-up antiques to create a secret escape.

A number of reports floated around, but the one that looked the most complete came from NBC Chicago, which reported that police had arrested thirty-eight-year-old Jeffrey Mundt and thirty-eight-year-old Joseph Banis at the Hyatt Regency when Mundt allegedly approached the doorman and attempted to break a phony one-hundred-dollar bill.

When the police arrived, they discovered that Banis had a weapon. Upon searching their room, police found more firearms, fake IDs, counterfeit money, and a glass container with "clear liquid" believed to be GHB, also known as a "date rape" drug.

The Cook County State Attorney's Office took the case. They charged Mundt with theft and possession of a fictitious or altered ID card. They charged Banis with aggravated unlawful use of a weapon, possession of a fake identification card, misdemeanor theft, possession of a controlled substance, possession of drug paraphernalia, and possession of a weapon without a Firearm Owner's Identification Card. Both were arraigned in Cook County Criminal Court, the judge setting

Mundt's bond at fifty thousand dollars and Banis's at two hundred thousand. Police reported they had no idea what the couple planned to do with the weapons, cash, drugs, or fake IDs. The higher limit for Banis must have been due to his previous run-ins with the law—and because he told police the bogus bills belonged to him.

After reading through several more reports I checked out a couple of online true-crime forums to see what people thought about the case. "Dakota" moderated one known as "Dreamin' Demon" and her avatar depicted a stereotypical white-headed granny, middle finger extended, who identified herself as "FORUM BITCH/Beloved Cunt." The thread, entitled "Joseph Banis was pissed at boyfriend, Spills beans about body in basement," had interesting comments in the days right after the story broke.

"TheMeaningOfItAll" said, "Mundt has 'crazy eyes,' but Banis is the one that I'd be afraid to be stuck in a dark alley with. It will be interesting to see how this plays out. It wouldn't surprise me to find out Banis committed the murder (or at least had a huge role in it) and tried to pin it on Mundt as revenge. Glad to see they are both being charged with murder. These guys make me sick."

"Kufismacka" said, "damn gangster gay dudes . . . doesn't get any more dangerous."

"I'd say hell hath no fury like a woman scorned . . . but there is no woman in this one," was the response from "Ninja0980."

"Misskittychaos" wanted to know: "Is it just me or does it look like the guy on the left used a marker to draw on all the hair on his face?"

"It looks like he has a matchbook striker strip glued there," said "FORUM BITCH/Beloved Cunt."

"This is going badly" rounded out that day's comments by saying "Well . . . he might be what we used to call a 'fussy queen' back before the world went all PC . . . but, seriously, I don't think revenge is gender specific. Wondering if the fucktard was high? I think he must have been to implicate himself just to get the BF in trouble. Can't wait to see what a defense attorney will do to 'spin' this confession . . . if my BF and I had ever 'accidentally' killed someone I sure as shit would have kept my mouth shut."

I sure as heck would have kept my mouth shut, too. But why on earth had Joey revealed the dirty secret in the basement to the police?

What did he have to gain? Was he so drug-addled that he didn't realize the implications of what he was doing? Were they both equally at fault, or was one more culpable than the other? Could Jeffrey Mundt have been the mastermind? Or had Joseph Banis, thinking he had nothing to lose, done it as an act of revenge? Even still, he had lots to lose. Was he so intent on destroying his lover that none of this mattered?

Joseph Banis and Jeffrey Mundt piqued my interest more and more.

After checking out several more chat rooms, I pulled up my emails and started reading. They came mostly from my summer students, with lame excuses for why they couldn't turn in their final papers on time, but one of the subject lines caught my attention. From someone identifying him or herself as "Hillbilly Hippy," it read: "I knew Jamie Carroll." When I opened it, I found no message—just a telephone number with an area code from the eastern part of the state. I grabbed my cellphone.

After the second ring, a female voice answered, without a greeting. "Wondered when you'd get around to calling."

"Hillbilly Hippy?"

"Yes, that's me. But you can just call me Mary." A bark of a laugh came from the other end. "I was in a chat room and saw that you were snooping around about Jamie."

"Yeah, trying to find out a little more. Did you know him?"

"Pretty well. From back home and he used to do my hair when I was in Lexington."

"Were you surprised when you found out he had been murdered?"

From the other end came a long sigh. Or maybe it was the lengthy exhalation of cigarette smoke. "Can't say that I was. Jamie was always getting into trouble. He was a sweet kid but problems seemed to dog him."

"What kinds? Drugs?"

"Yeah, mostly. I thought he had straightened out for a bit, but then he started selling and getting mixed up with the wrong crowd." Another pause, a definite exhalation, and this time I envisioned clouds of cigarette haze encircling a wizened flower child with long braids streaked with silver. "And this time he really got messed up with the wrong people," she said with a note of disgust. "I can't believe what those SOBs did to him, leaving him in that basement for all those months. That cold dark room. Bastards."

I murmured something sympathetic, while Mary fired up another cigarette.

"He was hoping to get a new start, maybe in Old Louisville. He loved all those old houses there. He really wanted to live in one of those big Victorian mansions on St. James Court." She coughed softly. "Poor Jamie. He didn't have it smooth. Growing up gay with all those hicks in the hills. Couldn't have been too easy. And then his family. Kind of fucked up. Lots of violence."

For the next minute or two, Mary painted a picture of the bleak childhood and turbulent adolescence that had shaped Jamie Carroll. Intolerance in the community and financial troubles and hardship at home. Domestic violence. Beatings and family members shooting each other. Substance abuse and addiction. Though he had had his issues, it reminded me that Jamie was the innocent victim in this case. Nobody deserved to die the way he had, and his murder had obviously impacted many people.

"And then when he started wearing dresses, that just made things all the harder," Mary said.

"Wait. What?"

"He started being a woman, you know. A female impersonator. Performing on stage and doing lip-sync."

I sat up straighter. "Jamie Carroll was a drag queen? Seriously?"

"Oh, yeah. He won Miss Gay Pride West Virginia just a couple of years ago."

"No way."

"Yes, way. Ronica Reed the Pageant Queen," said Mary. "Hey, listen, I need to run and get to work. Call me back some time and I'll tell you more. Whatever you hear, Jamie was a sweet kid. He had so much talent."

I thanked her and hung up. In my head, gears started to turn, slowly at first, and things came into focus. Joseph Banis. Jeffrey Mundt. James Carroll. Then the wheels began to pick up speed, whirr. Joey, Jeff, Jamie. Drag Queens. Lovers' triangle. Revenge. Body in the basement. Spooky old mansion. Drugs. Kinky sex. Counterfeit money.

Suddenly, my breath caught and I let out a tiny breath.

You couldn't make this stuff up.

# 7

## THE CITY THAT'S NOT TOO BUSY

A WEEK later, I found myself at the Judicial Center, standing over a large cardboard box full of files. I had already come once before, but the lady behind the counter hadn't been able to locate the records that day and suggested I call to find a good time to return. I had called and left various messages, but nobody returned my calls. Other departments didn't offer much help, either, when I contacted them. Law enforcement also didn't seem particularly interested in providing information. Finally, I decided to make another trip to the Judicial Center and try my luck. Fortunately, the files had reappeared.

Outside, a hot sun beat down. With me was my friend Carrie Sweet, who, upon learning I had decided to write the book after all, eagerly volunteered to be my girl Friday and research assistant. I had met the recent transplant from California through friends at a neighborhood get-together and she knew me through my books. She especially loved the ones documenting the reportedly true cases of hauntings and paranormal encounters in the area and we quickly bonded, united in our love for all things quirky or creepy. A freelance graphic designer, she had just purchased a large brick house on First Street, near the southern edge of the neighborhood, where Old Louisville petered out and the University of Louisville's sprawling Belknap campus began.

I handed her a file and then opened one of my own and we began poring through records from the night the police arrested Joey Banis and Jeffrey Mundt at 1435 South Fourth Street. The police reports indicated that when officers responded to the call from 1435 South Fourth Street the night of June 17, 2010, they had no inkling it dealt with anything more than a run-of-the-mill domestic violence report. It took them ten minutes to gain access to the sprawling residence, which they at first took to be "an apartment complex," and they circled it several times only to discover that real estate lock boxes made all the doors inaccessible. Through the dispatcher, who still had homeowner Jeffrey Mundt on the line, the patrolmen received permission to batter in a side entrance. They broke through and, guns drawn, made their way up the stairs into the murky interior of the house. A piercing alarm went off, and the police heard footfall on the elaborately carved staircase. Apparently attempting to flee the scene, Joseph Banis came running down, at which time they aimed their weapons at him and made him lie flat before handcuffing him and taking him into custody.

Once Jeffrey Mundt emerged from the locked bedroom, the officers, as protocol dictated, separated the two parties to get a clearer picture of what had transpired. In the process, one of them had alluded to "the body in the basement," which nobody took seriously at first. Only when the second man intimated he knew about the body as well did they start to wonder. There was conflicting evidence about which of the men had first actually brought this to the attention of the police. But, eventually, and at Joey's request, someone from homicide agreed to meet with him and hear his story. "I know where a body is and nobody even knows he's missing yet," said Banis. At first, however, they thought it was nothing more than a ploy to buy time and avoid going to jail.

Only after Banis provided a name—Jamie Carroll—did detectives start to call around. When authorities confirmed that a Jamie Carroll had indeed gone missing, Louisville police slowly came to the realization that the person in their custody actually knew something. Within a few hours they had secured a warrant and began digging in the basement, where they uncovered Jamie's body in the exact spot Banis had told them.

We sifted through several more documents and Carrie turned to me. "Did you find anything about what they were arguing about in the first place? I don't see anything about that."

"No," I said, shaking my head. "It's kind of weird. Just that they were responding to a case of suspected domestic violence." I riffled through several more reports, but nothing listed the cause of the argument. Just then my eye lit on several lines I had missed during the first read-through of the initial report drafted after the two officers first arrived on the scene. While searching the premises, police had encountered Ziploc baggies containing a viscous liquid in a refrigerator. When they asked Joey about the contents, they probably weren't expecting the answer he gave them.

"What?" Carrie had turned when she heard the catch in my breath and noticed the look on my face. "What did you find?" She leaned in to get a closer look. When I pointed out the paragraph in question, she began reading to herself, her lips moving ever so slightly. Suddenly, her eyes got wide and she drew back. "Ew." She looked at me in horror, but then she started to laugh.

"I know. Big ew." I chuckled as well.

Joey had informed the arresting officers that the baggies contained ejaculate collected while he and his boyfriend were apart so they could use it as a lubricant for their sexual encounters when they saw each other again.

"I bet that policeman dropped that baggie like a hot potato." Carried grabbed the report from me and returned it to its file. "And right as we were getting ready to go and have lunch. Ew."

"I'm getting the feeling there are probably going to be lots of 'ews' the more we find out about the personal life of those involved. God, I'd be mortified if people found out about my private life." We returned the cardboard box containing the files to the man who had signed them out to us and headed outside. "Maybe if we take the long way we can work up our appetites again before we get to the restaurant."

Ten minutes later we strolled along one of the blocks of towering storefronts that stretched shoulder-to-shoulder from First to Ninth Streets on Main. Most of them dated from the 1830s to the 1890s. Some of them would have comprised the Louisville that Charles Dickens encountered during his second trip to the United States in 1842. While traveling through North America, Dickens recorded his impressions in the book *American Notes*. After fans mobbed the twenty-nine-year-old superstar in Boston, he arrived in Louisville by steamboat, finding what he described as a well-laid-out city bursting at the seams, if not full of activity and commerce.

"Some unfinished buildings and improvements seem to intimate that the city had been overbuilt in the ardor of going ahead," he wrote. "The buildings are smoky and blackened from the use of coal." He stayed at the original Galt House Hotel, at Second and Main, which he described as "a splendid hotel," where he was "as handsomely lodged as though we had been in Paris rather than hundreds of miles beyond the Alleghanies." However, his stay lasted only a couple of days because the city itself presented "no objects of sufficient interest to detain" him.

Though the sleepy river town and its lackadaisical magistrates failed to impress Dickens, he did leave with one fond memory: "Here, as elsewhere in these parts, the road was perfectly alive with pigs of all ages; lying about in every direction, fast asleep, or grunting along in quest of hidden dainties."

More than a century and a half later, and despite considerable growth, Louisville would retain its unhurried air, something that would prompt visiting journalist Dan Hulbert of the *Chicago Tribune* to dub it "the City That's Not Too Busy."

Directly overhead, the blazing sun signaled that summer had arrived in the Derby City. On the sidewalk, a slow-moving figure— or figures—approached from the opposite direction, and Carrie laid a hand on my arm, her pace halting. "Am I seeing what I think I'm seeing?" A man in jeans and a red flannel shirt shuffled along, accompanied by a large knobby lump with clawed prehistoric-looking appendages struggling to make purchase with the pavement. A head with eyes like black marbles bobbed at the end of a wobbly neck. "Is that guy walking a *tortoise?*"

I laughed. "Yes, that's Spike. He's kind of the mascot at Wayside Christian Mission. They take him out for walks all the time, but you usually see him in the NuLu part of town." We stepped aside to let the animal and his handler creep by. "Last I heard, he weighs more than a hundred pounds."

We watched the unlikely duo continue to the end of the next block. The light in the crosswalk had turned red, so Spike's friend reached down to restrain him but as soon as the signal went green again they continued their journey.

On the next block, a tall thin man with white hair and a neatly trimmed beard stood amid a cluster of people. He had said something and the crowd was laughing.

"Who's that?" said Carrie.

"That's Tom Owen, a professor and a former minister who's in charge of the photographic archives at the University of Louisville," I said. "He's the pied piper of Louisville and he's famous for his walking tours. He also served on the city council and ran for mayor."

Mr. Owen shepherded the group to the next building and took something out of his pocket. "Watch this," he said, approaching the storefront, where he tossed a refrigerator magnet against what appeared to be a stone façade. It stuck. In the audience, a few people chuckled.

"Whatever is that?" asked one of the tourgoers with a German accent.

Laughing, Owen rapped his knuckles on the surface and a metallic "donk" echoed. "Cast iron." He rapped once again to produce another hollow sound. "Louisville teemed with forges and foundries, and this stuff was quick and cheap to produce for all the merchants who wanted to get in on the trade roaring up and down this, the busiest street in town."

Carrie and I walked past the group and Tom waved a greeting. "That's a cool trick with the magnet," she said. "I knew Louisville had one of the largest collections of cast-iron façades in the country, but I never thought of testing it out that way."

Chitchatting, we continued west toward the overpass at Ninth Street, passing the huge golden David statue in front of 21c Hotel and the gigantic baseball bat propped up against the side of the Louisville Slugger Museum. "Hey, have you ever seen the marker under the overpass?" I pointed straight ahead. Carrie shook her head and gave a quizzical look.

Traffic buzzing by overhead, we stopped in front of a large plaque. Black-and-white photographs encircled in brass frames showed two women in Victorian dresses identified as Mildred Jane Hill and Patty Smith Hill. Golden letters spelled out "HAPPY BIRTHDAY TO YOU."

I pointed at the marker. "Did you know that Louisville is known as Happy Birthday City?"

"Really?" Carrie wrinkled her forehead and began reading.

In 1893 sisters Mildred and Patty Hill published a book titled *Song Stories for the Kindergarten*. During a birthday party, Patty suggested that they change the words of the first song in the collection, "Good Morning to All," to "Happy Birthday to You." And that version of the tune went on to become one of the most popular songs in the English language. For years, the song had enjoyed copyright protection but that had recently ended when a judge ruled that the copyright claim was absurd. The plaque on the small concrete pedestal commemorated the spot where the teachers' school had once stood.

"Oh, wow," said Carrie. "This city's just full of surprises, isn't it?"

"I was here five years before I found that out," I said. "I was walking around one day when I stumbled across the marker here."

We turned and started walking down Ninth Street, where the square towers of the old train station loomed over Broadway. In its heyday, 120 trains had left the station every twenty-four hours, but the last passenger car departed in 1976, a sad reminder of the increasing dependence on automobiles in this nation. Fortunately, however, the grand building escaped the fate met by so many downtown architectural treasures in the '60s and '70s, and the wrecking ball spared it. Not too long thereafter it became the Transit Authority of River City. Now the busses could call one of the most impressive nineteenth-century buildings in the city home.

Constructed in 1891, the limestone colossus sported all the rusticated masonry and heavy rounded arches so typical of the once-popular Richardsonian Romanesque style. A huge circular stained-glass window looked down over Broadway as did an imposing dormered clock tower. Inside, patterned tile floors and Georgia marble walls gleamed. Above wrought iron balconies a massive skylight with almost a hundred panels of colored glass sifted rays of hot summer sunshine into bright speckles that danced on original oak benches.

On one side of the atrium, I pointed to a pair of swinging doors. "Here, take a look at this." I positioned Carrie at an angle so that the glow of the sun highlighted the vague outline of something stenciled years before on the glass of the transom overhead. "Can you read what it says? They removed it, but its ghost image is still there, just barely, if you study it."

Carrie tilted her head, stood back, and then gasped softly.

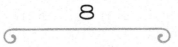

# 8

# FREEDOM RIDERS

THE FAINT shadows of old block letters identified the adjacent area as the COLORED WAITING ROOM. "Oh my god," she said. "Sometimes I forget that Louisville was segregated."

"Some say we're still segregated today."

"Yeah, I had heard that." She frowned.

"Louisville often ranks among the country's five most segregated cities and its history of blatant redlining is no secret. You can look at old city redlining maps, and the racism is obvious." City planners, real estate agents, and loan officers had ensured that Louisville would stay racially segregated for years to come—something borne out by modern-day trends in race, poverty, income, and vacant or abandoned properties.

Carrie and I found ourselves right at the edge of one of these redlined districts. The majestic and imposing train station that once served as the gateway for rail travel to the South also stood as a kind of gateway at the edge of the infamous "Ninth Street Divide," where it straddled the supposed invisible line that separated Black Louisville to the west from white Louisville to the east. In the Derby City, some people knew the "West End" as the literal "other side of the tracks."

Free Blacks started buying property west of Ninth Street in the 1830s, and by the 1940s West Louisville had an array of distinctive neighborhoods, including Russell, Parkland, Shawnee, Park Duvalle, Portland, California, Chickasaw, and Algonquin. Home to numerous prominent citizens of color in the late nineteenth century, it saw

Dr. Sarah Fitzbutler become the first Black woman to receive a medical degree in Kentucky, and her husband, Henry Fitzbutler, would gain fame as Louisville's first Black physician. In 1908, the Western Branch of the Louisville Free Public Library opened its doors as the nation's first public library servicing the Black community. Muhammad Ali, one of Louisville's most famous residents ever, would grow up in a small house on Grand Avenue.

In the West End, however, Black people lived alongside Jewish, German, and Irish immigrants and competed for jobs. The area between West Market Street and Broadway, effectively the northern and southern boundaries of the city center, down some twenty blocks from Ninth, teemed with Black-owned nightclubs, theaters, grocery stores, newspapers, and insurance agencies. Russell earned fame as "Little Harlem" because of the abundance of thriving Black businesses and entertainment venues. After World War II, however, white middle-class families began leaving.

Louisville writer and longtime state representative Jim Wayne assigned a great deal of the blame for this on white Catholics. "This sad history is found in segregated cities across the country where white Catholics settled. Had Catholics residing west of Ninth Street taken the lead in teaching the Gospel importance of the oneness of all people, Louisville today might not be one of the most segregated cities in America," said Wayne, the co-founder of Community Catholic Center serving that area. "Like the Jesuits at Georgetown University, our Kentucky religious sisters owned slaves. White Catholics owned slaves."

By the mid-1950s, the neighborhoods west of Ninth Street counted on larger populations of Catholics than many American dioceses. Some six thousand students attended twenty-one Catholic schools spread out over seventeen parishes, where there was a Catholic hospital, a Catholic home for the aged, and a home for troubled girls. But there was only a single Black parish, a single Black grade school, and a single Black high school. The rest of the parishes and schools excluded Blacks.

"Racial fear swept white neighborhoods in the late 1950s," wrote Wayne in the *Courier-Journal*, relying on information from Father Clyde Crews at Bellarmine University. "As a Black family 'broke' a block, white homeowners, including Catholics, panicked, put 'For Sale' signs in their yards, and fled East and South." Soon, once all-white working- and middle-class neighborhoods experienced drastic changes. "You can see it in the First Communion pictures of Catholic grade schools. The 1950s photos show no Black kids," explained Wayne. "By 1961 there's a sprinkling of dark faces among the white dresses, veils and shirts. By the mid '60s classes had shrunk, with a few white and African-American children." They would close all twenty-one parochial schools west of Ninth and only six struggling parishes would remain.

By the 1960s, bulldozers had started to demolish blocks of businesses to make way for public housing units. City leaders supported a widened and expanded Ninth Street, which became an expressway meant to facilitate the movement of motor traffic, but in the process, they also separated Louisville into two very distinct parts.

Even though many residents decried the Ninth Street Divide as a "fallacy," it remained a painful fact that the West End stood apart from the rest of the city in more ways than one. University of Louisville researchers, for example, found the life expectancy on the west side of Ninth Street was sixty-seven years, compared to eighty-two years for their neighbors to the east.

"Take a look at this." I steered Carrie toward an old trolley car, a remnant of the years after the Civil War, when mules provided the source of power for the city's once-extensive tram system. Painted in golden yellow with red trim and black stenciling, car 102 stood there, its immobility another sad reminder of the country's eschewal of public transit. On its side, painted letters identified it as a part of the Central Passenger Railway, the line owned by wealthy brothers Alfred Victor and Antoine Bidermann DuPont. They had once occupied a mansion that stood at the center of today's Central Park in Old Louisville. "This is one area where segregation failed."

On October 30, 1870, three Black men left the Quinn Chapel and boarded the trolley at Tenth and Walnut. John Russell, a white passenger, complained and the driver demanded the trio leave the near-empty car. But outside, a crowd of some three hundred Black men and women stood silently in front of the church, staring at the streetcar. Louisville's Black community had prearranged this action.

When one of the men, Robert Fox, an elderly mortician, quietly replied that he and his companions—his brother, Samuel, and their associate Horace Pearce—enjoyed the same right to ride as whites, the driver sent word to the main office. Soon, cars started backing up and nearby trolley drivers offered their assistance. Before long, a mob dragged the men into the street.

Author Maria Fleming wrote that the onlookers hurled stones and chunks of hardened clay. In the midst of the chaos, Pearce and the Fox brothers climbed back into the car, where they remained calm. When the superintendent of the Central Passenger Railroad Company offered to refund their fares if they disembarked, the men declined.

According to newspaper accounts, the crowd began chanting its encouragement. "Don't budge a step!" they shouted. "We'll pay your fines!" When police hauled them off to jail for "disorderly conduct," jubilant cheers followed.

The next day, the three men stood before the judge, defended by a prominent white lawyer. The judge fined the men five dollars. Backed by local leaders, Robert Fox sued the streetcar company—though he had to file his suit in the U.S. district court in Louisville because the state courts did not accept Black testimony. The Black community boycotted Louisville trams pending the decision.

The court's verdict came down on May 11, 1871, on the side of Fox, and though he received only token compensation—fifteen dollars—it represented an enormous victory. Emboldened, Black Louisvillians immediately began to assert their rights, but they knew they had an uphill battle.

The day of the ruling, a Black man entered a car on Jefferson Street and ignored the driver's demands to disembark. The operator derailed the trolley, and the two men sat in silence for half an hour. The Black demonstrator finally stepped down and disappeared into an anxious throng of onlookers, setting the precedence for many "ride-ins" to follow.

Editors of Louisville's local newspapers chastised the protesters and officials who refused to enforce the court's ruling now suggested separate cars for Black riders. The Black community rejected the proposal.

Sometimes employees and white passengers forcibly ejected the Black demonstrators. Often, drivers derailed the cars, which congested the streets and wreaked havoc. On several occasions, Black riders took the driver's seat after the operator and white passengers had fled. Crowds of cheering supporters roared when grinning protesters coasted by, leisurely smoking cigars with their feet kicked up on the plush seats.

The protests reached a climax on the evening of Friday, May 12, a day on which every tramcar line in the city experienced ride-ins. A furious mob assembled in front of the Willard Hotel, where a Black youth named Carey Duncan sat passively as whites swarmed around the streetcar. Chanting "Hang him!" they rocked the car back and forth but the teen hung on for dear life.

When white thugs stormed the car, Duncan just stared straight ahead. As they pulled the boy from the car and began beating him, Louisville's chief of police stood idly by.

When Duncan began to fight back, several patrolmen stepped in. They arrested Duncan for disorderly conduct, though the attackers went free. When rumors circulated that federal troops would come to restore order, Louisville's mayor and police chief arranged for negotiations.

The Black leaders refused to back down and the company owners finally gave in to the protesters' demands. Louisville's citizens of color would ride city streetcars restriction-free.

White Louisvillians tried over and over again to resegregate the trolleys, but citizens of color maintained their right to ride. Only in the Derby City did Blacks remain successful in keeping Jim Crow off city streetcars.

Carrie and I exited through a bank of doors topped with brass plaques and embossed black letters leading out "To The Trains" and returned to Broadway. We walked the several blocks to the Brown Hotel, the establishment that in 1961 denied admittance to two-time Kentucky Derby winning jockey James Winkfield—because of the color of his skin. And where a young Victor Mature had operated the elevator, until being fired one night for leaving his post for a quick dance with a young lady during one of the hotel's famous rooftop parties.

"Maybe my friend Kelly is working at the Brown today," I said. "You'll like him. We used to work together at the Seelbach. He's a hoot."

As we took the stairs to the second-floor lobby, my phone pinged and I saw an email with a disturbing subject line. I slowed and when Carrie noticed me trailing behind she gave a quizzical look. I slowly walked the couple steps up to her and held the phone out so she could see: "Jamie Carroll got what he deserved."

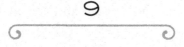

# 9

# THE PIE WHOSE NAME
# WE DARE NOT SPEAK

AN HOUR later, Carrie and I sat at a lobby table near the bar, look-ing down at empty ceramic skillets that ten minutes before had held thick slices of bread mounded with turkey breast and mornay sauce broiled with bacon, cheddar cheese, and tomatoes. We had ordered hot browns, the hotel's signature open-faced sandwich invented by Chef Fred Schmidt in 1926. "That was so good." Carrie wiped her mouth. "Could you imagine what we'd look like if we ate one of those every day?"

I put down my napkin, looked up at the elegant archways that framed the lobby, and let out a contended sigh. "It's definitely a special-occasion food." Overhead, coffered ceilings trimmed in accents of green and gold leaf soared. "Does that mean you're not up for dessert?"

"Oh, my goodness, no." Carrie pushed her plate away and took a sip of wine. "There's no way I could eat another bite."

"Not even if we share a piece of"—I dramatically looked over both shoulders and lowered my voice—"the Pie Whose Name We Dare Not Speak?"

"What kind of pie is that?"

"You know," I said, "*Derby* Pie."

"Ah, I see." Carrie giggled. "I think I'll pass."

What most people commonly referred to as "derby pie" consisted of a sweet and gooey filling enriched with bourbon and chocolate chips baked in a pastry crust—in essence a glorified pecan pie—and although many in the region used the designation in generic terms, one family did not. The Kerns.

Family members insisted Grandma Kern created the original version of derby pie for their restaurant, the Melrose Inn, in 1950, baking three pies at a time and leaving them to cool on the window-sill. It quickly emerged as the eatery's signature item, and when the restaurant closed in 1960, the Kerns kept the pie business. Not long after, Kern's Kitchen filed a registered trademark for "Derby-Pie" and they grew to make over eight hundred pies a day. The company went to great lengths to protect its technique, closing off the mixing area in the kitchen with a curtain so the production manager could make the secret filling unobserved. Ironically, their recipe forwent the bourbon and called for walnuts instead of pecans.

On NPR, Nina Feldman had just aired a story about the legend-ary dessert—and the legendary legal battles that it had engendered. In 1986, Kern's sued *Bon Appétit* for sharing a derby pie recipe in their magazine and a cookbook. The judge sided with the magazine, but Kern's appealed, and in the end the magazine settled rather than risk negative publicity from a drawn-out court battle.

In 1997, the company sued again: this time, Rick Paul, the cantan-kerous chef proprietor of the quirky White Light Diner in the state capital, Frankfort. When Kern's first demanded he stop selling a product named derby pie, he took it tongue in cheek and posted a sign that read: *Have a piece of 'I Can't Call It Derby Pie' pie.* Kern's sued Paul again in 2007, and at the time of the NPR story, he still hadn't paid off the fourteen thousand dollars in attorney's fees.

Now, when diners asked for a slice of derby pie, he always corrected them by saying, "I only make 'Kentucky bourbon pie.' I don't make a pie called derby pie."

And Kern's never let up. Throughout the region, employees serving anything resembling the official "Derby-Pie®" at restaurants such as the venerable Science Hill Inn in Shelbyville could share stories about obvious plants who had come in to catch unsuspecting servers in a slip-up and surreptitious phone calls enquiring "exactly what kind of chocolate nut pies" they had on the menu. More than one restaurant had received official cease-and-desist letters and threats from lawyers for the bakery.

The Brown Hotel, however, had the real deal on the menu, and the longer I sat, the more insistent my sweet tooth became. "Come on," I said. "Let's share a piece."

Carrie opened her mouth to decline, but then she stopped when a server walked by with a piece of the selfsame pie on a plate with dollops of whipped cream. "Well, I guess I could manage a bite or two."

I placed the order and pulled out my phone to see if I had a response to the email I had sent back to the person claiming that Jamie had gotten "what he deserved." There was no reply; instead my email had bounced back as "undeliverable."

"Did they write back yet?" asked Carrie.

"No, the message bounced back. Something wrong with the email address." I took a sip of coffee the waitress had just delivered and studied the message again. "I bet they just created the account to send the email and then deleted it after they sent it."

"That's so bizarre." Carrie leaned in so she could better see the message on the screen:

If youre writing a book about that little bitch, just make sure you don't make him out to be the victim. That bitch pulled a gun on me once and I saw him steal other peoples money on more than one occasion. Bitch fucked up my hair the last time I went and had it did and he still made me pay for it. Always cheated me on the meth too. Bitch. Glad the nasty ass bitch is gone. Have a nice day.

"Well, at least they told me to have a nice day." I moved aside my cup and saucer so the server could deposit the plate in the middle of the table. "Dig in, Carrie. Ladies first."

"Yes, I guess there is that." She popped a forkful of pie into her mouth. "But it's just so random."

"Not to mention bitter." I sheared off a piece of the dessert and scooped up some whipped cream. "I wonder how many other people out there felt the same way about Jamie."

"Maybe we'll find out tomorrow," said Carrie. "Hopefully, we can talk to some people who knew him." We had planned a road trip to the eastern part of the state the following day, to the places where Jamie had grown up and gone to school. And we intended to visit his gravesite as well.

"Well, so far, the handful of people I've come into contact with have been very reticent to talk about their connections to Jamie. We'll see. The only ones who had anything kind to say about him were the people who remembered him on stage as Ronica Reed. Ronica Reed the Pageant Queen."

"Oh my, don't turn around just yet"—Carrie stifled a chuckle with a hand to her mouth—"but in a few more seconds turn around and see who just came up the steps."

Perplexed, I waited the prescribed amount of time and then casually gazed over my shoulder. At the top of the stairs stood John Tan, the eponymous John of Little John's Pawn Shop, in a neat beige suit and bright tie. Hair slicked back, he strode to a nearby table and greeted someone who had been expecting him.

"He looks exactly like he does in those commercials," said Carrie.

"I'm kind of disappointed he doesn't have those Village People knock-offs with him. That would have made my day. Or Super Gold Man. I'd love to see him in person." For the next minute or two we debated which was the best of the Little John's commercials.

I finished the last of my coffee and had set down the cup when Carrie looked up, a concerned look on her face. Just then I felt something poke into my back, and a voice thickly accented with German said, "You are under arrest. Please stand up and slowly turn around."

# IO

## ROAD TRIP

I TURNED and looked over my shoulder. Then I released a sigh of relief. A waiter stood behind me, a long white bistro apron shielding his legs, a large silver soup spoon held out in one of this hands. "Kelly Atkins," I said, "you almost had me there for a minute."

"Mein Kapitän! Mein Kapitän! Wie geht's?" He smiled broadly, his cheerful voice echoing off the marble columns.

"You're nuts, you know that?" I bunched up my napkin and threw it at him. He dodged and missed it, then ran to retrieve it from the tile floor. "Carrie, this is my friend Kelly. The one who works here."

"Ha, I gathered as much."

"So, how's tricks?" Kelly tossed the napkin on the table and turned to Carrie. Grabbing her hand, he raised it to his lips and kissed. "Nice to meet you."

"Same here." Carrie laughed softly and smiled. "My, aren't you a courtly gentleman."

He released her hand and then raised his hand to the side of his mouth and twiddled his fingers. "Chivalry is not dead. Chivalry is not dead." He said it in a fair impression of W. C. Fields. Half of the time he spoke to me, Kelly Atkins imitated W. C. Fields.

"So, how are things at the Brown Hotel?" I said. "Enjoying the new job?"

"Got one of the most beautiful workplaces in town." He gestured at the towering coffered ceilings and the elegant double arcade framing the space. "So, what's up with you, chief?"

"Not much," I said. "We were just taking a break from the police records at the Judicial Center."

Kelly's eyes lit up. "Aw, man, I've got some stories about those two guys for you. My coworkers waited on the geeky one not too long before they found the body in the basement and they said he was an odd duck. Kept talking about rubber all night. And a bit condescending."

"Yeah, that doesn't surprise me. The condescending part, I mean. Never heard anything about rubber."

"And remember Andy, the one I used to wait on at the Seelbach, the guy who always came in with a one-legged whore? He followed me here and he knew the doctor's son, met him at their house or something, and said he's some kind of clean freak nutjob germophobe who's been causing the whole damn family grief since dangnabbit. You remember Andy, don't you? Remember the time his hooker escort got up to go to the bathroom but her prosthetic leg came undone and she tipped over and fell onto the floor?"

Carrie stifled a laugh and raised her eyebrows at me.

I did remember Andy, a regular of Kelly's when we waited tables together at the Oakroom, and I did recall the aforementioned incident, although I hadn't witnessed it myself.

"And that house on Fourth Street where those brokedick mother-fuckers lived! You know, I've been down in that basement." He turned maniacally and looked to Carrie and then back at me. "Remember that exorcism I told you about? That was down in that basement."

"Seriously?" A tone of skepticism edged my voice.

Carrie shot me a surprised look as a slight smile formed on her face. "A real exorcism in Old Louisville? No way."

"Yes, way. And they got some weird neighbors over there, too. Especially the cusswad flibbertigibbet who lives in the apartment building next door. They call him Duncan. Don't know if it's his first name or his last name, but he's a real asshole. Always looks like death wearin' a pantsuit." He paused and shook his head. "That whole block is full of hotheads and shitwads. Then there's that dickwad Christopher White who's just a general neighborhood asswipe."

"Hey, Atkins!" A male face looked down from one of the arches above. "Get a move on."

Kelly glanced at his watch. "Aw, shit and Shinola. Gotta go. I'll tell you more later. We're catering an event and Muhammad Ali is supposed to be there." He turned to leave. "The Louisville Lip loves his Derby Pie," he called over his shoulder as he made for the stairwell, where he disappeared.

"Wow, he's got some energy, doesn't he?" Amazed, Carrie stared at the empty stairwell as if she expected Kelly to bound back up and start up with a new line of chatter. Then she slowly shook her head and returned her attention to me. "Was he really involved in an exorcism here?"

I scrunched up my face before answering. "Maybe he was, but K.J. Atkins has—shall we say—a very active imagination."

"So you think he's making it up?"

"Not necessarily making it up, but I'm sure whatever it is, it is highly embellished. Kelly's a great storyteller."

Bright and early the next morning I picked Carrie up at her house. The sun cast horizontal shafts of light between the brick townhomes and stately limestone residences as we headed for the on-ramp that would take us to the eastern part of the state. On Oak Street two— presumably—trans sex workers in tight miniskirts and tube tops languidly strolled down the sidewalk. Nearby sat Mark Anthony Mulligan, fully clothed, on a bus stop bench. I tapped the horn twice as we passed. He smiled broadly and began waving furiously.

Carrie grinned and waved back. "I like him so much. I wonder what brings him down this way," she said. "He's usually in the Highlands but I've been seeing him downtown and in Old Louisville a lot recently."

"It might be one of the shelters down here. He gets around, though."

Soon, the Louisville skyline receded in the rearview mirror as the car coasted east. Nursing coffees from Day's on Bardstown Road, we sat in companionable silence for several minutes as the suburbs gave way to large copses of sunny green maple and elm trees and rolling pastures dotted with horses.

"So, do you think you'll hear from Joey or Jeffrey?" Carrie pushed back a strand of hair.

"Who knows? It's been a month since I wrote to them, and nothing yet." I fiddled with the screen on the dashboard and pulled up the Facebook message I had sent Joey. Carrie read the main paragraph.

> I met you very briefly at the bar downtown several years back. I'm a writer who specializes in the stories and histories of Old Louisville. I wanted to let you know I'm writing a book about the house you used to live in, and about the unfortunate case that is now playing out. I realize this must be a difficult period for you, but if at any time you would be interested in sharing your side of the issue, I would love to hear from you. I'd like to present this story as fairly and accurately as possible for all parties involved, but I fully understand if you'd rather not be in contact with me.

"Well, you were certainly diplomatic about it," she said. After watching the green countryside whiz by for several minutes, Carrie took out her phone. "Let's see if I can find anything new out there about Jamie or the guys. Things are always popping up." She began scrolling and then began nodding her head.

"Did you find something?"

"Yes, a new thread on his obituary page. There are many more comments today." Suddenly, her smile turned into a slight frown. "Listen to this woman," she said. "'James didn't just have ties to Floyd County, he grew up here, just outside of Martin. Went to school, church, played with us, laughed with us, etc. He graduated from Allen Central High School in '90.'" Carrie stopped and looked at me. "Geesh. He graduated high school the same year I did." Then she continued reading. "'He was a good person and friend and I am so heartbroken that his life has ended in such a tragic and violent way. I am sure he didn't deserve that. He was a victim. Please pray for his family while they deal with the shocking details of his murder.'"

"Funny you should find that all right as we're driving to see the places she's referring to."

"Well, it makes me feel better to know that there were people who genuinely cared about Jamie, especially after that crazy message you got yesterday." Bobbed black hair gleaming in a shaft of sunlight, Carrie gazed intently at the screen of her phone.

"Hey, have you checked Joey's Facebook page lately? Maybe there's something new there."

Carrie started scrolling and shook her head. "No, just the few things posted in the week after the body was found in the basement. On the twentieth, someone name Brian just wrote 'sick fuck' on his wall. And on the twenty-fourth, Kevin Asher wrote 'What a pathetic waste of a life.' And then on the twenty-eighth, a guy named Aaron says, 'Heard any good jokes lately?' That's wacko."

"Yeah, I saw those," I said. "I wonder if Joey has access to his Facebook account from the jail."

Carrie suddenly looked up from the screen and fixed me with a deadpan stare. "Oh, come on. You're not going to believe this."

"What?"

"Joey's Facebook says he most recently listened to New Order's 'Bizarre Love Triangle' on Spotify. I mean, really? It's too good. *'Bizarre Love Triangle'*?"

"Seriously? Maybe someone hacked his account. Or maybe he gave someone his passwords."

"Could be, but get this: that song is part of a playlist that was just made. The other songs are 'Die in Your Arms' by Justin Bieber and a song called 'Raise Your Weapon.' It would be too much to think he's sitting in jail listening to this stuff on the computer. Something is going on."

"Yeah, that's too coincidental."

"It also seems very incriminating. Maybe Mundt made it. Maybe he's trying to set Joey up. It wouldn't be surprising. Carrie took a sip from her mocha and gazed pensively out the window.

At that point, we were about an hour into the trip, and neatly manicured horse farms and old stone walls sailed by as my phone pinged. In an enigmatic text, the individual at the other end asked if I had some time to chat in person. At that moment.

I texted a quick reply in the affirmative before addressing Carrie. "This could be interesting," I said. "Maybe it has something to do with the murder." Less than a minute later, the person was calling, and I put it on speaker phone after answering.

"Thanks for taking my call," said a pleasant female voice. "My name is Ronica Reed."

My forehead wrinkled in confusion. "Excuse me. What did you say your name was?" I looked over and saw that Carrie wore the same expression.

"Ronica Reed."

I pinched the bridge of my nose with the fingers of my free hand and groaned inaudibly. "Probably another nutjob, or somebody pulling a prank." I mouthed the words to Carrie. Or somebody looking for attention.

I sighed. "Alright. What can I do for you?"

"I just found out that you're writing about the murder trials for Jeffrey Mundt and Joseph Banis," she said. "The Jamie Carroll murder?"

"Yes, that's right."

"Well, Jamie was a friend of mine. We're both from Martin, Kentucky. We went to the same high school."

Well, maybe she wasn't a nutjob, but that didn't explain the name. "You do know that Ronica Reed was Jamie Carroll's stage name when he was doing drag, right?"

"Oh, yes, I know that. He modeled his drag persona after me and took my name."

"You're kidding," I said. "So, your name is really Ronica Reed?"

"Yes, it is." A soft laugh came from the other end. "He spelled it differently sometimes, though."

"Seriously?"

"Seriously." She laughed again. "I know what you mean, though. I was surprised when I first found out he was using my name."

"You didn't know? Why did he take your name?" I slid my eyes sideways to Carrie. She had perked up but still had a look of disbelief on her face.

"Well, it was the late 1990s and Jamie was living in Huntington. I was living in Lexington and had gone back home for a family funeral," Ronica said. "There, I ran into a friend who told me Jamie had started doing drag, which didn't surprise me at all." What did surprise Ronica, however, was that Jamie had worked up a performance as "Ronica Reed, the Pageant Queen" and the whole show revolved around her, in her high school years, when the original Reed had won the Miss Kentucky Teen World Pageant.

I grunted softly. "And what did you think about that?"

"Actually, I was kind of flattered. Drag queens normally mimic famous people and I am far from famous."

"Well, you obviously made an impression on him," I said.

"I guess so. He must have liked what I wore because I later saw some pictures of him on stage and one really stood out. In it, Jamie had blond hair and a white beaded gown—just like the one I used to wear!"

Ronica Reed then went on to describe their high school years in a small town where "everybody knew everybody else." She was a freshman and looked up to Jamie, a senior. They loved watching drag shows. Although Jamie was openly gay, she couldn't recall him ever having been bullied or given a hard time for it. Instead, she remembered a confident and sweet young man who hung out with a popular group of people and had snappy comebacks.

"He was a very flashy dresser and often wore cowboy boots and tight jeans. He had the best walk of any man I knew." She had talked to Jamie most recently in 2002 and it was probably in 1997 that she had seen him last.

She had just found out about the discovery of Jamie's body in the basement. Stuck in Lexington traffic, she checked Facebook and saw that a friend had shared a link with the details about the grisly murder. "I was so shocked and I just started crying." Her voice turned heavy with emotion. "And right away I knew people would focus only on the gay thing. And that the drugs would take center stage, making everybody forget about Jamie the person. The sweet boy who had friends and family."

Ronica had sobbed for half an hour. "And the whole time, I couldn't get out of my mind that he must have been so afraid in that house. At some point, he realized what was going on. 'I'm not going to make it out of this house. I'm not going to make it out of this house.' That's what he must have been thinking the whole time."

A minute later, Ronica Reed announced she needed to return to work and she invited me to stay in touch before hanging up. Carrie and I sat in silence for the next quarter hour. Soon, we were entering the rolling foothills and lush green forests of eastern Kentucky.

\* \* \*

Jamie Carroll usually told people his home was Martin, a small town deep in the heart of coal country. With a population of well under a thousand, it had the air of so many small towns across the country, where downtowns struggled and few people strolled the streets. Every now and then, a disused building seemed to gape at us as we drove by, its vacant stare following the car until the next empty storefront could take over as sentry. Despite a number of dilapidated structures, the main drag had a new-looking fire department with a bright red roof and shiny new firetrucks parked in front. A brick school building looked clean and modern, as did the high school in nearby Allen City, where Jamie had graduated.

According to the funeral home that had handled arrangements, Jamie had been buried in Halbert Cemetery, in the unincorporated community of Printer, just south of Martin. When I asked for an exact address on the phone, the undertaker seemed somewhat taken aback that I didn't know where it was. "Oh, go over past the post office and it's up there on the hill behind the old Halbert Place," he had said. After a bit of snooping around online, I had come to the conclusion that Jamie's final resting spot had to be in what started off as family burial plot behind the ruins of the house where the Halberts used to live.

However, actually finding the grave site proved to be an impossible task. Printer appeared to consist of several neglected commercial properties and occasional clusters of houses that lined a two-lane road meandering through verdant hills. We located the post office, a small cinderblock building with a man repairing a motorcycle out front, and he pointed down the road and said we'd find the cemetery in about a half mile, on the right-hand side. But after a good deal of searching and lots of asking around, we still hadn't found it. The last man we asked informed us that we had come too far down the road and needed to head back the other direction. In the brief moment of small talk afforded us, I asked if he knew Jamie Carroll. "Oh, Jamie?" he said. "I went to high school with his brother."

Eventually, and by the process of elimination, we found what looked to be an overgrown pathway leading up the side of a low mountain. A small wooden house painted in white flanked one side and behind it stood a garage or outbuilding of some sort. On the other side stood another house, perhaps unoccupied. Beyond that, the rutted path seemed to end at an impenetrable curtain of green. I had pulled into the beginning of the path and Carrie and I sat in the car with the motor idling, gazing up into the forested hillside.

"That's got to be it up there." Carrie pointed and then lowered her head for a more expansive view through the windshield. "I wonder how far up it is."

"Should we try to find it?"

"I don't know."

The way she drew out her response reconfirmed what I already suspected. It probably wasn't a good idea to head into unchartered territory, especially one with so many snakes. "Watch out for rattlers when you go up there," more than one of the helpful locals had warned as we were asking for directions.

Not only that, the abundance of no-trespassing signs let us know much of the area consisted of private property. Louisville friends who hailed from this part of the state had given us advice before our road trip to the east: "Whatever you do, don't get out of your car and go knocking on people's doors. If you do, you're liable to get shot," they had said. "Wait out in the driveway in your car and honk the horn once. If they want to talk to you, they'll come to the front door."

And apparently nobody wanted to talk to us at this location. We had been sitting there for ten minutes, gently tapping the horn once every now and then, but nobody appeared. The same thing had happened at several other houses down the road, where the slight movement of curtains at one window suggested people had indeed been home.

"Yeah, probably a good idea not to brave the snakes," I said. "Hang on a sec." I got out of the car and opened the trunk. I took out the bouquet of yellow roses we had planned to leave at Jamie's grave and left it at the base of a towering chestnut oak that stood sentinel at the path.

"Well, at least we tried," said Carrie when I hopped back behind the wheel.

"Yeah, maybe we can come back some other time. Line up someone to help us."

"Yeah, we're definitely outsiders here. It seems like we've already aroused suspicions."

In our constant back-and-forth down the mountain road looking for the elusive entrance to old Halbert Cemetery, we had noticed more and more people peering through their front windows or standing at the ends of their driveways as we passed, as if a neighbor had called ahead to let them know strangers had arrived in their midst. The last time we had driven past the Martin City Hall, an incongruous metal outbuilding raised on stilts, the sheriff had been standing out front, arms resolutely crossed while his dark glasses followed us with an almost menacing glare.

"Well, I guess the trip hasn't been a total bust," I said. "At least we made it this far and know a little more about him." I started the car but we didn't move. Carrie and I stared out the windshield, up at the mountainside, at the thick blanket of green that covered Jamie Carroll.

On the way back to Louisville, I had a call from Frances Mengel. "Oh, darlin'! What are you doing this weekend? There's an event. Lucie and Louise are all set but I still need a date."

"Well—"

"And don't forget that you promised to attend the Fillies Ball with me. You know I was one of the founders of the Fillies back in 1958, don't you?"

"Yes, I remember."

"The Barnstables are hosting the bash this weekend. You know the Barnstables, don't you?" In Louisville, everybody knew identical twin sisters Patricia and Cyb Barnstable. The blond bombshells made a name for themselves in the 1970s as Wrigley Doublemint Twins and then on the short-lived sitcom *Quark*. Today they were famous for their philanthropy in general and their Derby Eve party in particular. Frances laughed but then cut herself short. "Your tux is clean, isn't it?"

"Well—"

"Oh, good. I'll pick you up Sunday afternoon."

I started to ask what time when she cut me off. "Say, I was talking to one of the girls in the Antiques Club and she knows Dr. Banis. They've already hired the hottest attorneys in town to defend their son.

Joey and Jeffrey are each blaming the other, though. This is going to be some trial, darlin'. They're calling it the trial of he-said/he-said."

"Any word on—"

"Gotta run. My rerun of *Lawrence Welk* is coming on. See you Sunday, half past five."

Laughing, Carrie shook her head as I ended the call. "That Frances is something else, isn't she?"

"Lord, I hope I've got that much going on when I'm in my eighties."

We made a detour and headed for Morehead, then south to Elliottville, where we navigated leafy backroads and gravel lanes in search of a secluded attraction Carrie and I had been wanting to visit for ages. After getting lost several times, we rolled to a stop in front of a green wooden sign edged with a red-and-white checked border that confirmed our arrival. In chalky handwriting it listed Bet Ison as "Executive Director" and Cecil R. Ison, F.A. as "Resident Forensic Anthropomorphologist" since 1987. A yellowing rubber doll's head had been affixed above their names and titles, and a dozen figurines and puppets of varying shapes and sizes had been nailed to the large wooden post supporting the sign. One of them, an infant with a cloth body and plastic limbs, seemed to glare at us, its pudgy face streaked with grime and mud.

"Welcome to the Home for Wayward Babydolls," I said to Carrie, maneuvering the car down a rutted lane. On a nearby fence, an assortment of plastic doll heads had been impaled on the wooden pickets, and below them, Virginia creeper ran rampant, tendrils reaching out to tickle the hem of a tattered white dress hanging from the body of a large armless doll. Empty black eye sockets stared out from a porcelain head.

Carrie looked around in wonder. "I can't believe this. We're finally here." Outside, she slowly turned and took in her surroundings. From the hollow trunk of a decaying tree, a cluster of kewpies followed us with their collective gaze as we made our way to a ramshackle cluster of buildings that included a two-story wooden house. On the other side of the lane, someone had strung a perfect row of tanned Barbies and Kens—all of them headless—along a length of barbed wire. In the grassy area on the other side, a crooked wooden sign with hand-lettering read: "Science goin' on."

A pair of snuffling hound dogs accompanied us past decaying dolls hanging from elm branches, strapped to rusty box springs, and mounted on the spokes of paint-flaked bicycle wheels. Framed by an artistic assortment of woven baskets, a life-sized female mannequin in patterned black capris and a floral-patterned blouse lounged on a porch swing, a hand raised in greeting. Leopard-print slippers and a flouncy straw hat rounded out her ensemble.

A screen door creaked open and on the front porch stood Cecil R. Ison and his wife, Bet, the owners—and inhabitants—of the Home for Wayward Babydolls. Cecil, in a green fishing vest and long-sleeved checkered shirt, polished a pair of wire-framed spectacles before putting them on. "Did you have a hard time finding us?"

"One or two wrong turns," I laughed, "but it wasn't too bad."

His wife, in jeans and a pink T-shirt, waved us up to join them. We had called ahead to schedule a tour and after a bit of small talk they showed us around.

We walked past a bright blue telephone booth with a flashing blue emergency light mounted on top. On either side of the device had been wedged two grungy plastic dolls.

As Bet and Carrie chatted amiably, Cecil told me more about being a forensic anthropomorphologist. "My official title is actually president of the International Assembly of Forensic Anthropomorphologists. Since 1987." He chuckled.

"And how did this all come about?"

"When I worked as an archaeologist at the Daniel Boone National Forest, I started noticing these discarded dolls in the woods," he said. "It made me curious about their past and how they'd met their demise." His first encounter occurred in 1984 when he discovered a baby doll with a tick pinned to its forehead. In an interview with reporter Pat McDonogh, Ison said, "Why would someone discard a baby doll and attach a tick to it? It piqued my interest on the affliction of trauma on these small objects of love."

Some had bullet holes in their heads or had been blasted with buckshot. Many of them, he noticed, appeared to be mutilated or defaced in strange ways. Ison began carrying the dolls back to his office.

At work one day, a law enforcement officer brought in two specimens for Cecil's inspection. "It was a Ken and Barbie, America's most famous couple, and the sheriff had found them at the end of a remote logging road, in the middle of nowhere. Simply discarded under a pine tree in the forest, both had been sexually molested," he said. "Ken had been burned and then someone pulled a condom over his body."

Carrie stopped and wrinkled her nose. "Who does something like that?"

"Yes, why would someone abuse them in such a heinous manner and then abandon them in the middle of the forest? I have no answer for that—yet," said Cecil.

Over the years, the home evolved into something of a folk art shrine.

We moved to another cabin, a wooden shack identified as "Curation Facility #1." Inside, on wall shelves, mounded a bank of oddly interesting objects that included a taxidermied bison's head, a Chucky doll, and a goofy Howdy Doody puppet. Nearby sparkled a new glitter ball.

I pointed. "Did you know that for a time in the '70s and '80s a company in Louisville produced most of the world's glitter balls? At least that's what they say."

"Doesn't surprise me," said Cecil. "It was a Kentuckian who made the disco ball famous."

My phone vibrated with a text. As Carrie chatted with our hosts, I quickly looked down to see who sent it.

It was from Margie. *Out of town today? Someplace in the hills?*

An hour later, I looked at my watch. "Carrie, we should probably head out if we want to make it home at a decent hour." She nodded and we thanked Bet and Cecil.

"Next time you come back, you can take a look at the scary dolls," said Bet.

"What do you mean? They all seem a bit scary to me."

"Well, we've got a handful of haunted dolls."

"A family moving to Florida dropped by one day, their car packed with all their belongings. They wanted to leave the little girl's dolls with us," said Cecil. "The father didn't want them anymore because they were possessed."

"Are you serious?" said Carrie.

"Totally," chimed in Bet. "The mother insisted there was something wrong with them."

"When I saw the little boy in the back seat, he frowned and said, 'They stare at me at night,' and he just shook his head slowly back and forth." Cecil grinned. "That's when I looked at the little girl—maybe three or so—and she said gravely, 'They're bad baby dolls.'"

Even with the warning, the couple took the dolls in. Theirs was *the* Home for Wayward Babydolls, after all. They kept those dolls in a special container, however, and visitors wanting to commune with them had to sign a waiver and wear a lead vest.

11

# DARK ROOMS

THE NEXT day, in my car on the way home from the Judicial Center, my cellphone twittered and I saw Kelly Atkins was calling.

"K.J., what's up?" I said.

"Mein Kapitän!" boomed his voice from the other end. "Got time for a stroll through Cave Hill? We've got more than an hour before they close the gates."

I laughed and checked the clock on the dashboard. "Sure. I'm on Baxter, just a minute or two away. Meet you at the main entrance."

Louisville buried its legends at Cave Hill Cemetery. With over 120,000 graves, it counted as the largest, not to mention most prestigious, burial ground in the city. Going back to the 1840s, its almost three hundred acres had become a repository of mausoleums, monuments, and historical markers honoring a slew of notable figures, including George Rogers Clark, the Revolutionary War general who settled Louisville in the 1770s. His younger brother, William Clark, along with Meriwether Lewis, would gain fame as a leader of the Corps of Discovery Expedition, which departed Louisville in 1804 and traveled across the Louisiana Purchase to the Pacific Ocean, where they claimed the Pacific Northwest for the United States.

After parking in front of a turreted red-brick Italianate mansion on Cherokee Road, I hurried to the steepled gatehouse, where Kelly waited—goose-stepping back and forth with his arm raised straight in a salute. He wore a comically oversized gray woolen coat that went down to the tips of his boots, and the hem jerked up each time he kicked out. On his head rested a Cossack-like fur hat with a strap that hugged his chin.

Immediately, strains of Mussorgsky's *Night on Bald Mountain* filled my ears and a scene from *The Wizard of Oz* came to mind, the one where the Cowardly Lion, the Scarecrow, and the Tin Man smuggled themselves into the castle by stealing uniforms from the Winkies and attaching themselves to the rear of the procession. Kelly looked like the Cowardly Lion, who wasn't able to conceal his tail as the guard marched into the Witch's Castle.

Sure enough, he was chanting something that sounded like "O-Ee-Yah! Eoh-Ah!" as well. When he reached the curb, he pivoted into an expert 180-degree turn and came in my direction. Nearby, a guard behind a grated window slowly moved his head back and forth. Seeing me, Kelly clicked his heels together and abandoned the goosesteps in favor of a more traditional gait.

"Mein Kapitän!" He smiled broadly.

I shook my head. "You're nuts, you know that?"

"Ja wohl, mein Herr!"

"Where'd you find that getup? You look like a deranged defector from the czar's Winter Palace."

Kelly broke character and looked down at his feet. "Aw, this old thing? I was just down at the Goodwill and I saw it and I had to have it." He said it in his W. C. Fields voice.

"It's ninety degrees out," I said. "You're going to die of heatstroke."

We walked through the huge wrought iron gates, under the suspicious gaze of the watchman in the guard's quarter, and left the hustle and bustle of Baxter Avenue behind us. Completed in 1892, the imposing Corinthian-style gate house once counted as the tallest structure for miles, housing a two-thousand-pound bell in its massive clock tower. A frequent target of lightning strikes, the five-story tower cut an impressive—and recognizable—figure along the busy Baxter Avenue/Bardstown Road corridor, the city's famous "restaurant row" that cut through the trendy Highlands neighborhood.

We proceeded down the formal tree-lined alley and into the oldest part, known by many as "the Victorian section," which arose in 1848 when they first chartered the cemetery. In front of us waited a vista of ornate mausoleums, elaborate funerary sculpture, and tombstones, all nestled among hillocks topped with soaring obelisks and granite markers.

Among the resting places of wealthy politicians and renowned artists and activists nestled oft-visited graves such as those of George Keats, brother of the poet John Keats, and the Hill sisters, who wrote the "Happy Birthday" song. But humbler graves, sad monuments for adults cut down in their prime and children who never made it that far, received their fair share of visitors as well.

In one quiet corner, an elegant statue of Saundra Twist, a fashion model killed in a car accident, presided over a stone tablet telling the story of her career and the realization of "all of this world's bountiful wonders." Nearby, a beaming bronze sculpture of three-year-old Samantha McDonald sat on a swing suspended from the verdigrised arms of Jesus Christ himself. The child had drowned after riding her tricycle into the family pool. Behind a large obelisk-topped monument for D. C. Parr, which contained the details to his safe deposit box, rested the family pet: Pretty Polly. At less than a foot tall, the parrot's modest stone marked the only animal known to be interred in Cave Hill Cemetery.

Arriving at the Parr monument, Kelly turned to me and said, "You know, that house on Fourth Street has some bad juju, right?"

I chuckled softly. "Well, a body in your basement will tend to do that."

"No, man, I'm talking before that."

"You don't mean the exorcism. Were you serious about that?"

"Serious as a heart attack, man. The Vatican was involved and everything. I was there for part of it. Saw a spoon fly from a little table and smash into the wall on the other side of the room."

"And was this recently?"

"Naw, it was like twenty years ago."

I stopped and gave Kelly a skeptical look.

"I swear, brother. A dark little room down in the basement. They had this guy strapped to an old wooden chair and he was speaking all kinds of gibberish and mumbo jumbo. The only thing he didn't do was spin his head around and spit up pea soup at everybody."

Kelly paused, took off his hat, and put it in the crook of his arm. A tiny rivulet of perspiration ran down his temple. "I think he actually lived in one of the houses nearby, where one of the hotheads or shitwads lives."

"Why didn't they do the exorcism in his house then?"

"Well, crap and crapola. I don't know why. There was something about that little room down there. They thought it had a special power or something."

"Oh, come on." Once again, I stopped and turned to give him an incredulous look. "Special power?"

We halted in front of a clunky Gothic mausoleum topped with wrought iron cresting and a boxy tower and stone cross. Built by noted Louisville architect Henry Whitestone for James F. Irvin in 1867, the tomb drew its inspiration from one designed by A. T. Brongniart around 1816, in Père Lachaise Cemetery in Paris. On April 16, 1871, the *Louisville Daily Commercial* had noted the elegant varieties of marble used on the interior surfaces of the mausoleum, which also boasted Scottish granite columns, dome, and exterior walls. The article described the main chamber as a crypt with "four depositories for coffins, with marble doors, awaiting their inmates."

Captain James E. Irvin had made his fortune captaining a steamboat on the Ohio River, but he also served on the board of Cave Hill Cemetery, which no doubt assured him of one of the choicest hilltop lots. His widow, Florence McHarry, who would go on to scandalize the city by marrying the much younger William Botto, and her father, Frank McHarry, shared the grand structure with Captain Irvin.

"Hey, did you know that old Frank McHarry, Irvin's father-in-law, was originally buried in a tomb overlooking the Ohio River?" Kelly changed gear and pointed to the entrance of the mausoleum. "This is his second resting spot."

"Is he the old man legend says was buried standing up, in a bluff along the river?" I asked. McHarry, they said, operated a ferry and was always coming into conflict with the steamboats. When he died, his will included a peculiar provision about his interment, one that would allow him to seek revenge from the grave.

"Damn straight! He made sure they buried him upright so he could hurl curses at all the steamboats passing by." Kelly grinned and rubbed his hands together. "He used to be a vertical stiff, but now he's a horizontal stiff."

"So, what about this room down in the basement having special powers?" I said. "Sounds kind of kooky to me."

"Supposedly one of the previous owners, one of the earlier ones, used to have an altar down there, a kind of shrine. Kept relics and stuff there. Holy water by the gallon. And that imbued the room with a kind of protection."

"Like a Catholic altar?"

"Yep. That woman who had the place since the '60s was a big-time Catholic." He gave me a knowing look. "We're a tight-knight group in these here parts." Kelly took off this coat and slung it over his shoulder. He used his free hand to fan his face. "Getting kind of hot under there."

"Well, duh," I said. "I can't believe you're wearing a full-length winter coat on a hot summer day. In a cemetery, no less."

Just then Kelly cocked an eyebrow and leaned forward to look around me. An elegant lady, perhaps in her early seventies, had emerged from behind a nearby mausoleum and stooped to lay a neat bouquet atop a large marble tablet embedded in the ground. She wore a black skirt suit with a ruffled white blouse. Her silver hair had been pulled into a neat ponytail. "My, my, what do we have here, my little chickadee?" He twiddled his fingers at the side of his mouth as he did his best W. C. Fields voice. Kelly had a thing for older women—much older women. If they could reminisce about the 1940s and '50s and knew how to dance to big band music, he was in all his glory.

A gleam in his eye, Kelly lasered in on the woman and started in her direction.

I grabbed him by the arm and held him back. "Ah, hang on there, sport. She's obviously in mourning and does not need a little K.J. Atkins in her life right now."

"Aw, man, I was just going to go and offer my condolences."

I pulled him away from the unsuspecting lady at the tombstone. "So, tell me more about this little room downstairs. I've been down in that basement and didn't see an altar."

"Who knows how that basement has changed over the years." He looked wistfully over his shoulder as I led him farther afield from the object of his affection. "Things change over time. Rooms come and go."

"Things do change over time, I'll agree with you there, but not so sure about rooms coming and going. That seems less likely."

"Dangnabbit," said Kelly. "That broad who used to live there? She owned half of Fourth Street. She rented out rooms to anybody. A high school friend of mine turned one of those rooms in the cellar into a kinky S&M kind of club. It was only there for a year or two, but I went once because he was so excited about it."

"Now, I did hear about some kind of S&M club down there." I halted mid-step and turned to stare at him. "Wait, you went to a kinky S&M club?"

"Sure, man. But I didn't do anything. Just went to see the freaks. People hanging from chains and tied to wheels and wearing spiked collars. A guy laying across a sawhorse getting spanked." Kelly pointed to a simple stone cross set back from the road under a thick canopy of leaves. "They even had a guy in a leather hood and harness pouring Pappy behind a bar at the door. His bar was a big barrel. Everyone took a shot before you went inside."

We were passing in front of the grave of Julian Proctor Van Winkle, better known as Pappy Van Winkle. Many distillers lay under tombstones in Cave Hill, but locals tended to consider Van Winkle the most notable. Responsible for the namesake bourbon that had earned a cult-like following through the years, Pappy, when he died in 1965 at the age of eighty-nine, counted as the oldest active distiller at the time.

Kelly swung the coat from his shoulder and crossed the grass to the Van Winkle grave. "Inside the club was another barrel with a big iron cage kind of built on top of it. A woman wearing nothing but a ball gag sat on a little purple velvet stool inside and waved at everyone as they entered."

"Well isn't that a fine howdy do?" I said. "How many people did they cram in? Sounds like it was Grand Central Station down there."

"Oh, not that many. A dozen and half, maybe, but they came and went, kind of in shifts."

"Hey, do you recall any glitter balls down there?"

He reached the stone marker, laid a hand on the crossbeam, and looked up, almost wistfully, into the low-hanging branches. "Why, yes, I do. Yes, I do, indeed." Back to the W. C. Fields accent. "There was one hanging in each corner, if I remember correctly. They weren't the huge kind, though. Just about the size of a basketball. Really pretty the way they sparkled. You could tell they were the good quality kind, not the cheap ones from China."

"You think they were the ones made here in Louisville?"

"Wouldn't doubt it. Probably from good old Omega National Products, right over there." He turned and pointed to a location outside the high brick cemetery walls. "Wouldn't be surprised if that doll Yolanda Baker didn't make it herself. They say she's the last one who makes them by hand in the U.S." He turned and gave me a sly glance. "But she's not a spring chicken anymore."

"So, do you prefer disco ball, glitter ball, or mirror ball?" I asked. "The more I find out about them and Louisville, the more I find myself calling them glitter balls. I like glitter."

"Kind of like glitter ball myself." Kelly took the coat and draped it over the cross, fitting one of the stubby arms of the cross into each of the sleeves. After adjusting the collar and fastening several buttons, he set the furry hat on top. Then he returned to the pathway and evaluated his handiwork. The coat perfectly fit the cross on Pappy Van Winkle's grave. He clapped his hands twice and then rubbed them together deviously. "Alright, chief. Let's set off in search of new adventures."

"You're not just going to leave that there, are you?" I gave him a perplexed look. "That's a pretty nice getup. Those Cossack hats are hard to find."

"Pappy can have it. I got two of those outfits at home already."

"Well, if you say so." We turned and headed back toward the main gate.

"Say, have you had any luck yet getting a bottle of Pappy twenty-three-year-old?"

"Not yet. Skippy's working on it, though. And let me know if you find someone with a spare bottle," I said. "It's crazy how it became such a hot commodity all of a sudden."

Ahead loomed a large domed structure supported by a ring of twelve Italian marble columns. The Temple of Love, one of the most famous tombs in the cemetery. We approached and ascended a short flight of wide steps to a graceful statue standing on a pedestal at the center of the monument. Carved by sculptor Sally James Farnham, the figure commemorated Florence Brokaw Martin Satterwhite, the wife of Dr. Preston Pope Satterwhite. The wealthy couple enjoyed an extravagant life of parties and relaxing summer getaways, but it all came to an end in 1927, when Florence died.

Her distraught husband purchased more than twenty-six thousand square feet in Cave Hill Cemetery for the princely sum of fifty thousand dollars and commissioned Horace Trumbauer to design a memorial befitting their love. The architect modeled the tribute after the Temple of Love built for Marie Antoinette at Versailles, the domed structure deriving its inspiration from the Roman Temple of Vesta. The Satterwhites had the largest grave in Cave Hill Cemetery.

Quietly, we circled the marble statue and paused to read the engraving in a marble tablet embedded in the floor: "Her ways are ways of pleasantness and all her paths are peace."

As we prepared to leave the monument, a sparkle caught my eye and I noticed something hanging from a marble hand of the statue. "Hey, look at this." I went in for a closer look. At the end of a silver chain glittered a small disco ball, about the size of a tennis ball. "Someone left a gift for Florence Satterwhite."

Kelly came closer to inspect the mirrored surface and smiled. "I think that's one of the good ones," he said. "Not a cheap one. See how perfectly spaced the individual mirrors are? It looks like they were laid there by hand."

"Who knows? Maybe it's one made by Yolanda Baker."

"I sure hope it is." Kelly lifted a hand and twiddled his fingers at the side of his mouth.

"You know," I said. "I could go for some bourbon right about now. How about you?"

"That sounds like a plan, chief. Let's ditch this fairytale world of funerary art and byzantine crypts and find a good bar." Kelly turned and I followed him down the steps to the road. "I know a place that sells Pappy by the drink, and it won't cost us an arm and a leg."

"Sounds good to me," I said. "We'll drink a toast to Glitter Ball City."

PART TWO

# 12

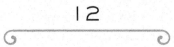

# GOTTA KNOW THE TRICKS

ALMOST THREE years had passed since the discovery of Jamie Carroll's body and after numerous delays and motions and much courtroom wrangling, the first of the accused murderers would go on trial. The trial of Joseph Richard Banis officially began on February 15, 2013, a cold, gray day in Louisville. I hadn't been able to sleep and was up early that morning, putzing around in the Magic Library. Lights twinkled on the ceiling, but outside all was pitch black. In the dining room, four melodious *dongs* from the grandmother clock signaled the early hour.

After checking emails and correcting a few student assignments, I straightened the room a bit. Studying the books and mementos on the shelves, I came to the realization that 2013 marked my twentieth anniversary as a Louisvillian. Had I really been here that long? What I had planned as just a couple of years at law school had now turned into almost half my life spent in Louisville. Glitter Ball City, it turned out, had a way of sucking people in.

Before moving to Louisville, I had lived in Austria for five years and qualified for citizenship, so the plan was to return to Europe that following summer and complete the naturalization process. I had applied to the diplomatic academy in Vienna and envisioned an ex-pat life in exotic outposts. I had all the paperwork in order and needed only to concentrate on improving my rudimentary French, fluency in which was a requisite for admission to the Diplomatische Akademie Wien.

However, as the first year came and went, tendrils of bluegrass began tickling my feet, slowly taking root as dreams of a career in far-flung locales began to fade. With its friendly people and laid-back attitude, Louisville started to feel like a favorite sweater or a comfortable pair of slippers. I met Ramon and we never left.

Louisville had a certain exoticism that satisfied my wanderlust for the time being. Granted, it wasn't Mongolia or Africa, but it was possessed nonetheless of a character that made it one of a kind. Perhaps it was the geographical schizophrenia, a kind of cultural and regional paradox, that always had outsiders asking, "Is Louisville in the North or the South?" but erroneously concluding, "It's in the Midwest, right?"

Kentucky was in the South; however, it lay at the very top, where the Ohio River served as a boundary, and across the muddy waters, Louisville faced the North. To add to the confusion, Kentucky declared its neutrality at first, but then sided with the Union in the War between the States—as long as it could keep its slaves. The ensuing romantization and victimization of the Lost Cause in the late 1800s would give rise to a tongue-in-cheek moniker that nicely summed up the state's political and social ennui: Kentucky, the Only State to Join the Confederacy *after* the Civil War.

Wherever you came from, Louisville was a gateway to somewhere else. From the North, it was a gateway to the South. From the South it served as the portal to the Midwest. Americans of the early 1800s regarded Louisville as a jumping-off point for the Wild West, but by the twentieth century this river city had become firmly rooted on the eastern side of the country. River traffic along the Ohio brought a constant influx of east-west travelers, and when railroad tracks crisscrossed the country, Louisville served as convenient stopover on the north-south route between Chicago and New Orleans.

"It's a Southern city to its bones but farther north than Evansville, Indiana. It can be as genteel as Charleston but as gritty as Pittsburgh," declared the *Chicago Tribune* in an article discussing the city's well-known—and often celebrated—personality disorder.

Some of this uniqueness stemmed from the obsession with horse racing and the deeply rooted culture of tobacco. Without a doubt, the love of whiskey and the legacy of generations of bourbon distillers and moonshiners had something to do with it. They loved their bourbon in Glitter Ball City, a city built on drinking, smoking, and gambling.

And they loved their quirks as well. Louisvillians reveled in claims to obscure bits of fame and they delighted in telling out-of-towners that their city not only gave the world the "Happy Birthday" song and the spelling bee and produced most of the world's glitter balls for a time, but it was also home to the Louisville Slugger, Muhammad Ali, actress Jennifer Lawrence, and nightly news anchor Diane Sawyer, as well as UPS World Headquarters. It also boasted the dubious distinction of having the most fast-food restaurants per capita of any city in the country, hardly surprising given that Yum! Brands, Inc.—owners of KFC, Pizza Hut, and Taco Bell—had its base here. And the list of often unknown badges of honor, such as having the most-delicious tap water in the country and being home to Papa John's Pizza, went on and on.

One of these claims to fame included the self-proclaimed honorific of having "America's Largest Victorian Neighborhood." In the forty-square-block area immediately adjacent and to the south of downtown Louisville, fans of late nineteenth- and early twentieth-century American architecture could find a wonderland of antique houses constructed mostly of local red brick and limestone. Architecturally speaking, it counted as the most exuberant historic district in the nation with postcard-perfect examples of Beaux-Arts, Renaissance Revival, Italianate, Châteauesque, Richardsonian Romanesque, and Victorian Gothic mansions, just to name a few of the styles represented. And with its secluded pedestrian-only residential enclaves such as Floral Terrace and the gas lamps flickering away twenty-four hours a day on Belgravia Court, locals boasted it was poised to be the new Savannah or Charleston any day now.

Despite the pride, however, many Louisvillians declined the honor of living in the largest Victorian neighborhood in the nation. It was too close to downtown and it had too many problems. "Let the students and the homos live there," an objector at a city council meeting discussing allocation of funds for beautification projects in Old Louisville once said. "I prefer the suburbs where the normal people live." And the murder of Jamie Carroll had only served to reinforce the already entrenched stereotypes many had about the neighborhood. The sensational trial starting that day would do little to rehabilitate Old Louisville's image.

Carrie and I had agreed to meet before the trial for breakfast at Burger Boy, a twenty-four-hour diner right around the corner from Carrie's house, and because I still had some time to kill, I packed up my things and headed for Old Louisville to do some work beforehand.

As I maneuvered the car down Eastern Parkway and through the university campus, only one other vehicle passed. At the entrance to the law school, two priests in dark cassocks caused me to do a double-take. What were they doing there at such an odd hour? I drove on, and in front of the university's signature Jefferson-inspired rotunda building, an original casting of Rodin's *The Thinker* seemed to raise its eyes from its musings and glower at me.

It was still dark as ink as I settled in at a small table next to a north-facing window at the diner. The only other customer, a young woman in a rumpled trench coat, sat at the counter. I ordered black coffee and orange juice to tide me over until Carrie arrived. At a neighboring house, it sounded like a bunch of frat boys still had a party going. I opened my laptop and started going through my notes.

Several minutes later, the door creaked open and another customer entered, but I didn't look up. It was quiet for a moment, but then the clip-clop of high heels started in my direction and before I knew it, I had a breakfast companion sitting down across from me. It wasn't Carrie, though.

"Well, hey, doll!" said the new arrival. "Look who's here. Mind if I join you?"

At first, I recoiled, but then recognition set in and I smiled. "Hey, Candy. How've you been?"

"Good, doll. How about you?" She wore a midnight blue sheath gown made of velvet with gold and black embroidery trimming the neck. A matching floor-length cape covered her bare shoulders. "See? I told you good ol' Candy don't always wear the same thing." Beaming, she gestured at her ensemble.

"Very nice. I like it. Looks like something Audrey Hepburn might have worn."

"Thank you very much. I think I look stunning, if I do say so myself." She turned her head both ways so I could admire the large turquois clip-on earrings and the blond wig that hung to her shoulders.

"Nice," I said, after a sip of coffee. "What brings you out so early?"

"Oh, nothing much. The old banshee is out visiting a friend in Tucson and I've got the run of the place—and her closet—till she gets back. Not for another week, though." Candy leaned back in her chair and seemed to luxuriate in the notion. I invited her to join me for breakfast and when the waitress came, Candy ordered the Burger Girl Breakfast Spread with ham, two eggs over easy, fries, biscuits and gravy, and a double side of bacon, in addition to a huge Belgian waffle with whipped cream for dessert.

"Somebody's got a hearty appetite," I said with a wink.

"Somebody sure does, doll, and somebody plans on eating well all this week." She took a noisy slurp from her coffee and grimaced. "Whores in hot pants. That banshee makes us eat hummus and raw cucumbers all damn day long. Once in a while I get a turkey wrap or a poached chicken breast, but that's about it. Been having a terrible hankering for smoked pork products."

"Well, bon appétit."

When the waitress set down the breakfast platter, Candy's eyes gleamed with delight and she immediately gobbled up the bacon and ham. "Now that's what I'm talking about, doll."

"So, have you heard anything about what's going on with the house on Fourth Street?"

"Well, looks like someone might be fixin' to buy it." Candy cut into one of her eggs and smeared the yolk around on the plate before lifting it to her mouth. That's when I noticed she had made up her face, unlike the previous times I had seen her. Deep burgundy lipstick seemed expertly applied, as did a bit of rouge on her cheeks and the deep blue eye shadow that matched her dress and cape. "People been going in and out, kind of like they're taking measurements and stuff."

"Have you been inside since the last time we met?"

"Maybe." Candy forked up half a biscuit smothered in gravy and started to chew. "How about you?"

"No. The couple times I went snooping around, it was locked up tight as a drum. The carriage house was open, but that was about it."

"Doll, you gotta know the tricks." With another noisy sip, she drained her cup and signaled the waitress for a refill. "I been in there alright."

"Tricks? What tricks?"

"Well, whores in hot pants! They're trying to sell the place and there's a lock box on the door. I called the agent and told them I wanted to see the place—which wasn't a lie—and he gave me the code and I been going in whenever I damn well please."

"Seriously?"

"Yeah, honey." Candy speared a fried potato and popped it into her mouth. "I don't know how long that will last, though, if someone's fixin' to renovate it." She slurped her coffee and polished off the last of her biscuits and gravy. "Hey, you seen the price lately? It just keeps tick-tocking its way down to nothing. And when they first put it back on the market, they wanted something like three hundred and fifty thousand for it. That's close to what Mundt paid for it. Last I saw, it was at a hundred and seventy-five thousand."

"Wow, that's a bargain."

"Yes, indeed." Candy finished up the rest of her breakfast platter and made room for the large waffle that had just arrived. She lifted her fork and prepared to decimate the large dollop of whipped cream but stopped. "But, you know what, doll? Something's been going on in that house." She fixed me with a peculiar gaze.

"Like what?"

"Well, I was there creeping around one night and I noticed that in several of the rooms somebody had pulled the mantels off the fireplaces. They had propped them up against the wall, turned around so the backside faced the rooms."

"You think they were refinishing them?" I watched in amazement as Candy ate half of her waffle in two large forkfuls.

After daintily wiping her mouth with a paper napkin, Candy removed a compact from a beaded handbag I hadn't even noticed and she checked her makeup. Satisfied with the reflection in the mirror, she stowed the compact and took another slurp of coffee. "That's what I assumed at first, but then I noticed something." She looked over her shoulder and then leaned in for a whisper. "There was writing on the backs of the fireplace mantels. In marker or thick graphite, like a carpenter's pencil, not sure what."

"Could you read it?"

"Sure, I could, doll. I'm not illiterate. I speak English, you know."

I sighed in exasperation. "That's not what I mean. Could you make it out, decipher it?"

"Sure, I could. It was pretty neat handwriting, nice and looping, in cursive, so I'm sure it wasn't young people who wrote it."

"What did it say?"

"You mean, what did *they* say?" Candy leaned in even closer. "They had scrawled tons of crazy-ass Bible verses on the backs of the mantelpieces."

"Oh, wow. Do you remember any of them?"

"Do I remember any of them?" Candy pushed herself back and resumed the task of devouring her Belgian waffle. "Doll, I was raised in a Pentecostal church in the hills of eastern Kentucky. All we did was memorize Bible verses when we weren't playing with rattlesnakes and drinking poison." She smeared the last chunk of waffle in chocolate sauce and tittered before eating it. "Sure, I remember, Nancy Boy."

"*Nancy Boy?*" I scrunched up my face. "That was kind of random. I think I like *doll* better."

"Gotta shake things up a bit. I like Nancy Girl, too."

"Well, anyway, what about the Bible verses?"

"Well, I don't think they were in the King James version, like we were used to, so I might have to paraphrase, but one of them was *Behold, I give unto you power to tread on serpents and scorpions, and over all the power of the enemy*, which is Luke 10:19. Whores in hotpants, we used that one all the time at my church." She paused and watched me for a reaction. "That one was down in the front room, but get the one they had upstairs in the room where they murdered poor ol' Jamie Carroll: *Be sober, be vigilant; because your adversary the devil, as a roaring lion, walketh about, seeking whom he may devour.* That's First Peter 5:8, if I remember correctly."

"Wow. Almost like they were trying to warn Jamie Carroll."

"I know, doll, but they were too late." Candy pushed herself back in the chair and waited for the waitress to clear away the dirty dishes.

"God, that was good. Last time I had waffles was two years ago at that tacky bed and breakfast on Sixth Street when the banshee and I joined her cousin for breakfast. Worst waffles ever. And that innkeeper is a real see-you-next-Tuesday." Candy grabbed the menu again and shook her head. "This neighborhood."

"So, were there more Bible verses?"

She turned the menu over and returned it to its holder. "Sure. They had creepy-ass verses down in the basement as well."

"In the room where they buried Jamie Carroll?"

"Yep. By the way, doesn't look like they've done much down there. That nasty-ass pit is still there, gaping like an open wound. You'd think someone would fill it in or something." Candy glanced longingly at the specials board. "Well, anywho, they had kind of a little altar set up, with a banner hanging on the wall above. It read: *And in the synagogue was a man that had the spirt of an unclean devil and he cried out in a loud voice. What have we to do with thee, Jesus of Nazareth? Art thou come to destroy us?* That one's in Luke someplace, too."

"You know, a friend of mine told me that they had conducted an exorcism in that room down."

"It sounds like something just like that might have been going on down there. But you know, it could have only been like that a day or two. The next time I snuck in, the mantels were back in their normal spots on the walls and that little altar in the cellar was gone." Again, Candy leaned forward for a whispered confidence, her tone becoming very serious. "I tell you what. That house has some bad energy and scribbling Bible verses on the woodwork will either take care of what's been causing all the problems—or it will just make it madder."

"Hmph. Let's hope it's not the latter."

"You know what's weird? I saw those very same verses scrawled on little papers tacked to the Witches' Tree later that day when I was out for my evening stroll. You know the Witches' Tree, don't you? That old tree on Sixth where they say witches used to—"

Candy suddenly stopped and slapped her knee with a guffaw. "Well, look at me, doll. Who am I to be telling you about the Witches' Tree? It's because of you and your stories that I even know about it!" After she stopped laughing, she reached for the menu again and began perusing.

"You still look like you're kind of hungry," I said. "Why don't you order something else?

"I was thinking the same thing, doll. The waffle and chocolate sauce gave me a hankering for something savory now." She patted her belly. "Well, let's see . . ." Candy ran her finger down the list of items and then called over the waitress and ordered a plate of corned beef hash.

While we waited, she took out her compact and a lipstick and touched up her mouth again. "Say, did you ever notice that bleached-out outline on the wall down there, like there was something pushed up against it at one time?" Candy spoke without looking at me, as she pursed her lips together for the mirror. "Looked like a more elaborate piece of furniture or something. It wasn't just a plain old cabinet or wardrobe. It had little spires on the sides and a peaked roof or whatever you call it."

I vaguely recalled such an outline. "Yeah, I do. But if it was a piece of furniture, I don't think it was there when Jeffrey and Joey were in the house. A lot of that basement was full of junk for years."

"Hmm. I don't recall it down there during the S&M club days either." Candy leaned back as a faraway look filled her eyes. "Of course, it was always pretty dark and I was usually hanging upside down from the ceiling," she said, half under breath. Then her eyes brightened and she straightened up again. "Say, have you made it over to that club I was telling you about on Sixth Street yet?"

"No, haven't gotten around to it. It's on my bucket list, though," I lied, glancing outside, where darkness was giving way to thin streaks of golden light on the horizon. "Whores in hotpants still the password?"

"Sure is, Nancy Boy." The waitress arrived and Candy greedily rubbed her hands together before digging into the large platter of corned beef hash. After her first mouthful, she looked up and swallowed quickly, struggling to get her words out fast enough. "Hey, did you see on the news how they found that old abandoned sex club down in the subbasement of those buildings they're rehabbing on Whiskey Row? Doll, that was Latex! My old stomping grounds! Talk about whores in hotpants."

"I saw that." For several weeks, Louisville had been titillated by the discovery of a series of secret warren-like rooms that had once catered to the needs of Louisville's S&M and swingers set. The underground spaces involved the block-long stretch from 101–133 West Main Street known as Whiskey Row, a collection of mostly nineteenth-century buildings with cast-iron façades that served as the de facto home to Kentucky's bourbon industry. On the list of Louisville's Most Endangered Historic Places, the buildings had been slated for demolition but an agreement between the city, local developers, and preservationists like Debra Richards had saved it.

Now, distillers, bars, and restaurants had plans of opening up shop and recent renovations in the subterranean levels had brought to light a side of life in Glitter Ball City that few knew even existed. Workers found the forgotten club hidden beyond a room filled with thousands of empty whiskey bottles.

"When you're demolishing an old building, you don't really expect to find a decades-old sadomasochistic swingers sex club. Sometimes it just happens," reported the *Huffington Post*. "If the club has any plans for a revival, now's probably the time, given increased interest in BDSM thanks to the erotic novel *Fifty Shades of Grey*. The book has inspired a boost in extramarital bondage in the U.K., while rope sales have reportedly surged in the U.S."

Candy sighed wistfully. "It would be so nice if they reopened it, but I'm sure they'll just put another boring restaurant down there or who knows what. Chains and whips are better."

"Well at least they didn't tear down those great old buildings like they were planning," I said. "Some of those were from the 1850s. It would have been a terrible loss."

"Yes, Nancy Girl, it's a good thing they saved them." Candy scraped up the last of her hash and cast a forlorn glance around the room. "Say, did you see that report WDRB just aired? About that guy they arrested at the fire station on the corner of Jefferson and Brook? The one they thought was trying to burgle the place, but turns out he was just a pervert?"

"You mean the one the firemen had to overpower?" On Saturday morning, police had responded to a call from a downtown station house and they arrived to find that several firefighters had captured twenty-seven-year-old Nicholas Gonzales, who had allegedly shattered a window to gain entry. But instead of stealing, they found him committing a sex act in a storage room near the firefighting equipment.

"What a freak. Jerkin' off on the hoses, I bet."

Several other patrons trickled in, and the chirps of songbirds punctuated the air outside. The horizon had come alive with a vivid blue. After studying the specials scrawled on the blackboard behind the counter, Candy retrieved the menu yet again and studied both sides.

"You're not still hungry, are you?" My eyes grew in amazement.

Taken aback, Candy looked up. She wore a hurt expression on her face.

But that quickly gave way to a sly grin. Then she returned her attention to the menu. "Well, doll, a girl's gotta eat."

# 13

# THE FIRST JURY

TWO HOURS later, after Candy had departed and Carrie had arrived to take her place, we parked and were trying to enter the Judicial Center. A line from the security checkpoint extended out to the sidewalk and news crews with cameras congested the entrance. News vans parked in a neat row flanked both sides of Jefferson Street. Although opening arguments wouldn't start for another week, the first days being consumed with jury selection and various motions, the first official day of trial had arrived.

Elected to the 30th Judicial Circuit, which includes Jefferson County, on November 7, 2006, Judge Mitch Perry presided. Described by colleagues as one "generally slow to anger," the gray-haired man cut an imposing figure at the bench despite his soft-spoken demeanor. From far western Kentucky, he had proudly remarked to more than one potential juror that his county was "famous for having won more state basketball championships than any other rural county in Kentucky."

In Louisville, the judge's face had become a well-known one on the television screen because of his involvement in another bizarre murder trial—also with a gay twist. Not too long before, a shy Indiana boy named Andrew Compton had gone missing. The aspiring culinary student had moved to Louisville to attend Sullivan University—but not even a couple of months later, he disappeared on a chilly October evening.

Surveillance video showed the eighteen-year-old leaving his dorm late that night but he never returned. An email led detectives to forty-year-old Gregory O'Bryan, someone Compton had hooked up with through social media. Dr. Phillip Johnson, a psychologist who examined O'Bryan for the Department of Corrections, reported that the Louisville man had emotional problems, psychological problems, and alcohol dependency issues.

According to the *University Herald*, O'Bryan admitted to getting the teen drunk and binding him with an electrical cord before having sex with him, but the Sullivan University student became unconscious and died. "I looked up and he was dead," claimed O'Bryan. He suspected he had broken the young man's neck while having sex "in an unusual position."

O'Bryan then had intercourse with the corpse before wrapping the boy's slim body in a rug, sealing it in a cardboard TV box, and stowing it in the trunk of his car before eventually tossing it in a garbage bin near Bellarmine University, next to Our Lady of Peace psychiatric hospital—just down the road from my house.

It was alleged that O'Bryan had murdered the teenager with the express purposes of engaging in postmortem sex.

Police believed the contents of that dumpster ended up at a landfill in Medora, Indiana, where they searched for almost two weeks. Several homicide detectives, fifty police recruits, and three cadaver dogs assisted.

They never found Andrew Compton's body.

O'Bryan was indicted for murder, sodomy, abuse of a corpse, and tampering with physical evidence. In his most recent appearance, Perry had found the defendant competent to stand trial and the prosecution announced they intended to seek the death penalty. O'Bryan, however, would avoid capital punishment by entering a plea deal in exchange for a twenty-five-year prison sentence.

The first day in the courtroom for Joey Banis's trial, attendance was very sparse and Carrie and I were some of the few in the gallery. Actual arguments weren't projected to start for another two weeks, and the judge spent the first day housekeeping and addressing several motions. I was shocked to hear the first one was about me.

"It came to our attention that there is a local author who is writing a book . . . and I have attached for the court's edification . . . the Facebook group page indicating who he is and what he is writing, as well as a post from last November," said the defense. Alleging I had improper contact with the prosecution, they went on to read several posts referencing various telephone exchanges with the prosecutor. My spine stiffened despite the urge to go limp and slink down beneath the pews and I grabbed my cellphone. Carrie's face went pale.

"Crap," I texted Beth, my friend and attorney. "They're talking about me in the motions. Saying I had improper contact. What do I do?" Half a minute later my phone vibrated with a return text: "Don't say or do anything! Let me know right away what happens."

I tried to look nonchalant as the prosecutor replied. "I can't control what people say about me. I can't control what people post on Facebook. The press is the press. That doesn't have anything to do with me. Reporters call all the time," she said, adding, ". . . This is sort of provocative in light of the case in Indiana, and the prosecutor signing book deals."

Carrie shot me a concerned look. The local news had been abuzz with allegations that Keith Henderson, the lead prosecutor in the murder trial of Indiana state trooper David Camm, accused of shooting his wife and two children to death, had secretly entered into a lucrative book deal about the case and should have recused himself. The Indiana Supreme Court would eventually impose a public reprimand against the Floyd County prosecutor, charging him with three violations of professional conduct rules, but even though they had removed him from the trial the year before, Henderson's story was still fresh in the minds of the local legal community. Did Joey Banis's defense really think that I had entered into an agreement with the prosecution for a book deal? I was years away from anything like that.

Fortunately, the prosecution easily convinced the judge that this was not the case, and Mitch Perry quickly dismissed the motion. After several tense moments, I let out my breath. Trying to remain inconspicuous, I reached for my phone. "Whew, I think we're good," I texted Beth. Two seconds later, I felt the vibration of a return message. "Good. Stay out of trouble!"

"Everything's fine," I whispered to Carrie. She let out a breath.

After entertaining several additional motions, the judge wrapped up the "housekeeping" portion of the trial, and the lengthy process of jury selection began. As prospective jurors began filing in, one by one, I took a seat in the waiting area while Carrie went off to Gavi's in search of coffees to go. Sitting nearby was a nice-looking lady, maybe in her sixties, with a serene look on her face.

I wondered if she was in the jury pool and I scooted over to talk to her. Just then, my phone vibrated with an incoming text. It was Beth, in lawyer mode, as if reading my mind: "And do not even think about talking to any of the prospective jurors!"

I stowed the phone in my coat pocket and prepared to turn on the charm. "You're not in the jury pool, are you?" All the people entering and exiting the courtroom as potential jurors sported clearly numbered paper labels near their lapels, and this lady had none, so I took it as a safe bet that she wasn't there for jury duty.

"No, a longtime friend of the Banis family," she replied, adding that she had come to show support. "Sligar is my last name. Rhymes with tiger." She had known "Joey, as I've always called him" for a long time and had visited him a number of times in jail. "He's doing well, all things considered," she confided, "and he's a different person from the person he was on drugs."

We chatted for at least twenty minutes. In that time she mentioned that Joey had "always been very talented, artistic, a wonderful writer" and that the whole case was proving understandably hard for his family. Being a social worker, Mrs. Sligar suspected that Joey probably had a personality disorder and the fact that his parents weren't supportive about "the homosexual thing" might have compounded "his other issues." She also confided that Joey had pretty much confessed to it all, but she believed he hadn't acted alone. "Mundt was responsible as well."

Just then, Adam Walser, the investigative reporter from WHAS11, saw us and headed in our direction, eager to find people to interview about the case. Mrs. Sligar declined, but I agreed and went to a bank of cameras along a far wall. I told her we'd probably be seeing more of each other and she smiled as I turned to go. "We are all children of God" were her last words.

After the interview, I told Walser more about the book I had in mind and he perked up when I mentioned my interest in Old Louisville. He was working on a story about a rash of thefts in the neighborhood and said he would have some breaking news soon. "Old Louisville," he laughed. "That's got to be one interesting place to live." When I pressed for more details, all he would divulge was that "it involved Little John's Pawn Shop."

I tried to stifle a chuckle. "Have you seen his commercials? Each one's better than the last." He agreed and for a minute we exchanged tidbits about our favorite aspects of the commercials, but his phone started ringing and he had to run to the cameras.

Just then, a prospective juror exited the courtroom and walked over to where his presumed wife or girlfriend waited and said, "Let's go." When the bleached blonde asked how things had gone and what would come next, he pulled out a pack of Marlboro's and sniggered. "We'll see if I get called back or not." The overweight man put a cigarette to his lips and prepared to light it, but the woman slapped him on the shoulder and pointed to the no-smoking sign behind him. He shrugged and as they headed to the elevator, he muttered, "I lied and said I had nothing against faggots, but if I get on the jury, that homo better be worried."

I made a mental note of the man's appearance in case he were seated on the jury.

Just then, a man in a linen suit and round spectacles emerged from a nearby cluster of people and introduced himself as Mr. Shouse, an attorney for Jeffrey Mundt.

He didn't need to introduce himself, though. His was another face often seen on the evening news. Ted Shouse was a well-known face in Louisville's legal community, having been recognized by his peers as one of Louisville's Top Lawyers in *Louisville Magazine* and serving as directing attorney of the Kentucky Innocence Project.

Some, however, harbored a deep-seated resentment against him. He had represented Father Stephen Pohl, a local priest involved in a child pornography scandal at St. Margaret Mary School, a school with more than seven hundred pupils. A mother became suspicious after seeing the priest photograph her two children, and when she confronted him, his nervous reaction put her on edge. When the seven-year-old boy started showing signs of defiance and behavioral issues, she discovered that Pohl had directed the child to pose in provocative positions. The child's parents eventually confronted the cleric and notified the authorities after discovering more photos of young boys on his phone. Police discovered many more incriminating photos, as well as child pornography on the priest's computer. With Shouse's representation, the priest received a prison sentence of less than three years.

Comparatively speaking, Pohl's was a minor scandal in a long line of Louisville's clerical sexual abuse scandals. In 2003, the Roman Catholic Archdiocese of Louisville agreed to pay a settlement of more than twenty-five million dollars to people sexually abused by priests and employees of the archdiocese going all the way back to the 1940s. It was the largest settlement ever paid directly from the assets of a diocese.

The financial impact and the scandal itself rocked Louisville, a small archdiocese of around two hundred thousand Catholics with 115 active diocesan priests. The plaintiffs had accused thirty-four priests, two religious brothers, and three laypeople of abuse.

Most considered Louisville's Rev. Louis Miller the worst serial abuser of all the clergy held to account anywhere in the nation. Ninety of the 243 plaintiffs had identified "Father Lou" as their abuser. At St. Elizabeth of Hungary, the fourth and final of Miller's churches, he enjoyed a reputation as a strong leader in the working-class Schnitzelburg neighborhood. A former council member described him as "a caring man, but also a man's man—a tough character who didn't come across as a pushover." Miller would spend hours at the bedside of the sick and dying and he made regular house calls on parishioners in need. A former council president said, "He worked like a dog and always seemed to have a smile on his face." Many fondly remembered him stirring turtle soup at church picnics, and in 1997 Schnitzelburg named him its "No. 1 Citizen."

He was known "to follow the rules and do all the priestly things right"—except when it came to children. For child sexual abuse, reported the *Courier-Journal*, the court sentenced Louisville's "notorious ex-priest pedophile" to thirty years in prison, where he would die in 2017.

That day in the courtroom, if Ted Shouse seemed bothered by the grudge some people held against him for defending a pedophile priest, he didn't show it. He was a defense attorney after all.

He shook my hand and leaned in. "So, are you writing a book about this?" When I replied in the affirmative, the lawyer smiled and nodded his head. "I guess I'll be seeing you around then."

Jury selection wouldn't wrap up until the last week of February 2013. Upon learning that the jury pool for the Banis trial consisted of a total of 143 candidates, Perry said, "Wow," and then started the collective voir dire to determine the suitability of potential jurors. When asked if those assembled knew any of the defense, prosecution, or courtroom staff, one man replied that he thought he might have known attorney Justin Brown of the defense from somewhere, but he wasn't sure how.

When Brown asked the individual where he had gone to high school, Perry shook his head and chuckled. "You know, in another life I was a military guy and I roamed all over the world. This is the only city where people always ask: 'Where did you go to high school?'"

At this, the courtroom erupted in laughter. "It is the darndest thing," concluded the judge with another shake of the head. Then, he continued to poll the members of the jury pool for circumstances such as physical conditions, felonies, or hardships that would excuse them from jury duty.

Then, the individual voir dire began, and Bailiff Michael Brown ushered in prospective jurors, one by one, for more intense questioning from the judge, prosecution, and the defense. Mitch Perry asked the first candidate a series of three questions, the first one laying out the allegations and asking about prior knowledge of the case.

"This case has received quite a bit of attention from the media, and it's important to know if that attention has influenced you in any way," Perry explained. "The case itself involves a murder, a homicide, in Old Louisville. It's alleged that Mr. Banis and another man, Jeffrey Mundt, were engaged in a consensual sexual relationship with a third man, James Carroll; it's further alleged Mr. Carroll was shot and killed during the encounter and that Mr. Carroll's body was discovered buried in the basement of an Old Louisville home." Then he asked, "Do you recall hearing, seeing, or reading any media coverage about this?"

The next question involved the candidate's personal thoughts on homosexuality. "The defendant's sexual orientation is homosexual. Do you have any prejudice or bias for or against that particular sexual orientation?"

And the final question, in essence, dealt with the potential juror's thoughts on the death penalty. "If this jury were to find this defendant guilty of murder with a statutory aggravating circumstance, there's a range of penalties for the jury to consider in the penalty phase," said Perry, explaining that the range could cover a term of years, twenty-five to fifty years life imprisonment, life without parole for at least twenty-five years, life imprisonment without the possibility of parole, and the death penalty. "The question to you is: Could you consider that full range of penalties?"

The individual voir dire continued over the next several days and a version of these questions was repeated to all the subsequent prospective jurors. After securing the fifty-ninth prospective juror for the pool, all parties agreed to cease the individual voir dire and randomly select fifteen from the fifty-nine to serve as jurors. Of those excused, a good number belonged to individuals who had strong views on homosexuality and the death penalty. About twenty percent said they had "reservations" about the death penalty, and a good ten percent were stricken when they firmly said they could never consider the death penalty as a punishment.

Of the jurors polled, about ten percent admitted they had biases toward homosexuals, but most said it would not affect their impartiality and they remained in the pool. Prospective juror 823254, an older woman who boasted she never watched the news, said of homosexuality, "I disagree with it. I think it's a sin," but added, "I'm a Christian and I try to love the person." Prospective juror 822971, when asked if he had anything against homosexuals, responded, "Not unless they would come on to me or something like that." Prospective juror 823163 explained he "was raised with a prejudice towards that [lifestyle]," but living here in Louisville, he got used to it. Prospective juror 823214 didn't "believe in it religiously or morally" while prospective juror

823031, a middle-aged man in a University of Kentucky sweatshirt, said, "Honestly, I don't have nothing against 'em; they do their things, stay behind closed doors, but I just feel like God woulda made two Adams and no Eves or two Eves and no Adams, I mean. And that's just the way I've always looked at it."

Prospective juror 822825, an older, white-haired veteran said, "I feel very uneasy when I'm around them if I'm aware they're homosexual. And I would just try to get away from them as quick as possible." Prospective juror 822867, a Black man said, "It's not right in God's sight." Prospective juror 822867, a male, said, "I'm just old-school. I'm not into that thing."

But prospective juror 823119, a middle-aged male who claimed he could remain impartial and wouldn't punish Banis for being gay, was stricken when he admitted that he would have a hard time being exposed to homosexual details during the trial. "I think it's wrong," he said. "Bible says be fruitful and multiply." Prospective juror 822978, an Asian woman who said, "If you normal, you don't do things like that," was stricken for admitted prejudice.

When prosecutor Ryane Conroy asked prospective juror 823183 about "the lifestyle" Banis had "chosen to lead," the woman also admitted she was "biased against homosexuals," and that she did "not condone that kind of relationship." She was excused as well. "I have very strong biblical beliefs," she explained.

Prospective juror 822789, an old man hard of hearing, who said "I don't like homosexuals, the way they live and all that. I just don't think, as a Catholic, I don't think that's the right thing to do," was excused from the jury when he admitted he "might" punish Banis for being homosexual.

Prospective juror 822745, an older white male, said, "I do have a problem with that type of activity" and "I am not in favor of that." When asked by the judge if he would punish Joseph Banis for that, he said, "Possibly. Like I say, that's against my religion and upbringing. Honestly, that may play a part." He was dismissed as well. So was prospective juror 823394, an older, gray-haired man with a flannel shirt and glasses, who paused when asked, then responded gravely, "I am very disgusted by homosexuals. I believe they're people, they have rights, but it just, it bothers me."

After the individual voir dire, the court entertained various motions for several days before conducting a final round of collective voir dire, the prosecution asking if those assembled had specialized legal knowledge or prior criminal jury experience. Ryane Conroy also asked if anyone had been a witness to a crime or the victim of a crime, and so forth. Finally, they ferreted out the last unsuitable potential juror and they had a whittled-down pool from which to randomly select the final jurors. On February 25, 2013, the fifteen-person jury was sworn in and seated.

The next day, the trial of Joseph Banis began.

# 14

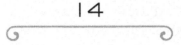

# OPENING STATEMENT FOR
# THE PROSECUTION

GLOOMY, GRAY skies clouded that Tuesday morning when I picked up Carrie. By eight o'clock we had passed through security and had seats in a waiting area with large windows overlooking downtown Louisville. A disgusting guy next to us kept clearing his throat and coughing up phlegm, so we moved, and that's when Ryane Conroy emerged from an elevator. Not wanting to incur the prosecutor's wrath, I steered Carrie to a large window and we watched as news vans pulled up and parked down below. Excitement permeated the air and animated those milling about, and a grinning passing attorney rubbed his hands together and commented to a colleague that he was "there for an all-dayer."

Carrie and I found seats in the courtroom and soon the IT people came in and started setting up camera equipment, followed by Ryane Conroy, who organized and tested her audiovisual aids. An aerial view of Old Louisville popped up; after that appeared a close up of 1435 South Fourth.

In the almost three years since the discovery of Jamie Carroll's body and the arrest of the suspected killers, neighbors informed me the house had been sold to a bank and found itself in an extreme state of disrepair. Any improvement work Jeffrey Mundt had done on the premises seemed unnoticeable. Box gutters sagged at the roofline and the front porch sported an abundance of rotting wood. White paint flaked and peeled away in long ribbons and patches of red brick showed signs of weather damage and erosion.

Two people passed by and squeezed into the bench further down, and when we looked up it became apparent they were Joey's mother and brother. About the brother, Carrie said, "He looks just like Joey." A *Fortune* magazine resting in his lap, he wore black slacks, brown scuffed-up shoes, a gray sweater, and a light blue collared shirt. His hand seemed to shake as he checked his phone. As one of the defense attorneys slid into the bench to greet them, I felt a hand on my shoulder and heard a friendly "Good morning." Turning around, I saw Mrs. Sligar and greeted her with a handshake before she joined Mrs. Banis.

When Bailiff Brown called to have the defendant brought in, only about ten people sat on the defense side and about twenty on the prosecution's side, many fewer than I had anticipated. Several seconds later, Joey Banis emerged from a side door with a stack of files and his computer held in his outstretched arms. Before taking the chair between his two attorneys, he gave me a long stare. A long, pointed stare.

Mitch Perry called the court to order. Josh Schneider, a lanky, tow-headed assistant prosecutor who had joined the team several years before, delivered the opening statement on behalf of the Commonwealth of Kentucky. A graduate of Northland College, he had earned a master's in education from the University of Vermont and his law degree from the University of Louisville Brandeis School of Law, the school that had brought me to Louisville. Schneider, for a time, taught English as a second language to high school students in the Czech Republic and high school English to Iñupiaq people in Alaska. Just the previous year, he had made the news when courtroom video captured him rushing to the aid of a bailiff after a six-foot-four, 260-pound inmate in an orange jumpsuit burst through a side entrance and attacked the man.

Schneider began. "Three men entered; two men left. Jeffrey Mundt, Joey Banis, and Jamie Carroll entered into a bedroom in 1435 South Fourth Street in mid-December 2009 for the purposes of having group sex. The next day Jeffrey Mundt and Joey Banis left that bedroom. Jamie Carroll didn't leave that bedroom, didn't leave that house until homicide detectives dug his body out of the basement on June 17, 2010."

I leaned over to Carrie and whispered, "Not a big deal, but it was actually the next morning when they found the body, June 18, 2010."

"I know. I'm surprised they missed that." Carrie returned her gaze to the front of the courtroom.

Schneider walked over to the tarp and lifted the container high for jurors to see. After a moment, he set it back down. "Jamie Carroll spent approximately six months in a fifty-gallon Rubbermaid container covered in lime, sealed shut with foam, strapped with duct tape, so no one could smell his corpse. Stripped naked with only a few personal items, hog-tied, his knees broken by a sledgehammer so he would fit inside. His body was stabbed numerous times and a bullet remained lodged in his chin." Behind me, somebody softly gasped.

"You see, it took six months for someone to find Jamie because Jamie Carroll was the kind of guy that no one would miss. And Jeffrey Mundt and Joey Banis knew that fact," said Schneider. "In 2009, Jamie Carroll was in his late thirties. He'd been in trouble most of his life, most of which were drug-related charges. In fact, in mid-December of 2009, he was facing drug charges both in Lexington and Louisville. More than likely Jamie Carroll was going to prison in mid-December 2009 and he knew that." The prosecutor turned and fixed his gaze on Banis. "And so he was going to spend his last moments of freedom partying, living life while he was in Louisville waiting to go to court. And who better to party with than Jeffrey Mundt and Joey Banis? So, Jamie met up with Banis and Mundt at the Old Louisville apartment for the purposes of group sex and smoking meth."

At that moment, there was a shuffling noise from the bench behind us and a young female voice whispered, "Gay guys are so creepy." Carrie and I exchanged glances before the prosecution continued.

"Eventually, they ran out of meth. Jamie tells Mundt and Banis: 'I've got more meth in my hotel room. I'll go get it.' So he leaves to get the remaining meth. And Banis and Mundt stay in that room. And they plot."

Schneider walked back to his table and then turned to face the jury. "Carroll comes back to the Old Louisville home with the meth. And they again engaged in group sex . . . and at this point the party is over for Jamie Carroll. Because the last thing that Jamie Carroll will ever remember is lying naked on that bed as he is stabbed and shot numerous times to his death." A cough came from one of the jurors as the prosecutor took a moment to let everything he had said sink in. He lowered his voice when he continued.

"Banis and Mundt take the remaining meth, and whatever money they can find on Mr. Carroll, and they carry out the rest of their plan. First, they clean up the blood—and there's a lot of it. Next, they go to a hardware store to buy a fifty-gallon Rubbermaid container and some rubber foam." Schneider turned from the jury to look at the defense table. "Now, when they get back, rigor mortis is starting to set in on Jamie Carroll and so they can't just put him in the container. They have to take a sledgehammer, they have to break his knees to wedge him inside." When the prosecuting attorney returned his attention to the jury box, a gray-haired female slowly shook her head back and forth.

"Next, they take lime and they pour it all over Jamie's body. Then, they take foam sealant and seal it, and finally they take duct tape and wrap it around the container, all to conceal the smell of Jamie's corpse." Again, Schneider paused, and there was barely a sound in the courtroom. "They take hours digging a hole, five feet deep by five feet wide, and they take the container and they stick it in the hole. And they fill up that hole with the dirt and they walk away. Because Jamie Carroll was the kind of guy no one would miss."

Mrs. Banis blinked once and slightly raised her chin before the prosecution continued. "On June 17, 2010, approximately six months after the murder, Detective Jon Lesher gets a phone call. Officer Trey McKnight has responded to a domestic violence call at 1435 South Fourth Street. It involves two individuals, Joey Banis and Jeffrey Mundt." Raising an eyebrow, Schneider took a step toward the jury box. "And the interesting thing is that Trey informs Detective Lesher, who is in homicide, that Mr. Banis has some information on a body. A body that no one . . . had been looking for. And he can tell Detective Lesher where that body is."

At the prosecution's table, Conroy unwrapped a piece of candy with a soft crinkle and popped the sweet into her mouth. "Detective Lesher tells Officer McKnight to go ahead and bring him down, and Detective Tommy Miles, Detective Collin King, and Detective Jon Lesher sit down with Mr. Banis," said Schneider. "Well, his story begins with the fact that he can tell them about this body and the fact that nobody was going to know that this body was missing, this person was missing. Now, at this point, Detective Lesher is thinking, 'This guy is full of BS. He just wants to get out of his charges. He's more than likely going to spend the night, at least, in jail,'" continued Schneider, "because Officer McKnight had found counterfeit money on him and methamphetamine. But, as any good homicide detective will do, he's going to listen to the story, to see where it goes."

After glancing over his shoulder at the defendant, the prosecutor went into more detail. "So Banis starts feeding him tidbits of information. The first of which is that the victim is a Jamie Carroll, and that no one would be looking for Jamie because he was due to go to prison in the next couple days, right before his death. He also tells them that the plan, initially, was that Banis and his boyfriend Jeffrey Mundt were going to rob Mr. Carroll of his meth—and of his money." Schneider turned and glared at the defendant again. "So the first thing that Detective Lesher does is that he enters Jamie Carroll's name into a database. And he finds—lo and behold—that, yes, there is two outstanding bench warrants for a Jamie Carroll, one in Louisville, the other in Lexington. And, they're from mid-December 2009."

Joey Banis looked straight ahead, no emotion registering. "Now, this entire time, at least initially, Banis is wanting to strike a deal with Detective Lesher: 'I give you this information, you let me go home. I tell you about this body, you let me out of here.' He wants to get out of there, and he will give him this information in order to do so. So Detective Lesher enters into another database and he pulls up a mug shot of Jamie Carroll. And, he enters into a homosexual dating website and finds that there's another picture of Jamie Carroll. And he takes these pictures and he presents them to Mr. Banis and he says, 'Is this Mr. Carroll?' And Mr. Banis says, 'Yes, that's the one I'm talking about.'"

At that moment Joey leaned in and loudly whispered something to his attorney, Darren Wolff. Casting a sideways glance in their direction, Schneider skipped a beat and then carried on. "So, he does some further research into who this Jamie Carroll was. And he finds out that there are three addresses in Lexington connected to Jamie Carroll. He calls Lexington police to check out those three addresses—and nothing. Next, he enters into a database to see if in fact James Carroll is in prison. He looks into it. Nothing."

"Well, how about a missing person report? Maybe he's just out there and no one knows where he is, so he looks into a missing person report database. Nothing. Finally, Detective Lesher is able to locate a phone number for James Carroll's mother," he said. "So he calls his mother and makes contact with her. And asks the question: 'When's the last time you saw Jamie?' 'Well,' she says, 'I think the last time we saw him was around Thanksgiving of last year, that would be Thanksgiving of 2009. But you're not gonna find him. He's in prison.'"

At that, Schneider adopted a graver tone. "'He was supposed to go to prison.' Now, some red flags are starting to really pop up on Detective Lesher's radar. So he goes back, starts up the conversation with Banis, and Banis says, 'I witnessed his death. I saw my boyfriend, Jeffrey Mundt, stab and shoot Jamie Carroll and together we took that body and we buried it in the basement of that home.'"

Just then Carrie leaned over. "Oh, wow," she whispered. "Do you think it really happened like that? That Mundt killed him? Everything in the news made it seem the other way around."

"I know," I said, out of the corner of my mouth. "Joey is supposed to take the stand, so it'll be interesting to see what he has to say."

Josh Schneider continued. "And also he gives some information about the fact that they would be able to—they being homicide detectives—would be able to locate the gun that was used to shoot Jamie Carroll because it had been confiscated in an arrest that following April when Mundt and Banis were arrested in Chicago with possession of counterfeit bills and guns."

At the defense table Joey seemed to shake his head slightly. "So, Detective Lesher makes a phone call to Chicago. Lo and behold, those two had been arrested in April for those charges, and, yes, those things had been confiscated, including guns. Well, now it's time to see what's going on at this house. So, Detective Collin King makes contact with Jeffrey Mundt, and informs him, 'Hey, we've been talking to your boyfriend and he's been saying these crazy things about a body being buried in the basement of this house.' Well, Mundt acts shocked, horrified that could possibly happen. So, Detective King says, 'Would you mind coming down to homicide?'"

At the prosecution's table, another soft crinkle of candy unwrapping punctuated a momentary pause in Schneider's statement. "'And we could talk to you about what's going on with this story.' And he agrees. So, he goes down to homicide with Detective King. Now, Detective Lesher, Detective Kevin Thompson, and Lieutenant Barry Wilkerson go to the house. They go to the basement. And the basement floor is made of dirt. And, lo and behold, there's a spot that has a fresh pile of dirt. So, they dig. And they dig. And they dig. Eventually, a shovel hits something solid. And the mystery of where Jamie Carroll has been the last six months is answered."

"Wow, great line," murmured a voice nearby. I turned and saw it was Sally Bean, the victim advocate, who had come to sit right behind us. "That would be a great closing line."

But Schneider went on with more details. "They locate a blue fifty-gallon Rubbermaid container in that hole. And in that container is the body of Jamie Carroll. Detective Lesher then calls Chicago to verify the items are there—and he goes back after the body is located to see what is going on with Mr. Mundt and Mr. King."

The prosecutor turned and fixed the jury box with an intense stare. "Well, Mr. Mundt has denied and denied and denied. And they said, 'Well, would you be interested in taking a polygraph test?' and he said, 'Yeah, I'll take a polygraph test.' So, they sit him down for a couple of hours and they start to prep him and at that moment Mr. Mundt decides, 'Well, it's time to tell the truth.'"

Schneider now turned his gaze to the defense table. "'I know about the murder. I can tell you everything you want to know about it.' And the story that he tells mirrors the story that they've been hearing from Mr. Banis, except the roles are different. 'No, no, no, I didn't kill him,' says Mr. Mundt, 'He killed him. I was just there. He killed 'im.' Now we have two stories but two conflicting involvements."

Joey Banis slowly moved his head back and forth, the first clear sign of movement or emotion from him since the defense started their opening statements. "The next week Detective Lesher goes up to Chicago and collects all the items that Chicago police have collected. There's computers, there's phones, there's video recorders, there's GPS, and there's guns. In fact, there's a revolver that they test. And once they extract the bullet from Jamie Carroll's face—lo and behold—the gun that they find, confiscated from Chicago, is the same gun used to shoot Jamie Carroll. At this point, the investigation is over. Detective

Lesher has located a body that nobody was looking for and he has two suspects that claim to be telling the truth, but with two different stories as to who did it."

For several minutes, Schneider expounded on the technicalities of the case, but then he closed his arguments. "And make no mistake, at the end of this trial, when you've heard everything and everything's been presented to you, the choice as to this individual will be clear: You will find him guilty of complicity of illegal possession of drug paraphernalia. You will find him guilty of complicity of possession of a controlled substance, methamphetamine. You will find him guilty of complicity of criminal possession of a forged instrument. You will find him guilty of complicity of tampering with physical evidence. You will find him guilty of complicity of robbery in the first degree. And most importantly, ladies and gentlemen, you will find him guilty of complicity of the intentional murder of Jamie Carroll."

At that, the gangly prosecuting attorney returned to his team and briefly conferred with Conroy, whose expression seemed to indicate approval of his opening statement. Although nobody else moved or said a word, an electric buzz seemed to pervade the courtroom.

I was reminded of my brother Paul and thought about calling him. I decided against it.

# 15

# OPENING STATEMENT FOR
# THE DEFENSE

AT ABOUT ten to eleven, Justin Brown rose to deliver the opening statements for the defense. Born and raised near Knoxville, Tennessee, Brown moved to Louisville in 2002 to take a staff attorney position with the Louisville Metro Public Defender's Office. After taking a moment to compose himself, the ginger-haired, bearded attorney turned and addressed the jury.

"Joey Banis. Joey. He is not guilty. Joey is not guilty of murder. He is not guilty of robbery. He is not guilty of the laundry list that Mr. Schneider informed you of. Joey Banis, that man," he turned and pointed, "he is innocent. And he is an innocent man."

Brown grabbed a book, which he held up for inspection. "Good morning. I'm reading this book here. It's a biography of Billie Holiday. She is a, was, a fantastic, infamous—yes, infamous—jazz singer. And as I began reading this book here—"

Just then a voice behind me hissed, "Jesus. H. Christ. Where the hell is he going with this?" before the attorney continued.

"—I turned to a page before the title page. There was a quotation on the page before the title page, which leapt off the page. It might as well have been flashing in neon, staring directly at me. And it's a quotation from Voltaire, a French philosopher and a French writer," said Brown. "Now, I don't think I have ever in my life quoted a French philosopher or a French writer, and I don't think I ever will again. But this quotation spoke to me. I hope it speaks to you. Because it speaks directly about this case: 'To the living, we owe respect. To the dead, we owe only the truth.' To the dead, we owe only the truth. To the young man, Mr. Carroll, we owe only the truth."

For the next minutes, Brown laid out the defense's strategy, and he caused several eyebrows in the jury box to rise when he said, "And, I'm here to tell you that Joey is guilty. He is guilty of tampering with evidence . . . he assisted in moving Jamie's body . . . and, yes, helped Mundt to bury Jamie's body . . . and those actions, they do haunt him every day." But then the defense attorney went on to explain, "He will also testify, however, about what he is absolutely not guilty of. And that is assisting in anyway—or carrying out on his own—the brutal and senseless and horrific stabbing and shooting of James Carroll. James Carroll, his friend, and his other lover at the time."

Carrie leaned in and whispered. "You know what? I can see where this is going already." I raised my eyebrows, but didn't say anything. "Just wait and see. They're going to paint Jeffrey as the woman scorned." She nodded her head sagely and returned her attention to the front of the courtroom.

Justin Brown paused to look at the clock before he continued. "The evidence will show that on June 17 of 2010, that Joey insisted—and that Joey was persistent—with Officer Trey McKnight, who we will probably hear from later today. He asked again and again, 'Please, let me speak with someone in homicide. I know where a body is that y'all don't even know about.' He insisted and he was persistent. You will hear that Joey again asked that, again and again. He did not give up his desire to speak with someone in homicide. Please. Till, finally, yes, he was finally transported to homicide. And he began to talk. And Joey began to talk and he was fully aware what he was saying was being recorded."

Banis was fully aware that what he was saying could be used against him in a court of law, Brown insisted, but "he continued to talk. And he continued to talk. And, as I promised, he will talk, in just a few short days from now . . . It was Joey who told the police that the man in the basement was Jamie Carroll. He, he told them the identity of that young man. Listen to Mundt's answers, when asked to identify Jamie, when shown a picture: 'He looks familiar.'"

Joey Banis had voluntarily provided the phone numbers, addresses, Gmail accounts, and passwords, which they used to finally track down Jamie Carroll's mother. And, insisted Brown, it was Joey who told the police "the details of that senseless act. About the stab wounds around the neck. He told the details of the burial. It was Joey who told Detective Lesher and the other officers the caliber of the gun . . . And it was Joey who told them where to find the gun."

One of the male jurors fidgeted loudly in his seat and the lawyer stopped for a second to collect his thoughts. "Detective Lesher and the other members of LMPD homicide thought that he was crazy, that he was full of it. And, just like before, y'all are going to hear, Joey was insistent, and he persisted about his friend. And you will hear that Detective Lesher and others went down to that terrible, dungeon basement in the home of Mundt. And that they dug and they dug and they dug, until Jamie was rescued from an eternity in Mundt's basement."

After informing the jury about an especially interesting witness they planned on putting on the stand—a contractor hired to do work in the basement—Brown confirmed again that Banis himself would tell his story. "He will speak to you about how he met Jamie on a dating website—October, September of 2009—and they hit it off immediately. Him and Jamie, two peas in a pod. And they became fast friends. Joey will testify and you will hear about their relationship, about how special Jamie made him feel."

Just then Carrie nudged me in the side. I nodded my head once. "And how that friendship over time became something even more meaningful. They became lovers. Now, they were not exclusive. They were not monogamous, but they were lovers, and they were friends . . . another thread that connected Joey and Jamie . . . is crystal meth . . . but . . . there's so much more between the two."

Then Brown got to the crux of the matter. "Joey refused to cut ties with Jamie. He wouldn't do it. Joey did not wish to settle down. He did not wish to be exclusive or monogamous with anyone, be it Jamie or be it Mundt. What Joey did not know and what he could not have known . . . was that his other lover, Jamie, would brutally be removed from his life forever," he said, adding that sometime in mid-December of 2009 Jamie had come over to Mundt's home—and never left. But "Mundt was left out. Mr. Mundt was ignored by Joey and by Jamie.

Mr. Mundt was ignored in his own bedroom, in his own bed, in his own house. By his lover, who was focused solely on his other lover."

I turned and gave Carrie a look. "Yep, you were right." She nodded briefly and we both directed our gazes back to the opening statements.

My phone vibrated in my pocket, and when I retrieved it, I found a text from my brother Paul. He wanted to come to Louisville and was wondering if he could stay with us for a while. I groaned inwardly. He had stayed with us a number of times already, but he usually wore out his welcome rather quickly. Late-night comings and goings, inviting total strangers over for early morning parties, drinking everything in sight, drunken brawls—these were just a few of the things that made him a less-than-ideal houseguest. Later, after I got home, I'd text back a tactful reply that now wasn't a good time.

"Folks, sympathies or personal opinions, feelings of shock or disgust, they don't matter," continued Brown. "What matters most is whether or not at the end of these next several days the government has proven to each and every one of you beyond a reasonable doubt that Joey is guilty of these terrible, senseless, and brutal acts."

Brown pivoted on his heel and looked out across the gallery before returning his attention to the jury. "Mundt was also arrested for murder. And also been arrested for robbery. And they say here in Louisville— when I moved up here it was one of the first things I heard—if you don't like the weather, if you don't like the weather in Louisville, wait five minutes and it will change. The same goes for Mundt's stories."

He paused and looked at the ceiling. "It was Mundt and Joey and Jamie. And who ends up dead? Joey's other lover. Who ends up in an unthinkable Rubbermaid container for six months? Joey's other lover, in Mundt's house, in Mundt's basement . . . Mundt had everything to gain, of course, by telling police that Joey did it."

Brown painted a duplicitous picture of the co-defendant and his deal with the Commonwealth before taking a long pause. Then he turned and gravely eyed the jurors. "Joey Banis is an innocent man. This man is not guilty. He did not take a life. He did not do these unimaginable things to his friend and to his lover. And, ladies and gentlemen, we ask that you return a verdict after hearing the evidence—the only verdict—a verdict of not guilty, on behalf of Joey."

At the defense table, Joey Banis sat expressionless and unmoving.

\* \* \*

That evening, Ramon and I attended an event at the Little Loomhouse in the South End. Actually a collection of three summer houses from the 1800s, it gained fame in the 1930s when renowned weaver Lou Tate opened a shop in the complex and resided there until her death in 1979. A weaving demonstration, followed by a book signing, took place in the Esta Cabin, the former weekend retreat for the Hill family.

"I bet hobos used to live here." Ramon looked around the room and narrowed his eyes in skepticism. "This old shack is falling apart."

"According to legend, Patty and Mildred Hill first sang the 'Happy Birthday' song here," I said. "And it's not falling apart. These were rustic summer retreats never even meant to last this long. It's amazing they're still around and that's why they have events like this—to raise money to help preserve them."

"Did I hear somebody say the word *hobos* or am I imagining things?" A dapper silver-haired gentleman approached us and extended his hand. It was James Segrest III, who lived at Linden Hill, a beautiful two-hundred-year-old estate overlooking the city. He had spent his younger years in Old Louisville, before moving to Butchertown and establishing himself as a staunch preservationist who fought to save dozens of endangered houses.

"Hi, Jim." I shook his hand. "No, you're not hearing things."

"Oh, good, because I just love hobos. My grandmother had them asking for handouts at her back door in Old Louisville all the time in the '20s and '30s. Hobos had their own communication system, a series of symbols and characters carved into wooden gates and fenceposts to let fellow hobos know how hospitable folks were at a certain household—did you know that?"

"Actually, I did, Jim. I believe we had some of those carvings on the old backyard gate for our house on Third."

"Third Street? You know that's where the Mapothers used to live, two blocks down from your old place. My grandmother was quite a dear friend of theirs. The Thomas Mapothers were always very accomplished." Jim stopped and considered for a bit. "There was Thomas Cruise Mapother I, Thomas Cruise Mapother II, Thomas Cruise

Mapother III—and then, of course, Thomas Cruise Mapother IV! Everybody knows him simply as Tom Cruise today, but Thomas Cruise Mapother IV is his given name."

"Yeah, and he doesn't really talk up his ties to Louisville, does he?"

"No, he doesn't." Jim shrugged his shoulders. "Louisville—the Town that Tom Cruise Famously Ignores. There's another nickname for you."

After the fundraiser, Ramon and I drove to Old Louisville for a late dinner at Amici. At the next table sat Herb and Gayle Warren and the Tripletts, regulars who belonged to the neighborhood association responsible for the block where 1435 sat. We chatted for a bit and they mentioned that the price on the Murder House, as locals now called it, had just dropped again. Intruders had broken in on numerous occasions, most likely associates of Mundt and Banis's attempting to remove any last bits of evidence. "Pretty soon they'll just give it away to the first person who asks," said Hank Triplett.

After finishing our pizzas and salads, we left the restaurant and had started for the car over on the next block when Ramon suddenly patted his pockets and realized he had left his wallet on the table. "Go on ahead," he said, tossing me the keys to the car. "Let me run back to the restaurant. I'll catch up in a bit."

"Who's the hobo now?" I called after him.

I began walking, but out of nowhere the bright flashing of red and blue lights exploded on the dark street, and a police car zoomed in front of me and cut me off at a driveway. The driver's side door opened and a deep voice demanded, "Stop right where you are."

# 16

# WITNESS FOR THE PROSECUTION

AS ITS first witness, the Commonwealth called Officer Jacob "Trey" McKnight, who in June 2010 worked as a patrolman in the 4th Division, which covers mostly Old Louisville. Lead prosecutor Ryane Conroy, a graduate of Bellarmine University and the Brandeis School of Law, started off with the night that police arrested Joey Banis and Jeffrey Mundt. McKnight described the night of the 911 call, arriving at 1435 South Fourth Street shortly before fellow beat officer Kris Pedigo, and was convinced it dealt with an apartment building, not a single-family home, because of the size. Pedigo would be called to the stand himself shortly to back up his partner's account of the night of the arrest. After walking around the premises and scouting out the situation, the patrolmen eventually located a side door under a set of scaffolding, pried it open, and entered. At that point the security alarm screeched to life, and the two men heard noise somewhere in the house. Feeling their way around the gloomy foyer, they heard footsteps, and several seconds later, Joey Banis came running downstairs. That's when McKnight drew his gun and made him lie down.

Pedigo then went upstairs, wending his way through hallways and a disorienting set of rooms, to find Jeffrey Mundt, shaken, in a bedroom. The officers separated the two parties then, Joey Banis taken to the backseat of McKnight's squad car, and Jeffrey staying in the house with Pedigo. McKnight found drug paraphernalia in Joey's backpack, and as he filled out the requisite paperwork in the front seat, Banis kept interrupting him, "trying to bargain his way out of going to jail." Banis insisted he had information about "a homicide they knew nothing about." McKnight didn't take the allegations seriously.

On cross-examination, defense attorney Justin Brown established that Jeffrey Mundt showed no signs of injury the night in question and that the police actually had to break in to gain entry. He also had McKnight admit that Banis did not have a knife on him, as had initially been reported, and that authorities had dropped the domestic violence charges of terroristic threatening and burglary against him. He also admitted a potentially important messenger bag was never taken into evidence, just drug paraphernalia consisting of pipes, hollow cigarettes, and syringes with nothing more than residue, and there weren't three counterfeit fifty-dollar bills as alleged.

After the questioning of the two officers wrapped up, the court adjourned for a lunch break.

Carrie and I made our way down the block to Gavi's, the breakfast and lunch hangout for downtown prosecutors and defense attorneys. "So, that's crazy about last night and that police officer," she said, bundled against the cold in a pea coat and a pink and white crocheted hat pulled down over her dark hair.

"And that's the third time it's happened now." I opened the door and we scouted the room for a free table. "The last time was several years ago, but I doubt she remembered it." The previous night, Officer Janet—a name I assigned to her because of her resemblance to a friend of mine by the name of Janet—had emerged from the vehicle and demanded to see my ID, which I had left in the car. When I told her I didn't have it and pulled out the lone credit card I had taken with me, she took it brusquely and went to radio my name to dispatch.

Once again, I fit the description of somebody they had received a complaint about, but they cleared it up quickly and let me go. Before she returned the credit card, Officer Janet shook her head condescendingly and told me to carry proper identification next time. "You should know better than that," she had said.

"What is it with that woman? It's so bizarre." The smell of cooked vegetables permeating the air, I shrugged. "At least she didn't scare me to death with a gun in my back like she did the last time." Carrie and I zeroed in on two empty places at the Formica-topped counter.

Once described by a judge as a "local institution that is part of the extended courthouse family," Gavi's began cooking up Russian and Jewish favorites like borscht, stuffed cabbage, and matzo ball soup in 1982, but they also offered standard fare like burgers and fries, grilled cheese sandwiches, and quick plate lunch specials. Patrons came as much for the tales as they did for the food, however. The namesake founder Iosef Gavi had fought Nazis as a kid and earned some fame as a skilled mountain climber—and though he had already passed on, his family still liked to tell stories about him.

Before emigrating with his wife, Ida, to the United States in 1978, Gavi had served in the Russian navy as a teenager, trained as a champion Greco-Roman wrestler, and guided Soviet soldiers in the Caucasus Mountains. He had also earned a doctorate in physiology. Gavi, who stood less than five feet tall as an adult, could squeeze through gaps in walls and fences as a child, leading hundreds from the Minsk ghetto into the safety of a nearby forest. Though he rescued his mother and brother, some thirty other relatives, including his father and grandparents, didn't make it out.

He found a second family in Louisville and his diner would become so much a part of the legal community that it was the scene of a famous sting operation in 1998 when undercover agents filmed a local attorney as she allegedly passed on one hundred dollars to bribe a police officer into fixing a drunken-driving case. Although the lawyer was acquitted, the episode sealed Gavi's reputation as being the lunchtime hangout for the legal set in Louisville.

Ida burst through the swinging kitchen door just then, barking orders in Russian—a sure sign something had upset her. Half the courtroom seemed to pack the main dining area, and overheard snippets of conversation indicated the opening statements had made quite an impact. We claimed the last two stools as the matriarch handed over a hot roast beef sandwich glistening with dark gravy to a solitary bailiff next to us.

Carrie seized a menu. "I don't know what to believe now. This is going to be such a strange case, I can feel it." Just then, Gavi's daughter Zina zoomed over and scratched our orders on a pad before disappearing into a back room.

"I know. Why would Joey bring up the body in the basement if he really had something to hide?" I shook my head and moved my laptop aside so the server could set down two bowls of chicken noodle soup. "It doesn't make sense." I wondered what the next witness had to say. We dug into the steaming broth and hardly said a word until two BLTs with extra bacon and tater tots arrived. We wolfed those down and rose to leave.

While Carrie took a quick bathroom break, I went to the cash register to pay. The front door opened and in walked Kelly Atkins, heralded by a gust of cold air. He stopped and stood, hands on his hips, surveying the room for a free table. When he saw me, he smiled and saluted. "Mein Kapitän! Mein Kapitän! Wie geht's?" He sported a pair of shiny military jackboots and a black leather trench coat cinched tightly at the waist. In the crook of the arm not raised in salute rested a billed officer's uniform cap.

Cringing, I took my credit card receipt from Gavi's wife and made my way over to where Kelly stood. "Please tell me you're not wearing what I think you're wearing." I mumbled under my breath as he reached out and crushed me in a bear hug. "Please, please, please, let it not be another Nazi getup."

He released me and patted me on the back. "But, Herr Doktor Professor. Was ist los?"

"You know *was ist los*," I whispered, reaching out and pulling apart the lapels of his coat. Sure enough, under the heavy leather trench coat, he wore a black woolen jacket with an SS insignia on the collar. I quickly pulled together the upper parts of his coat and fastened the topmost button to ensure that nobody could see the offending paraphernalia. "I don't believe you." I shook my head and chortled, despite my misgivings.

"Ja wohl, mein Herr!" He grinned and started humming, still scouting the room for a free table. When he spied Zina hurrying by with a tray mounded high with platters of meatloaf and mashed potatoes, he waved and cried out, "Zdravstvuyte!" The frazzled woman knit her brows in vexation and reluctantly returned a greeting in Russian as she doled out the daily special to a table of attorneys next to one of the big plate glass windows looking out onto Seventh Street. As she whisked the empty tray under an arm and made ready to return to the kitchen, she did a double-take at Kelly. Her eyes slowly narrowed to suspicious slits as she gave his outfit the once-over.

He stopped humming and began singing the "Horst Wessel Lied" under his breath. My eyes widened. "Kelly! Oh my god, you're going to get us killed." I grabbed him by the elbow, then pushed him out the door onto the sidewalk. "Are you crazy? Half their family was murdered by the Germans."

He clicked his heels together. "Well, shit and Shinola, I'll go and change and come back without the kraut army gear. Had a hankering for stuffed cabbage and Gavi's has the best in town."

"More like you've got a hankering for getting the living crap beat out of you." I turned to wave and let Carrie know where I had gone. She exited the door and approached warily. "You're something else," I mumbled before she arrived.

"Hi, have you been following the trial as well?" Carrie withdrew the hand Kelly had ceremoniously lifted to his lips and kissed. "I see you're still the courtly gentleman."

"Oh, yes, I have indeed, but just on the news," said Kelly. "Maybe I'll come sit in on the trial with y'all one of these days. Saw Mundt on the news. He looks like death eatin' crackers."

I glanced at the time on my cellphone and, realizing the lunch recess was over, I signaled to Carrie with a nod that we needed to hurry. "Catch you later," I said. "And if you do decide to join us, don't you dare plan on entering the courtroom in that getup!" I yelled over my shoulder as we raced for the courtroom.

Carrie started laughing as we stopped at the corner and waited for the light in the crosswalk to change.

"Now you know why everyone calls him Crazy Kelly. He was like that when I first met him waiting tables at the Seelbach Hotel."

"Does he always dress like that?"

"Fortunately, no." I rushed and pulled open a door to the Judicial Center, letting Carrie pass through. We emptied our pockets and proceeded through the security check.

"It almost looked like he was wearing a Nazi uniform with that coat and those boots."

"He was." I collected my things before we headed for the elevators.

"He was?" Carrie asked, eyes wide in horror.

"One of these days I'll tell you more about him, but we just don't have the time right now."

We made it to the courtroom just in the nick of time.

The third witness Ryane Conroy called to the stand was Jon Lesher, the lead detective in the murder. Originally from a small town in Pennsylvania, the dark-haired thirtysomething had served in the U.S. Army and worked at the Jefferson County Department of Corrections before joining the Louisville police in 2001. Although he described himself as "kind of a rookie" the night he became the lead detective in the murder, Lesher had earned a degree of respect from his colleagues and rivals during his relatively short time in homicide. "He could cut through the BS faster than any other detective I've ever known," said criminal defense attorney Julie Kaelin, who represented several defendants accused of murder in cases cracked by Lesher. "He never treated me like an enemy and we had a mutual respect for each other because we each knew that the other was doing their job the best they could."

On the stand, Lesher described the situation leading up to murder discovery as "bizarre." He interpreted Joey Banis's offer to take them to the location of a body they knew nothing about as an attempt to avoid arrest and return home, a not altogether uncommon reaction for suspects in this situation. "He was continuously saying, 'I want to go home.'" But, there was no way to make a deal in this instance, explained Lesher, because in domestic incidents in Kentucky, "there is zero tolerance and they go to jail." Over several hours, the detective only managed to tease out "bits and pieces" from Banis. At first, "I thought he was full of it," said Lesher, but "he eventually provided a name to us, Jamie Carroll."

Banis claimed to have met Carroll through crystal meth connections and that he went by the username "Cruising Not Using" on the popular gay hookup site Adam4Adam. Carroll's family probably didn't have a clue he'd gone missing as they thought he had turned himself in and gone to prison. Lesher ascertained that Carroll had missed a court date in Jefferson County in December 2009. When shown a picture of Carroll, Banis identified him only as "the guy who missed court." He went on to say that Jeffrey Mundt had killed him and buried the body in a part of the basement with a dirt floor. At about four-thirty that morning, when officers went back to 1435 South Fourth Street, Lesher said Mundt was "shocked" to hear the claims of a body in his basement.

After a brief recess, the prosecution had Jon Lesher back on the witness stand and he narrated as Ryane Conroy showed a silent video of the inside of 1435 South Fourth Street, filmed as the police entered and made their way first to the basement and then through other parts of the house. As the person behind the camera wended through gloomy interiors and hallways, my mind went back to the wee morning hours when I had explored the darkened rooms and corners of the mansion. I recalled mostly empty spaces, but the video showed random pieces of furniture, storage bins, pet carriers, and framed artwork here and there. Much more than I remembered. No doubt, the police had snatched up evidence, but had people entered and carried items away as souvenirs in the couple of days between the discovery of Jamie Carroll and my late-night rendezvous with Candy in the basement?

The camera continued up the elaborate grand stairway, past a bank of leaded-glass windows, and down a long corridor. Somebody opened the door to room six and then eleven, where a large bed occupied one corner. Dull light reflected in a number of framed prints on a bookshelf. The camera panned to a wooden mantel and it went in close to show a photo of Joey Banis in jeans and a sweater, standing and giving the photographer a cheeky grin. His ginger hair was spiked in a slight mohawk. On a nearby nightstand stood an arrangement of several other pictures, all of them of Joey Banis. Then the camera zoomed in on several surfaces, including the top of a cat carrier, where smallish dark stains might have hinted at the presence of blood.

For several more minutes the courtroom audience watched as police walked through empty rooms and hallways, and up and down several flights of stairs. Then they reentered the mazelike ensemble of spaces that comprised the basement, the hazy light of a flashlight beam guiding them from room to room until they went down a couple of steps to a packed dirt floor. The camera slowly panned the area and then moved to a patch of disturbed earth.

Lesher then described the tedious, back-breaking process of digging down through more than four feet of hard dirt until, hours later, their shovels struck something that made a dull thud. After another hour of scraping and working to dislodge the object, the officers beheld a blue rubber storage bin wrapped in tape. Under normal circumstances the container would have been sent unopened to the medical examiner; however, in the process of unearthing it, Lesher said they inadvertently knocked into the lid and loosened it. "At that time, we smelled death," he explained.

When the defense rose for the cross-examination, lead attorney Darren Wolff went to question Lesher. Once described by a female colleague as "equal parts dashing and debonair," the California transplant had served as a captain and JAG officer for the United States Marine Corps before joining the Kentucky Bar in 2002. When the tall lawyer first appeared in the local news as the defense the Banis family had hired for their son, many Louisvillians knew his face and name already. They had seen him on national news outlets such as CNN or they had read about him in the book *Black Hearts* by Jim Frederick—all in connection with one of the most heinous war crimes perpetrated by U.S. forces since the Vietnam War.

In March 2006, in a region of Iraq known as the Triangle of Death, Private First Class Steven Green and three fellow soldiers from the fabled Black Heart Brigade got drunk at a lightly defended checkpoint, where they hatched a plan that stemmed from their hatred of the locals—and the heavy losses sustained by their platoon. Green and his co-conspirators disguised themselves in long black underwear they called "ninja suits" and slipped away. Just a couple of hundred yards down the road they entered a one-bedroom farmhouse and attacked the family living there.

While two of the soldiers savagely raped fourteen-year-old Abeer Qassim Hamza al-Janabi, Green held the family at gunpoint in the next room. He shot her mother in the chest, her father in the head, and her six-year-old sister in the face—all at point-blank range. Then Green entered the room and raped the child before shooting her several times in the head. One of his cohorts doused her with gasoline and set her body aflame. They "celebrated" their depravity with a meal of chicken wings. Green described the crime as "awesome."

The soldiers returned to their post and convinced the local police Sunni insurgents had orchestrated the massacre. For months, the army and many locals attributed the murders to Iraqi-on-Iraqi violence—until a whistleblower came forward. Military courts convicted Green's co-conspirators, doling out sentences of ninety years or longer, but because the army had already honorably discharged Green due to "anti-social personality disorder," the FBI arrested him and transferred him to Louisville, as he had been assigned to the 101st Airborne Division, based in Fort Campbell, Kentucky. Federal prosecutors charged him with rape and multiple counts of murder.

It was the first time a former soldier had faced trial—and the death penalty—in a civil jurisdiction for crimes committed in a war zone. Public defenders Scott Wendelsdorf and Pat Bouldin had brought Wolff to their team because of his previous experience as a judge advocate general with the Marines.

Given the strength of the evidence and Green's own confession, Wolff concluded that just keeping their client alive would constitute a major victory. Instead of opting for an insanity defense, they focused on the "context of the crime" by highlighting the awful conditions in Iraq, Green's horrible upbringing, leadership failures, and the repeated warning signs of his derangement and murderous obsession. Nine female and three male jurors found him guilty of all counts of murder, rape, and related charges; however, when the time for sentencing came, the jury tied at six for and six against the death penalty. This triggered an automatic life sentence with no chance of parole. Darren Wolff had proved a valuable asset to the defense team.

Locals saw even more of Wolff's face on the news a week after the trial when camera crews flooded the very same courtroom where Wolff now stood. In what proved to be a raucous and dramatic session, relatives of the Janabi family had flown in for the preliminary sentencing trial in Louisville.

Hajia, the grandmother, wailed as an interpreter translated. "This man has no mercy in his heart, he does not have honor, and yet you let him breathe air until he dies naturally?" she shouted from the witness stand. "He is a stigma on the United States. He is a stigma on the whole world. He is a bastard, and a criminal, and a dog!" Ululating, the keening woman suddenly stood and made for the defense table where Green sat. "Show him to me, I want to see him!" It took nearly a dozen court officials to wrestle the grandmother to the ground and carry her away, still kicking and screaming.

Abu Muhammad, the mother's cousin and the last relative to speak, pointedly criticized the jury for not doing its due diligence. His final words echoed in the silent courtroom as he turned to Green: "Abeer will follow you and chase you in your nightmares. May God damn you."

Five years later prison officials would find Green's body hanging in his cell at a federal penitentiary in Tucson, Arizona.

On his cross-examination, Wolff established that when questioning Joey Banis the police had someone in custody who was insistent about talking and providing information. He also pointed out that Lesher referred to himself as a "rookie" with only thirteen months of experience in his particular position and he questioned the detective's claim that he kept no written documentation. He also brought up that his client had been very generous in the information he provided, providing names and passwords that helped them track down Ellen Carroll and ascertain that her son was missing.

Lesher, who had been sitting at the prosecution's table since the trial began, proved to be a star witnesses for the state and over the course of four and a half hours, Wolff attempted to chip away at the quality of the detective's investigative work—and that of the entire homicide unit as well. They waited for almost a month before calling in blood experts from the Kentucky Crime Laboratory who used Bluestar, an effective blood reagent, to collect evidence, and during that time the house was not sealed off as a crime scene. "There's no telling how many people could have gone into the house during that time," said Wolff.

The attorney also took issue with the handling of evidence, especially the weapons and electronic devices seized after police arrested Mundt and Banis in Chicago. Lesher claimed the Secret Service had possession of several laptops but that they handed over copies of the hard drive with more than 700,000 files. "You didn't look at them all, did you?" said Lesher.

"Yes, I did," responded the detective.

Wolff stopped and gave him a quizzical look. "Really? 700,000-plus files?"

"I clicked on every link I could go through, yes."

In the back of the courtroom, somebody chuckled loudly and Carrie and I looked at each other. I took out my cellphone and pulled up the calculator. "Let's be generous and say he only needed a second to open each file," I whispered, tapping numbers into the keypad. "That would mean 700,000 files took"—I turned the phone so she could see the screen—"194.44 hours."

"Hmmm." Carrie shook her head. "I don't think so."

At the witness stand, Wolff shook his head as well.

Changing tack, Wolff brought up *The First 48* filming the night of the incident and how star-struck detectives had left the door to the interrogation room open wide so the cameraman could film them and their interrogation process. The defense attorney implied that Lesher had acted differently because he knew the cameras were on him, in essence being derelict in his duty. The detective staunchly refuted this.

During her questioning, Ryane Conroy had produced photos of Banis posing with a Glock, but before ending his cross-examination Wolff established that the registered owner of the Glock used to kill Jamie Carroll, as well as the others seized, was Jeffrey Mundt, not Joey Banis, and he drove home that it wasn't a gun that killed Carroll anyway. Referring to the coroner's report, he asked Lesher one final question: "The cause of death, that stopped Mr. Carroll's heart from beating back and forth, was a knife, is that correct?" Lesher reluctantly agreed.

Next to the stand came Detective Roy Stalby, employed by LMPD for twelve years and assigned to the 2nd Division as a patrol officer. The night of the incident he had assisted Lesher by conducting surveillance from an unmarked Crown Vic on the street in front of 1435 South Fourth Street while police obtained the search warrant. Conroy established that the premises were under control the whole time that evidence was secured.

After that, the prosecution called two witnesses from the local crime scene unit. Patsy Richards had collected evidence such as a sledgehammer, spent casings, and shovels, and she had video recorded the unearthing of the blue Rubbermaid container. Marilyn Chynoweth

Butts, trained in Bluestar latent blood detection, commented on the blood evidence, or lack thereof, found in the rooms where Joey and Jeffrey had lived and in the adjoining hallway on the second floor. On cross-examination, she ascertained that the crime scene hadn't been preserved per se and that twenty-five days would pass before they carried out the tests for chemiluminescence.

The judge adjourned for the day, and as spectators exited the courtroom I saw that he had called the prosecution and defense attorneys aside for a hasty conference.

As I prepared to walk through the door, I said goodbye to Bailiff Brown. That's when he turned and pointed up at the judge and the assembled attorneys. "Looks like you're in trouble again."

# 17

# GAY GUYS ARE
# SO CREEPY

I STOPPED and stared at the bailiff. In return, he arched a skeptical eyebrow at me. I returned my gaze to the front of the courtroom where the lawyers huddled with the judge. "Seriously? What did I do now?" I continued out the exit.

"I don't know," he said, "but they're talking about you." Brown followed me into the waiting room and locked the door. "I'm sure you'll find out if it's important enough."

It wasn't that important, but I did find out eventually. My daily presence in the courtroom had simply piqued the judge's curiosity.

"Who is the person—he sat behind you yesterday and you today—very large and blond hair?" Mitch Perry had asked the prosecution and defense teams.

Justin Brown answered, "He's the guy writing the book."

"Book Guy," said Darren Wolff. "Why, is he doing something?"

The judge chuckled and said, "Ah, okay."

Ryane Conroy eagerly cut in then and said, "Can we kick him out?"

Answering in the negative, Mitch Perry laughed softly. "He's just been particularly attentive, which I've noticed. So, alright."


I had dinner plans that night. I picked up Frances and we joined my friend and fellow writer Jerry Rodgers at Buck's, a popular Old

Louisville restaurant on Ormsby. At the piano, Rick Bartlett played the soft strains of a jazz song. A multitude of vases overflowing with white stars of Bethlehem crowded the bar, where patrons waiting for tables nursed their cocktails.

Seated at a table in the corner, we had ordered bourbon old-fashioneds and sipped them as the waiter took our ticket to the kitchen. "Oh, you know Joey Banis's family is very prominent, don't you? His father is a very well-known plastic surgeon," said Jerry. "They're not from here originally, from back east somewhere, and I think it was the Binghams or one of the old-money families that brought them to Louisville. So he could do their facelifts and tummy tucks."

"Oh, darlins, I could tell you about some of the facelifts he has done," said Frances. "If some of my friends get their faces any more lifted they're liable to float away." She gave us a knowing look while she smeared butter on a piece of bread. Then she lowered her head for a dramatic whisper. "Good lord, some of my friends are starting to look like Michael Jackson!" She laughed and popped the bread into her mouth.

"Oh, Frances Mengel, you're terrible," said Jerry with a stifled chuckle. He lifted a fork and started in on the salads the server had just delivered. "You know, it's a good thing this Jodi Arias circus is consuming all the national attention, because otherwise our murder trial here in Louisville would be dominating the news." The Arias trial, which had started in January, would drag on for over four months. A scorned ex-girlfriend, Jodi Arias stood accused of murdering Travis Alexander in his Arizona apartment. He had suffered multiple stab wounds, a slit throat, and a shot to the head.

"Well, thank goodness for small blessings!" said Frances.

"So, David, how is your brother Paul?" Jerry put down his napkin and looked at me expectantly. "What new mess has he gotten himself into lately?" Unfortunately, my brother's antics had become a popular topic of conversation among my friends, most of whom knew him from the times he had stayed with us.

Recently he had passed out on the side of the road while hitchhiking to a family reunion. I hadn't been invited because the organizer didn't approve of my "lifestyle." When a passing motorist alerted authorities, an ambulance arrived to discover Paul had lain unconscious on an ant hill for at least an hour and angry insects had taken their revenge. They were surprised he survived. Not long before, at a regional airport where exasperated family members dropped him off so he could travel on to avail himself of the next household's hospitality, someone called security when Paul suffered a panic attack brought on by drugs and a fear of flying for the first time. They had to close down the airport while he was brought under control.

"He's okay, as far as I know. He moved to Louisiana not too long ago. No new stunts to report." Our main courses arrived and the conversation lagged as we inspected our plates and waited for the server to pour glasses of wine.

"Oh, I just love the pork chop and cheese grits here." Frances smiled after her first mouthful. "Darlin', did I ever give you the recipe for Mrs. Mengel's pork and cheese grits? You know, my late husband's mother. The one who lived in the big mansion right around the corner. Well, not that she cooked very often, because they had a whole staff of servants, you know, but still, it's a tremendous recipe."

"No, I don't—"

"Lordy, that was a house. Have you been in it? Oh, of course, you have, you know the current owners, I forgot about that." A look of surprise suddenly washing over her face, Frances clutched the beads around her neck. "Oh, darlin', I totally forgot to tell you this! The Mengels were friends with a doctor who had a practice in Old Louisville back when they had the mansion—the '30s, I believe—and he ended up in some trouble. He was brought up on ethics charges and ruined. They said he had killed some of his own patients, kind of like an angel of death, and you'll never guess where he was practicing!"

Jerry swallowed a bite of his crispy fish with sweet chili sauce and inadvertently clattered his fork when he set it on the rim of his plate. "You're not saying he was in the house where the murder—"

"That's exactly what I'm saying, darlins, there was a mad doctor in that house at one time! And quite a few people have died in that place. No wonder something awful like a murder happened there. That house has some bad vibrations, I am telling you. When I first saw that house pop up on the news, I wondered why it looked so familiar. Well, that's why!"

"My, how exciting," said Jerry. "That house really does have a spooky pedigree."

"You know, there are a lot of stories about what used to go on in that place. It will be interesting to see how much turns out to be true." I took a sip of wine and mulled over my next words. "In Old Louisville there always seems to be a fine line between fact and fiction."

"Nothing wrong with that, darlin'," said Frances. "Nothing wrong with that."

The next morning began with testimony from the coroner, Dr. Donna Stewart, describing the state of Jamie Carroll's body when they brought him in on a gurney in "a fifty-gallon, plastic blue storage container" weighing a total of two hundred and seventy pounds, of which Jamie Carroll constituted just one hundred and twenty-eight pounds. Lime poured over his body accounted for most of the rest of the weight. "So, it's not a very large container," said the medical examiner. When they removed his body, which had "concretized," they found him "hog-tied in a crouching position."

The defense objected when Conroy prepared to show the jury the autopsy photos, claiming one of the images was particularly prejudicial and irrelevant. "It is a ghastly image," insisted Justin Brown. The judge overruled him and the prosecution began its slideshow.

A collective gasp sounded in the courtroom as the picture in question flashed on the screen. A large face loomed in front of the jury, eyes closed but with almost a hint of a smile on his lips. Patches of decay were visible but much of the flesh was intact, tainted by a blue-gray pallor. Despite the decomposition, it was still easily identifiable as Jamie. In the jury box, a head turned down and looked away.

According to Stewart, death had come as the result of three downward stab wounds that damaged Jamie Carroll's brachiocephalic vein and caused hemorrhage. It would have taken several minutes for Jamie Carroll to bleed out and die. The toxicology report indicated the presence of methamphetamine and alcohol in his blood. When asked if she had an opinion as to the cause of death, the coroner said, "Mr. Carroll died from the stab wounds to the neck and this was a homicide."

Jessica Silveria, also present at the autopsy, took the stand next. From CSU, she had documented and packaged various pieces of evidence, including a metal bracelet, a Fossil-brand watch, a silver cross pendant on a chain, two rings "worn on hand," as well as "two sexual-type devices," namely "a penile ring and a penile-scrotal harness removed from the body of Jamie Carroll."

"Ewww," hissed a familiar voice from somewhere behind us. "Gay guys are so creepy."

Carrie and I looked at each other.

After that, Ryane Conroy called a witness from the Chicago Police Department, a thirteen-year veteran officer, Hysni Selenica, who on April 11, 2010, responded to a call about a "deceptive action in progress" from the Hyatt Regency Hotel at 151 East Wacker Drive. A valet had received a counterfeit hundred-dollar bill from two guests who had just checked in. As the hotel employee was giving the details to the officer, he spotted Mundt and Banis coming down the elevator and pointed them out. Selenica and another officer followed and "stopped both of the offenders" in front of Mundt's blue BMW parked outside. When they patted them down, they found a fully loaded Glock in Joey's coat pocket, the weapon used to shoot Jamie Carroll. The officers arrested him and then Jeffrey when the doorman confirmed Mundt as the one who had given him the fake bill.

On cross-examination, when Justin Brown asked the policeman about Joey's reaction to the arrest, Selenica said, "He said he wanted to self-admit that it was all his fault and the counterfeit bill was his. And that he had over fifty-four thousand dollars in counterfeit bills in his bag." At this, an angry Darren Wolff stood and approached the bench, where he requested a mistrial over the "fifty-four thousand dollars" statement. It seemed that nobody knew what had happened to all the bogus bills and that had raised some suspicions. "To our knowledge, they do not have fifty-four thousand dollars," he exclaimed. "I have not seen it; it's not in the property room back here. Clearly, it wasn't there when I went down and looked at the evidence." Wolff alleged there was no way to know the money was counterfeit if they didn't have the chance to examine it.

When the judge looked to Conroy for clarification as to the whereabouts of the money, the prosecuting attorney just shrugged her shoulders and said it had been "seized, was in possession of the Secret Service in Chicago." Although Wolff insisted the inability to have seen the actual—and alleged—counterfeit bills "hamstrung" the defense of his client, Perry denied the mistrial and the prosecution returned to its witness. When asked for more details about items in Joey's bag, Selenica said they had found additional firearms and counterfeit money—in addition to ammunition and magazines, computers, credit card decoders or readers, and random personal property, "some Indiana ID that didn't belong to him, and a fictitious Washington ID."

For the next three witnesses, prosecutor Conroy called officers Bradley Woolrich and Denise Elliott to discuss the drug evidence, and firearm and toolmark examiner Leah Collier to establish that the bullet extracted from Jamie Carroll's body came from the gun in Joey Banis's possession. The three witnesses that followed—Erin Redfield of Louisville CSU and Shannon Phelps and Robert Thurman of the Kentucky State Police—all provided testimony linking bodily fluids samples they had collected or analyzed to DNA matching Joey Banis and Jeffrey Mundt.

Conroy's next witness to the stand, Detective Collin King had assisted Jon Lesher the night of the arrest and he described a Jeffrey Mundt who appeared genuinely "shocked" when told about the discovery of the body in the basement. But the detective sensed "something wasn't being fully conveyed" and suggested Mundt submit to a polygraph.

On cross-examination Darren Wolff took the detective to task for what he considered sloppy police work and pointed out his lack of experience as a homicide detective, not even having worked for a full year at the time of the incident. King hadn't kept the written notes he'd taken during the interview, he hadn't even taken the time to review the recorded interview before taking the stand, the defense emphasized. Nor had the detective taken into evidence a small knife in Jeffrey Mundt's possession the night of his arrest. Things began to get heated when King denied having any recollection of such a knife, and he only begrudgingly admitted there was a knife that night when Wolff produced video showing him asking Mundt about the knife. Given a knife had been used to kill Jamie Carroll, Wolff insisted a more responsible detective would have immediately taken it into evidence.

Implications of sloppy detective work continued, but at a less vociferous tone, on the cross examination of the prosecution's penultimate witness, Officer Chris Middleton, a thirteen-year veteran of the LMPD. After that, the jury had the chance to view the videotaped interview of Joey Banis for the first time.

At 1:25 in the morning of June 18, Jon Lesher, in the presence of Officer Tom Miles, had begun the interview of Joey Banis, who gave 1435 South Fourth Street as his address, the place where he had resided the prior seven to eight months with his boyfriend Jeffrey Mundt. When asked to recount the incident leading up to that night's arrest, he said, "I obviously felt violated because my boyfriend had lied somehow and gotten police there and had me arrested for something I didn't do, and, then, evidently, had told the officers there I killed somebody. And . . . it, it just shocked me because I'm not the one who killed anybody." When he spoke, Banis came across as articulate, if a bit tired, and calm.

"The guys came downstairs and said, 'Man, your boyfriend is mad at you. He said you're a murderer.' Or something like that. And I just—you know—I was crying. I didn't understand. Why was I in handcuffs? Why was I being told I had burglarized this place when I lived there?"

Lesher then asked if he knew Jeffrey's date of birth, and Joey responded that he "thought it was February 28th," 1972. But then he went on to make an enigmatic statement. "I don't know if it is or not. There's a lot of things I don't really know about him . . . He's got several different identities, passports. I've seen another passport with his face on it, with a different name."

Carrie and I turned and looked at each other. "He's got several different identities?" we whispered in unison. Detective Lesher didn't seem to think multiple identities and fake passports warranted more in-depth questioning, however, and he urged Banis to continue with the details leading up to the supposed homicide. "As detailed as possible, could you go over that again for me and Detective Miles again?" he said. "You witnessed everything, all the events that took place? And it's not secondhand information. You personally saw it all happen, and the aftermath, right?"

"I wish I hadn't, but, yes, I did," responded Joey. "I knew Jamie through drug use. Jamie was a drug dealer. I had recently met my boyfriend, Jeffrey Steven Mundt. He was a drug user. Jeffrey wanted to get some drugs so he invited Jamie over to the house on Fourth

Street. And, ah, Jamie came over and we basically used some drugs for a while." Soon, they had used up all the drugs and Jamie returned to his downtown hotel to get more, and during his absence Jeffrey, who Joey often called "Jase," floated the idea of killing and robbing Jamie when he came back.

"And, you know, I really thought he was joking or pushing my buttons to see where I stood on this whole thing. And Jamie came back to the house, at probably—I assume it was at least five or six o'clock in the morning." Joey recalled a very rainy night. "Jamie came back with the drugs. And . . . God knows how much money he had on him, and . . . we started to get high." According to Joey, "Jamie and Jase were in the bed naked and there was porn on the TV . . . and I was, basically, getting high and watching porn. And before I knew it, Jase had stabbed Jamie. Jamie jumped up. There was blood flying. There was a lot of yelling."

When Detective Lesher asked if Joey recalled where Jeffrey had stabbed Jamie, he responded, "it was somewhere around the upper neck, torso. I don't know exactly where. Really, this all happened so quickly that I was freaked out." Joey claimed he then ended up against the wall, hyperventilating and in shock. "Jamie was yelling my name, for help, and Jase had pulled a .38 Smith & Wesson revolver out and before I knew it, had shot Jamie, what it appeared like, to be through the heart, at least twice. I remember hearing *pow*. I thought at that point that he was going to kill me." Carrie and I exchanged puzzled glances because the coroner had said there was a single gunshot wound and that the bullet had lodged in Jamie's chin.

Joey's voice quavered. "Jamie fell to floor and was gushing blood. Or there was blood everywhere, I don't know if it was still gushing. This was in the corner of Jeff's room, near the door, where he had gotten Jamie buttonholed. There was blood all over the Oriental carpet, and on the walls, and on the wooden floor. And, just every-where. There was lots of broken glass . . . I guess Jamie had fallen into a glass-fronted cabinet in the room."

Joey then described a scene in which his boyfriend wrapped Carroll's body in bed linens and forced him to help clean the room. "Jase acted like he had done this before. He took Jamie's cellphone and broke the SIM card and destroyed about every bit of that. He eventually took Jamie's computer and he got into it and he removed the internet access—but he kept the computer, he used that for the other illegal activities as an anonymous computer that wasn't registered to him." When the detective asked about the location of the computer, Banis responded it was one of the computers seized in Chicago—used by his boyfriend for scams and modifications of counterfeit bills—and added, "Jeffrey said he would kill me—and my family—if I did not keep my mouth shut" and that "Jase was running around, acting maniacal."

When Lesher interjected and asked what motivated Joey to come forward now, he said, "I wasn't able to tell anybody in the beginning, because I was scared for myself, scared for my family, and I was also in love with this guy. But, over the past seven or eight months, I no longer love him and somebody's just got to know the truth." And he added, "I want freedom from this person. Jase has basically held me prisoner for a long, long time and it's just been one thing after another. And I'm not at all interested in being in a relationship with him nor being threatened or scared anymore . . ."

Lesher then changed course and asked if Joey knew about other murders that his boyfriend had committed, to which he replied: "Just stuff that he's told me in the past he has supposedly done for the U.S. government. And I do not know the specifics on very many of them. I've seen news stories on bombings but I don't know what's true and not true half the time with what he's told me. All I know is he scares the hell out of me." The detective then brought up a previous statement by Banis, claiming Mundt was responsible for thirty-five other murders. "Yes, that's what he told me," said Joey. "He told me he had a hat, a baseball cap, that he—and I guess somebody who he used to work with in the past—used to put little gold stars on, like 'good job,' each star was for people, a person who had died. From what I understand, how he became involved in all this was through government work."

"What the hell?" murmured a male voice behind us. "This gets more and more fucked up by the day."

"Gay guys are so fucking creepy," responded his female companion.

Carrie and I exchanged glances. The prosecution stopped the interview not long thereafter, and Judge Mitch Perry adjourned for the day. The weekend lay ahead, and on Monday, the prosecution's star witness would take the stand. Jeffrey Mundt.

# 18

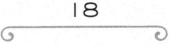

# REDHEADED STEPCHILD

**THAT NIGHT,** conversation about the trial buzzed at a party on St. James Court. "Oh, Jeffrey Mundt? He appears to be something of a kinky boy," said Louise Cecil. "He came in for costumes once, and he only showed an interest in leather and shiny black rubber suits." Something of a local legend, Louise had a huge costume shop on the upper floor of an old red-brick warehouse nearby. Shelves along the walls burst with bowlers and top hats, a multitude of masks, jewel-encrusted scepters, angel wings, and turbans. Bolts of colorful fabric lay heaped in the corners and racks groaned under the weight of elegant gowns and period attire. She hand-stitched many of the costumes—rumored to be over 10,000 in all—herself and kept track of everything with a simple system of receipts and tickets, refusing to use a computer to track the inventory. "And hoods with no eye or nose holes," she added.

"You don't say?" said Lucie Blodgett. "My, that does sound interesting." The octogenarian had arrived to cover the event for the *Voice of St. Matthews* in her weekly column The Social Side. "I remember once, when I traveled to London in 1953 to photograph the coronation of Queen Elizabeth, seeing a man in a pub—wearing a leather hood with just a big hole for the mouth and nose."

"Oh, Lucie, you saw no such thing!" laughed Louise. "I know you were at the coronation as a journalist, but really."

"I swear I did. Goodness gracious. I saw that exact thing," she retorted with a chuckle. "He just sat there, lifting his pint for a sip every now and then. If I had had the time, I would have stopped and asked him about it. There were so many things I wanted to know." Her eyes got wide as she scanned the faces of those gathered around her. "Did he wear it all the time? If so, how did he walk to the pub?" A speckle of laugher worked its way through the crowd and she paused to sip from a wineglass.

"My, Lucie! The things you see when you travel the world taking photographs," said Louise.

"And you know what I did before I went on that trip?" Lucie took another sip. "Well, I was in Oxford, Mississippi, so I decided to visit William Faulkner at his home—unannounced. I had heard he was traveling to the coronation as well, so I popped in to ask him what I should pack for the upcoming trip."

"You're a hoot, Lucie."

"Well, we sat on his porch with his hound dogs, and he was perfectly charming and got me something to drink. 'Mr. Faulkner, what are you going to take to Europe?' I said, and he just matter-of-factly wrote out a list of what he would pack: 'four oxford shirts, two pair of black pants, razor, razor strap, and plenty of sharpened pencils and notebooks.' I swear, that's exactly what he did."

Before her trip to Europe, Blodgett, originally from Mississippi, had covered the Kentucky Derby for the *Jackson Daily News*. She fell in love with Louisville, moved here, and never left. She quickly landed a job reporting for the legendary Barry Bingham Sr. at the *Courier-Journal* and her photography earned her a reputation as a trailblazer for women.

Suddenly, Lucie's tone became somewhat serious. "But, all joking aside, this trial just has everyone in a tizzy. Those boys come for such good families. I mean, Dr. Banis? He is salt of the earth. Humble and kind. I just cannot fathom the anguish."

"Oh, I know. It must be just awful." Maria Eckerle, the hostess, had joined the circle to greet new faces. "My late husband, the judge, really liked him."

Frances Mengel and I had just arrived a few minutes before, and it was the first time she had finally stopped her chatter to listen. "Oh, Maria, the house looks just wonderful—and I love your newest trophies!" Frances pointed to the entry hall, where a wooden pedestal supported the taxidermied shoulder mount of a zebra. Flanking it on either side stood the busts of an impala and a kudo. Farther down, a huge salmon gleamed from a wooden cartouche on the wall. Beyond that, the head of a large deer seemed to gaze on with disapproval.

"Thanks, that just arrived. I shot it in Zimbabwe." With her petite frame and training as an opera singer, the bouncy blonde had caused more than one eyebrow to arch in surprise when she announced her hobby as a big-game hunter. She had just returned from another African safari. "You know, I saw a picture of that Jamie Carroll on the news—the one they dug out of the basement—and I'm positive I saw him here on the court before, and more than once. He looked kind of shifty, lurking in front of the house."

Maria lived in the stately Alice Hegan Rice House, one of the largest on St. James Court, the celebrated residential enclave of Old Louisville. Completed in 1910, the Classical Revival structure was home to one of Louisville's most influential writers of the day—and her poet and playwright husband Cale Young Rice. Alice's most enduring work, *Mrs. Wiggs of the Cabbage Patch*, became an immediate bestseller upon publication in 1901 and the royalties had paid for the house.

A thinly veiled social commentary, the story presented a fictionalized account of Mary Bass, a real-life resident of Old Louisville, who resided just a few blocks from the grand mansions of Millionaires Row and St. James Court in a shantytown "where ramshackle cottages played hop-scotch over the railroad tracks." The single mother of five struggled daily to provide for her children all on her own, because, as the author wrote, the woman's husband "had gone to heaven by route of the alcohol highway." Her story made it to Hollywood, where it was filmed four times, the last with W.C. Fields and Shirley Temple in supporting roles.

"Do you think he was looking to sell dope or something?" said Lucie. "I heard he was a drug dealer."

"I don't know," said Maria, "but he seemed like he was up to no good."

"Well, it wouldn't be the first time there was someone up to no good down here in Old Louisville." Debra Richards, bemoaning another preservation failure in the vicinity and munching on a cheese straw, had joined the circle. "But usually it's not the homeless people or drug dealers. It's usually one of the sneaky developers wanting to chop one of these mansions up into cheap apartments or one of the churches looking to tear down old houses so they can have another parking lot or put in a soup kitchen."

"Well, it is getting better." Lucie Blodgett lifted a chocolate from a tray and took a dainty nibble. "I remember when I moved here eons ago in the 1950s how shabby the court was, but look at it today." She gestured to the front window, where the soft glow of gas lamps outside silhouetted the elegant fountain at the center of the green.

"Yeah, since they recast the statue of Venus rising from the sea and put back the old streetlights, it's come a long way." Debra Richards popped a cube of cheese in her mouth and chewed. "Y'all remember Gussie Smith? How she'd get up every morning and put on her Victorian dresses and lace up her tall heeled boots and just stroll up and down the court like she owned the place? They don't make 'em like that anymore."

"Oh, I remember her!" said Frances. "She cut quite a picture standing on her front porch under those incredible archways." Up through the 1980s, Gussie Smith had resided in one of the most photographed houses in the city, the Hindman Briscoe House. Completed around 1899, the large Italianate brick structure had lavish Venetian Gothic arches in terra cotta that anchored the ground floor. Delicate window caps accented the second level, while on the third floor, windows encased in faux parchment scrolls gazed out from beneath a majestic band of acanthus leaves resting atop a horizontal bundle of reeds. Legendary ceramic artist Mary Alice Hadley had begun making her famous stoneware in the hayloft of the carriage house.

"That's for certain," said Lucie. "She was one of a kind. We owe a debt of gratitude to her and the other grande dames who really fought to keep this neighborhood going."

"Even if so many still refer to Old Louisville as the redheaded stepchild of the city," said Debra. "Fuck 'em."

"Oh, my." Frances tightened a clawlike hand on my forearm.

"Well, Old Louisville is a diamond in the rough," proclaimed Lucie, "but that's what many people like about it. It's very diverse. You've got a little of everything down here."

Old Louisville did have a little of everything. Racially, it constituted a good mix of Black and white, as well as all strata of socioeconomics. "Some Old Louisville residents are wealthy, others barely make ends meet. Jefferson County Judge-Executive Harvey Sloane lives on South Fourth Street, only a few blocks away from a Salvation Army shelter for homeless people," explained a 1989 *Courier-Journal* article outlining Old Louisville's progress at the time. "In recent decades it has taken on a distinctive personality—an almost paradoxical identity."

"In short, Old Louisville can best be described as 'neither,'" said a Second Street apartment dweller. "It is neither white nor Black, neither rich nor poor. It is just Old Louisville. That's what I like about it. It is sort of like the real world; you can't put a label on it."

Early on, however, Old Louisville was easily labeled—and *posh* was usually the word. Located just south of the central business district, it became Louisville's first suburb, an affluent district that locals knew as the most exclusive part of the city.

The area people referred to as Old Louisville arose at the outskirts of the city in the mid 1800s, remaining largely rural until the 1880s. It consisted of scattered country estates, slave and free-Black tenements, and a farmhouse or factory here and there. Major change came in 1883, when the city hosted an industrial and mercantile show, which Henry Watterson, editor of the *Courier-Journal* and driving force behind the event, insisted would "advance the material welfare of the producing classes of the South and West."

Touted in newspapers far and wide as "the hundred days that Louisville would open its doors to the world," the Southern Exposition covered forty-five acres south of Central Park, on land belonging to the wealthy DuPont family. City dignitaries boasted that the main exhibit hall counted as the world's largest wooden building at the time. President Chester Arthur came for the opening ceremony, where he flipped the switch for thousands of softly glowing incandescent lamps that illuminated the main exhibit hall and adjoining areas. There were five thousand incandescent bulbs in all—forty-six hundred lights for the exhibition hall and four hundred for the adjacent art gallery—which was more than all the electric lamps in New York City at that time.

The incandescent light bulb was a very recent invention of Thomas Edison, who had worked in Louisville as a Western Union telegraph operator in the 1860s, and the novelty contributed to the exposition's huge success. In the first eighty-eight days, more than a quarter million tickets were sold and instead of the planned one hundred days, this series of early world's fairs spread out over five years. The city experienced an unprecedented period of growth and prosperity and a building boom ensued. New construction and planned communities sprang up in the areas surrounding the fairgrounds, and when the immense wooden structure was cleared away, it left behind a large empty space ready for a savvy builder.

William Slaughter led the development of St. James Court, which he envisioned as a haven for the upper class. His Victoria Land Grant Company touted it as a London-inspired neighborhood with deed restrictions ensuring only brick or stone construction. The elite poured in and began building comfortable residences. Within several years, city dwellers came to refer to "the Court" as the most sought-after address in town. As the neighborhood grew, so did Louisville's reputation as a comfortable and gracious place to live; and house-proud Louisvillians proclaimed themselves "the City of Beautiful Homes."

Old Louisville's heyday was short-lived, however. After World War I, a better-developed streetcar system made commuter neighborhoods more accessible and the once-grand mansions became passé. The end of World War II saw city dwellers across the nation flee to the suburbs, and in Old Louisville, as elsewhere, residents began abandoning the downtown areas. People such as St. James Court homeowners Mae and David Salyers were considered "eccentric" when they decided to stay.

Areas west and east of downtown Louisville saw the destruction of vast swaths of tenements and working-class housing, especially along Walnut Street, once thriving with Black-owned businesses. Displaced residents began moving into Old Louisville mansions—but only because they had been divided into small apartments or turned into rooming houses. As crime went up, the desire to live in certain parts of Old Louisville went down. By the 1970s, urban renewal, which many hoped would help the downtown area, had contributed to its blight instead.

When urban affairs reporter J. Douglas Nunn penned a series of articles likening Old Louisville to thriving districts such as Georgetown in Washington, D.C., and Beacon Hill in Boston—areas also teeming with old mansions and university students—people began to sit up and take note. Nunn joined with attorney Eli Brown and formed Restoration Inc., a corporation that renovated almost a dozen homes on Belgravia Court.

This stimulated the rehabilitation of St. James Court and other parts of the neighborhood. In the 1970s the neighborhood received official recognition from the National Register of Historic Places, which generated more grassroots organizations and zoning ordinances to preserve the residential character of the neighborhood. By the 1980s Old Louisville's business and residential groups had earned a reputation for being well organized and tenacious.

Old Louisville enjoyed a reputation for other things as well. Residents often had a difficult time finding parking, and noisy University of Louisville students tended to overrun parts of the neighborhood. Homeowners and activists came across as a cantankerous lot, lamenting the lack of amenities such as grocery stores and retail shops but then banding together to ward off companies like Walgreens and Whole Foods when they announced plans to open businesses nearby. "We want it, but we don't want it," said a former director of the prestigious St. James Court Art Show. "We don't want to change the Victorian aura of our neighborhood, yet we clamor for the services of more retail."

And then there was the crime problem—or at least the perception thereof. Even if statistics didn't support it, the perception was that Old Louisville had a rampant crime problem—almost as bad as the West End, the literal other side of the tracks. Neighborhood residents argued that, given they lived in the most populous zip code in city, with nearly fourteen thousand people per square mile, this would naturally account for a higher crime rate, but that when you averaged it out on a per capita basis, the numbers indicated a statistic commensurate with most other neighborhoods.

"But try to explain that to an East End hausfrau in her cookie-cutter McMansion who might come down here once a year for the St. James Court Art Show and it's like banging your head against a brick wall," said a former president of the South Third Street Neighborhood Association, the organization representing many of the homeowners along the city's historic Millionaires Row. "I had a friend from the Polo Fields stop by for coffee one afternoon with her teenage daughter and she wouldn't let the girl go outside to get a gift out of the trunk of the car because she was terrified something awful would happen to her! It was broad daylight and we could see the car twenty yards away through the living room window."

It didn't help, either, that local media often got things wrong when it came to their crime reporting, something that caused many Old Louisvillians to pull their hair out in clumps. News anchors tended to report shootings and muggings that occurred outside the confines of the historic district as actually happening in Old Louisville, thereby inadvertently contributing to its image problem. "The rest of Louisville has been looking down on this neighborhood since at least the 1950s," complained David Williams, a longtime resident of Second Street who worked for the *Courier-Journal* and often criticized news outlets for their mistakes. "Most recent case in point: a murder on Preston Street. The media reported that it happened in Old Louisville. It did not. It was in Shelby Park."

"I have friends who wouldn't come down here to save their lives and it infuriates me," said Louise Cecil. "How narrow-minded."

"Lord, I can't abide those people." Lucie Blodgett lifted her glass in a toast. "They don't know what they're missing."

"Hear, hear." I returned the toast.

Frances tugged my arm and I said my farewells as she led me away from the group. At the bar, Frances leaned in for a conspiratorial whisper. "Bless her heart, she's a mess, but I still love her to death!" She erupted in a gale of laughter and pressed a hand to her heart. "Yes, I tell you, that Lucie Blodgett is a character!" She grabbed my forearm for support while she dabbed a tear from the corner of her eye with her free hand.

"Darlin', did I ever tell you about the Mengels, my husband's family, who had two chimpanzees they kept as pets? In the 1930s, I believe." Frances had, in fact, told me the story many times before. "What were their names? Ike and Mike or something like that. Or was it Ikah and Mikah? Well, one day those monkeys got loose and they were scaring the entire neighborhood and they eventually ran all the way over to Eastern Parkway, where the sheriff had to shoot them. It was in the newspapers and everything. Well, I tell you, they never kept monkeys in the house after that."

\* \* \*

That night I was watching the eleven o'clock news when my phone buzzed. The number was unfamiliar so I ignored it and returned my attention to the screen. WHAS11 was rehashing the story of the "Trinity Murders," one the most notorious murder cases in Louisville history, one that involved rape, murder, and the kidnapping of two high schoolers.

On September 29, 1984, Scott Nelson and Richard Stephenson became lost while headed to a Trinity High School football game at DuPont Manual High School near Old Louisville. The pair stopped at a Moby Dick restaurant to get directions, where they met cousins Victor Dewayne Taylor and George Ellis Wade, who offered to lead them to the stadium in exchange for a ride.

Instead, the men kidnapped Nelson and Stephenson and directed them to a vacant lot in the 300 block of Ardella Court near the stadium. The perpetrators—both in their twenties—forced the teenagers to remove their clothes before binding and gagging them. Taylor sexually assaulted one of the boys, and then the men shot each of them in the back of the head.

The murders gripped the city. Police arrested the men after a relative reported receiving a Trinity High School jacket from Wade, who, in turn, implicated Taylor. The men had supposedly joked about their crimes to family members. Wade received a life sentence at the Kentucky State Reformatory in LaGrange, and Taylor was sent to death row at the Kentucky State Penitentiary in Eddyville.

In 2000, the controversial clothier Benetton incensed many in Louisville when they featured Victor Taylor in a new advertising campaign titled "We, On Death Row."

Now, George Ellis Wade Jr. had made the headlines, having just been indicted for robbery and being a persistent felony offender. The son of the convicted murderer had a criminal history dating back to 2001. The news station had interviewed Scott Nelson's father for his take on the matter. "A family that could tolerate one of their children coming in laughing about having murdered two Trinity boys thinking that's funny and the parents didn't do anything or say anything about it. It tells you a lot about them," said Emory Nelson.

My phone buzzed again. The same number as before.

When I answered, an anxious voice asked if I had a moment to chat. "I'm Jerome," he said. "I found out you were writing about Jamie and I just wanted to touch base. I've been following the Banis trial the best I can." A quiet but sharp intake of breath came from the other end. "I still can't believe he's gone."

"Oh, thanks. Did you know Jamie?"

"Yes, but not that well. I knew him from his days in Huntington, in West Virginia." The caller went on to explain that the two had met in the local club scene, where Jamie enjoyed an established stage presence in the local drag community. And that Jamie had been the first person to encourage him to perform in drag. "I was terrified the first time I tried—it was amateur night—but I survived. Jamie helped me with my wardrobe and makeup and he was in the audience cheering me on. I'll always remember how supportive and encouraging he was."

"When was the last time you talked to Jamie?"

"Well, that's the thing," said Jerome. "I think I might have been the last person to talk to him. That's why I decided to call you."

"Oh, really?" My ears perked up. "So, this would have been late November 2009?" Conflicting information had surfaced in the courtroom, but Jamie Carroll might have already been killed in late November and not mid-December.

"It was right after Thanksgiving. We were on the phone and he was in Lexington. I was still in Huntington at the time. He called to say goodbye because he planned on going to Louisville and turning himself in the next day."

"Did you know he had been in trouble?"

"Yes, he had told me a couple of things over the years, so I wasn't surprised. It wasn't until he got involved in drugs that things took a turn for the worse."

"But, he was selling drugs, wasn't he?" I said. "He wasn't just using them."

"That's right, but he was trying to straighten out his life. That night we talked, we kind of had a heart to heart. He was tired of everything the way it was and wanted to change things. He said he was tired of being an outsider all the time and not fitting in." Jerome coughed softly at the other end and cleared his throat. "You know, we knew a little about each other's lives and we always called each other 'redheaded stepchild' because we felt like outcasts in our own families—and because I have red hair."

"And did he say anything else the last time you talked?"

"Yes, he did. He said he was tired of being a redheaded stepchild. He said he was going to do his time and then try to come out a different person, be on the straight and narrow." At that point something that sounded like a sniffle came from his end. "Jamie had met some of the drag queens that live down in Old Louisville and they said he always had place to stay with them when he got out. He really loved all those Victorian homes and dreamed of buying and living there himself one day. He was planning on a new start in Old Louisville."

I hung up and headed into the Magic Library to do some work when the phone buzzed again. Kelly was calling. I answered.

"You're never going to believe this, Herr Professor," he said without a greeting, ice tinkling in a drink on the other end.

"What? You finally find me a bottle of Pappy twenty-three-year-old?"

"Nope. Try again. Guess what they found at 1435 South Fourth Street?"

"I give. What?"

"Another body."

## 19

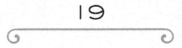

# STAR WITNESS

IT WAS going on eleven o'clock Monday morning when Ryane Conroy called Jeffrey Mundt to the stand. In a dark suit and steel-gray tie, the now forty-one-year-old described himself as a "former boyfriend" of Joey Banis. Mundt was born in Louisville, where he attended Atherton High School, had a BA in Computer Science from Indiana University at Bloomington, and worked as a technology consultant. "My last job was vice president of an IT firm based down in Florida," he explained, which landed him the stint as consultant at the University of Louisville. He had also worked at Northwestern University, George Washington University, and LLP Global Star Systems Corporation.

In a serious tone, Mundt told how he had bought 1435 South Fourth Street "right after Election Day 2008" and that he was the sole owner. He didn't actually move in until May 2009; Joey, whom he'd met in September 2009, moved in with him in November 2009. He described Jamie Carroll as "someone with whom someone has sex, but no emotional relationship." Jamie, Jeffrey, and Joey had had sex on one prior occasion.

When prompted about the night of the killing, Mundt portrayed a Jamie Carroll on "quite a bit of drugs" and as having a hard time finding the house on Fourth Street because he was so high. "He kept missing the I-65 exit and ending up out at Gene Snyder." Questioned about his own drug use, Mundt explained, "Meth makes me intensely focused and very sexual. It's very sexually liberating effectively."

When Jamie finally arrived, the three ended up in bed together. "We were playing with each other. We were jacking off," said Mundt, when suddenly, "I feel a jerk. I'm thrown off of Jamie and thrown into the table that's at the bedside, where I hit my head. And I thought they were doing some type of scene—I didn't know what was going on. I didn't realize it, because Jamie started screaming, 'No, Joey, no, no, no, please, no.' And they started struggling."

Mundt thought "this was some type of sex scene that was going on because that was one of the things we did, involving role play. You know, sort of the typical—well, I don't know about typical, it's probably not the right word to use, yes—sort of a sex scene that you would invent."

"I don't understand. What do you mean?" interjected Conroy, which elicited a groan from someone behind us.

"Well, I mean, this is part of the fantasy world of sex, where you use sex as a release. The best example I can come up with is a heterosexual couple may be into, you know, the naughty nurse and the patient, or the naughty nurse and the doctor, or a woman who likes to dress in certain types of lingerie because it, you know, makes her feel sexy," Mundt explained. "It's sort of a role-playing experience, where you add excitement to sex. And, it went particularly well with the use of meth." When asked about the use of meth again, Mundt replied, "It's a hypersexual kind of thing. It basically makes you incredibly horny."

Mundt claimed he had been "hit pretty hard in the head" and had a hard time getting up, then saw the other two struggling. "Joey had a knife and was slicing at Jamie's throat," he said. "You could actually smell the blood."

Next to me, a female observer raised a hand to her mouth to stifle a gasp.

"Remember, we were all naked," continued Jeffrey. Then Joey shot Jamie. After, he pointed the gun at Jeffrey and made him lie on the bed. Mundt said Joey gave him a choice: either help or be killed.

Joey then gave Mundt GHB "to calm" him down and the two dragged Jamie Carroll's body down into the basement. Past a wooden door with hasp and padlock, past a deep freezer, washer and dryer, and then up two steps into the old wine cellar. Banis then locked his boyfriend in that room to keep him from contacting anybody and ordered him to get to work. With Jamie Carroll's body lying nearby,

Mundt began to dig a hole. When Joey came down to check on him, he expressed his displeasure that "adequate progress" had not been made in the digging of the hole. On more than one occasion Jeffrey mentioned how "not strong" he was.

It took three days to dig a hole deep enough and large enough, and during that time the pair made a trip to Lowe's to get a large Rubbermaid storage container, duct tape, foam, and other items. Joey cleaned the body with mineral spirits to get rid of DNA evidence and Jeffrey came up with the idea of using lime to cover up the smell because he had once seen something on television about that being used for a pauper's grave.

When the prosecution repeatedly established that along the way Jeffrey had numerous opportunities to contact the police, but chose not to act, he responded with "I did nothing. I did nothing, out of fear, you're quite right. And, I live with that regret every day." Mundt claimed to have been terrified of Joey because he had threatened to kill his family and pets. And even though Joey made him go to work to avoid arousing suspicion, he surveilled him in a car parked outside.

Soon thereafter, Mitch Perry gaveled the courtroom to attention and called for a lunch recess. As I was exiting, I heard a man in front of me mumble something to his female companion. "Did you hear the tone of Mundt's voice? Except for the kinky stuff, I don't believe a word that comes out of his mouth. Do you?" At that, the woman burst into laughter and shook her head twice.

"What's so funny?" he demanded as she raced on ahead of him.


An appointment had prevented Carrie from sitting in on the previous hour and a half of testimony but we still agreed to meet for lunch. She waited for me at Gavi's, where a lively crowd filled the main room with chatter. Behind the counter, Zina and Ida appeared to be quarrelling in Russian. Above the cash register, somebody had hung a pink glitter ball.

After ordering, I filled Carrie in on what she had missed. Then, over grilled cheese and tuna salad sandwiches with tater tots, we talked about the latest development at 1435 South Fourth Street.

"So, where did they find the body?" Carrie popped a tot into her mouth and chewed. "I haven't seen anything on the news about it."

"That's because it might have been accidental," I said. "Or a suicide. They don't report things like that on the news, usually."

"So, what exactly happened? How did you find out?"

"Kelly called last night and told me. He listens to the scanners all the time."

"Ah, Kelly the courtly gentleman?"

"Yep. And I called my EMT bartender friend and he filled me on the few details they have." A body hadn't actually been found inside of 1435 South Fourth Street, he informed me, but rather on a concrete walkway to the south. It divided the property from the lot with the large apartment house next door.

"Oh, you mean where Duncan lives?"

"Yeah, Kelly calls him the Grand Poobah of the neighborhood hotheads and shitwads."

Carrie muffled a laugh. "Was it an overdose?"

"Most likely, but intentional or unintentional is the question. My EMT friend said it appeared the person had been dragged outside and left there. They think the drug supplier lived in the apartment building and that's where the poor girl overdosed. The dealer or whoever didn't want to get in trouble and left her outside."

"Oh, no." Carrie started in on the second half of her sandwich. "Do they know who it is yet? Someone from the neighborhood?"

"Well, I can't say for certain, but Kelly said it's the daughter of the guy who lives down the block. A different hothead and shitwad."

Carrie put down her sandwich and frowned. "Seriously? You mean the girl with the drug problem?"

I nodded and washed down a tater tot with a mouthful of iced tea. "The sad thing is the EMT guy said they could have saved her if someone had called 911 in time."

"That's such a shame." Distractedly, Carrie finished the last of her grilled cheese.

"You know what else is a shame? It only adds to the sinister reputation of the house."

Carrie nodded. "The poor people living on that block."

Zina approached the table and I moved aside so the woman could clear the empty plates.

Suddenly, Carrie cracked up, shaking her head. "Hotheads and shitwads."

I chucked and soon we were both howling.

The laughter was subsiding when we both looked over and saw Zina at the cash register. Nonchalantly, she reached up and twirled the pink glitter ball. Sparkles from the florescent lighting overhead flew out and went dancing across the room. Everybody looked up from their tables and smiled.

Carrie's gaze drifted to the dessert case on the counter and she leaned forward suddenly, laying her hands flat on the table. "Hey, let's have pie for dessert."


When we returned from Gavi's, I got on my laptop in the waiting area and had a quick Skype interview with Chuck Goudie, an investigative reporter for ABC News in Chicago. In the Windy City, Mundt had been a well-known name because of his leadership in Project Café, a program to upgrade the computer and financial accounting infrastructure at Northwestern University. When news of his arrest for the counterfeit money incident broke, it had titillated the academic and tech communities, especially when it was reported that, according to the *Chicago Tribune*, Mundt had been in the company of somebody covered in tribal tattoos "who sported a blue-tinged Mohawk hairstyle with matching nail polish when he appeared . . . in the Cook County Criminal Courts Building." A couple of months later, when Chicagoans learned of Mundt's arrest for a murder in Louisville, outlets jumped on the story and many in Chicago wanted to know more from the Louisville end.

Unfortunately, and unbeknownst to me, as I was wrapping up the interview, a passing juror heard me discuss the case and felt obligated to inform Bailiff Brown, who in turn, reported it to Judge Perry. "You did it again," said the bailiff to me as I entered the courtroom for the afternoon session. "You're getting in trouble with the judge."

My jaw dropped. "What did I do this time?"

"One of the jurors heard you conducting that interview with the news station in Chicago and ratted you out."

"How was I supposed to know a juror would be walking by?" I said. "I tried to find the most secluded corner on this floor."

"Well, that corner just happened to be right next to the secret door the jurors use to come and go," said Brown severely. "You were in the best place of all to be overheard."

"Good grief." Sheepishly, I returned to my regular spot, but when I saw Bailiff Brown grin, I knew it couldn't have been that serious.

The judge called counsel to the bench and briefly discussed the matter. He determined that nothing substantive had been overheard and that was that. I let out a sigh of relief.

Within minutes, Conroy had Mundt back on the stand and she projected a large photo on the screen for the jury. Taken in the front hall of 1435 South Fourth Street in December, it showed Jeffrey and Joey in front of a rather bare-looking Christmas tree. They had their arms around each other and were beaming. "At the time of this photo, is Jamie Carroll buried in the basement?" asked the prosecutor. A solemn Jeffrey Mundt answered with a simple *yes*. At the time, they would have been standing right over where Jamie Carroll's body lay in the earthen floor of the wine cellar. The pauper's grave

In all, Jeffrey Mundt spent more than three hours on the stand and Conroy had him talk about a slew of subjects, including his sex life and partners, the items stolen from Jamie Carroll, the altercation the night of the 911 call, the counterfeit money operation—and how he had met Joey through Adam4Adam, a gay hookup site. Claiming to be emotionally susceptible, having just come out of a long-term relationship, Mundt found Joey attractive and different from his regular boyfriends. "He had that bad-boy look. Dyed hair, jewelry, tattoos, and all of that. It was very attractive."

Observers in the courtroom seemed to sit up especially straight and take note when the prosecution started off with an unexpected line of questions. Conroy asked if Mundt had ever worked for the U.S. government and if he had killed thirty-five people in his line of work for the U.S. government. "No, ma'am," he replied.

"What if the jury hears from Joey Banis that you said that? How do you explain it?" she asked.

"That was a sex scene. Role play, creation of a fantasy world," said Mundt. "You let your sexual fantasies run wild. It adds interest to the sex. In that scene, Joey was the criminal and I was the government agent." When asked if the two wore costumes in their "role-playing,"

Mundt responded in the affirmative, adding "I happen to be into rubber and latex and vinyl. Things that are tight and shiny. It's just one of the fetishes I have. Spandex."

Mitch Perry adjourned for an afternoon break, and Darren Wolff was champing at the bit when Jeffrey Mundt returned to the witness stand for cross-examination. Taking a long drink from a bottle of water, the attorney seemed to steel himself with a slight jerk of his head to the side, almost like a prize fighter entering the ring. Facing the jury box, a blown-up photo on an easel showed a smiling Joey Banis, held in an embrace by Jamie Carroll, who rested his head on the other's shoulder.

As Wolff approached, Jeffrey Mundt lowered his head nervously and studied his folded hands.

"Mr. Mundt. Big day for you today, isn't it?" said the defense attorney.

Jeffrey Mundt blinked and lifted a hand in a gesture of *I don't know* before answering. "It certainly is an important day, yes."

"And the most important thing, of course, for this jury to understand is that you're telling the truth today, right?" Ever so slightly, Wolff's tone became more adversarial. "So, if I get something from you, after talking to you today, that we know is not the truth, is it fair to say that none of your testimony should be believed and that you're lying to us?"

Attempting to remain non-expressive, Mundt said, "I can't make that judgment." He looked down briefly.

"You can't make that judgment, but you're going to tell this jury that nothing you tell me today is going to be a lie, right?"

"I am telling the truth." Mundt's voice quavered.

"And nothing you told Ms. Conroy was a lie, correct?"

"I am telling the truth," insisted Mundt, his voice small.

For the next quarter hour, Wolff grilled the witness about his lack of honesty, as proven by numerous inconsistent statements and lies made during different interviews, pointing out that Mundt had needed to meet with the prosecution and his lawyers before taking the stand to go over statements that needed clarification because he had "lied and lied and lied." He also brought up Jeffrey's deal with the prosecution—at which point he displayed an enlarged document on an easel—and had Mundt admit that nowhere in the deal had he agreed to tell the truth.

When Wolff brought up that Mundt had no bruises or other signs of injuries the night of 911 call, he called into question whether Joey really attacked the witness at all. He also hammered home the point that Mundt had ample time to tell the truth but chose not to. The witness, he insisted, could have very easily said there was a body in his basement and that he'd been afraid of Mr. Banis for all those months. "They treated you with kid gloves," said Wolff. "They treated you like the victim."

Mundt, who displayed a talent for parsing his words and evading direct answers, gathered his thoughts and then said, "Well, first, I cannot agree with your supposition that I was considered a victim."

"You don't think that they treated you like a victim when you got in there?" Wolff's tone was incredulous.

"Unlike Mr. Banis, I don't have a long history of interrogations to fall back on," responded Mundt.

Darren Wolff flew off the handle. "What? Wait, wait. What did you just say? What did you just say to this jury? Did I ask you a question about that? Did I ask you about anything in Mr. Banis's history?" His voice had risen significantly.

"No, sir, I'm sorry," said Jeffrey Mundt, surprisingly contrite.

"Are you saying whatever you want to say to infuriate this jury and trying to get evidence in front of this jury about Mr. Banis in an inappropriate way? Is that what you're attempting to do?"

"I'm sorry. I thought it was relevant. I apologize."

After raking Mundt over the coals for another minute or two, Wolff said, "You will agree with me, that nowhere—until you actually walked up to the edge and saw the polygraph guy—did you make this claim that you were afraid of Mr. Banis and had been terrorized by him?"

Jeffrey Mundt shook his head. "I can't make that statement. I don't recall."

A quarter hour later, Judge Mitch Perry decided to adjourn for the day because one of the jurors had been nodding off to sleep.

# 20

# WEIRD RUBBER STUFF

THE NEXT day, defense attorney Justin Brown seemed to be looking on with glee when Bailiff Brown ushered in Jeffrey Mundt. In a turquoise suit, Ryane Conroy fidgeted with an easel as the jury entered and took up seats in the box.

A smile on his face, Darren Wolff resumed the cross-examination of the witness, beginning by highlighting many of the "inconsistencies" in previous testimony, including assertions that Mundt had only started using drugs after he met Joey Banis. Darren Wolff produced screenshots from a profile on one of the hookup sites Mundt had frequented where he had admitted to a predilection for drugs—well before he had even met Joey Banis. After a good deal of hemming and hawing, Mundt finally conceded he had indeed done drugs before.

At that, Wolff produced a large picture of Mundt from the website. It showed Mundt standing—stern-faced and in a black rubber suit—and listed his turn-ons as "rubber, rubber, rubber, pvc, leather, bondage—all types, restraints, cuffs, collars, hoods, gags, sensory deprivation, etc."

"Sensory deprivation. What is that, Mr. Mundt?" said Wolff.

"Ah, putting on a hood, putting hands over your eyes, putting hands over your mouth. It's something I enjoy, having my senses deprived."

"What does CBT mean?"

"Cock and ball torture. It means I like having my penis and my testicles played with—hard, hit." At that, Mundt quickly lowered his head and kept his gaze averted.

Wolff looked down at a sheet of paper in his hand. "What's WS?"

"Water sports. That's primarily, I guess, a gay term for urine."

I turned to Carrie. "Straight people are into that as well. Why's he making it sound like a gay thing?" She shrugged her shoulders and shook her head.

I must have whispered too loudly because Darren Wolff abruptly turned and glanced into the gallery before continuing with his questions. "SM?"

Mundt tensed on the stand. "Sadism and masochism. As I said, I like being hurt, within a set of limits."

Wolff consulted his list again. "Flogging?"

"Yes, it's the same, along the lines of getting hurt. There are multiple ways in which somebody might get turned on sexually by being hurt. Those are some of the ways I enjoy being hurt." In the silence that followed, Mundt looked down uncomfortably.

"Alright. Chastity?"

"Same thing, you know, preventing . . . from ejaculating, basically."

"Alright. BB?"

"Bare back. Which dates this profile." Mundt fixed his gaze on the attorney. "That is a sign that this is something that happened after I was with Mr. Banis. It means sex without condoms."

"OK. So, that's something you didn't starting doing until after you met Mr. Banis?"

"Yes, because Mr. Banis did not originally identify that he was HIV positive—"

Darren Wolff cut him off. "Say that again?" He turned and looked at the jury before returning his attention to the witness box. "You understand we have a copy of your computer, don't you?" On the computer, Wolff pointed out, videos showed Jeffrey and Joey having unprotected sex. This proved that Mundt did not have an issue with his boyfriend's HIV status.

Carrie inclined her head in my direction. "You know, I'm having a hard time understanding how well the guys actually knew each other."

"I know. And the other thing is what really happened the night of the 911 call—who said what. Was it Jeffrey who told the police about the body in the basement or Joey? It seems like Joey brought it up first."

Carrie let out a soft sigh before returning her gaze to the front of the courtroom.

"So let's move on," said Wolff. "Toys?"

"Sex toy."

"OK. So, what's this next one?" Wolff glanced up from the list in his hand, a feigned look of confusion on his face. "What in—?" He stopped abruptly. "What is *mummification*?"

From behind me came a soft gasp. Then an *ewww*. Jeffrey Mundt raised his chin an inch and tried to maintain an even tone of voice. "Ah, it goes along with rubber. Effectively, it means, basically being"—he gestured with his hands around his body—"fully covered in rubber or fully enclosed in some type of constraining environment. It's the same thing that I like in bondage."

Wolff then indicated that Jamie Carroll had been "constrained" in a box but Mundt disputed any connection between mummification and Jamie Carroll.

A message popped up on my phone at that moment.

*Are you in the courtroom?* Margie wanted to know.

*Stop that!* I replied.

A few seconds later another text appeared. *I haven't seen you in ages. Stop by sometime.*

Ahead, Darren Wolff paused and ruffled the paper in his hand. Jeffery Mundt swallowed.

I quickly shot off a response. *OK. I need your expertise on something anyway.*

*Okey dokey. About what?* she asked.

*Your old job.*

A minute passed before she got back to me. *Goodie goodie!*

Wolff's voice had a cheery edge to it as he continued. "Alright. Smoking and chems. And then you've got in parentheses: PNP. Let's talk about that. Exactly what does that mean?"

Mundt swallowed again. "That refers to drug use, particularly methamphetamine. 'Party and Play' is PNP."

"Alrighty, let's move on. Breath control—what is that?"

"It goes along with sensory deprivation and the mummification. I like having people hold my head, put a hood over my head and smother me. Obviously, only . . ." Mundt appeared to stop and think. "To a certain degree."

Acting flabbergasted, Wolff shook his head as the witness went into more detail, claiming that his online persona often involved "fantasy" situations instead of real-life ones. Taking a swig from his water bottle, Wolff then brought things full circle. "And rubber."

Over the prosecution's objections, Wolff then had Mundt read aloud passages from online chats in which he, "Rubberjase," and "stiffy69" had discussed their mutual interests and sexual propensities. Later texts would show that Mundt, who had portrayed himself as something of a sexual ingénue and emotionally vulnerable after being dumped by a long-term boyfriend, had no problems finding interested partners in internet chat rooms. And he knew exactly what he wanted.

In one exchange on Adam4Adam, a potential hookup had said, "Sounds like we would have a lot of fun. So, the punk dude is your boyfriend?" The "punk dude," Joey Banis, went by the handle of RadSexBoy.

"Well, we have an open relationship," replied Mundt. "He's never really been a slut like me so it's rather interesting. He started out verse, is now tending to be a bottom bitch and loving it. He really wants a gangbang, which I'd love to set up."

At the defense table, Justin Brown smiled, enjoying the grilling of Jeffrey Mundt.

Then Mundt tried to explain text messages he had sent Joey, which the defense insisted demonstrated that he had not lived in terror of Banis, as claimed. Wolff had him read the texts out loud and the jury heard Jeffrey refer to Joey as "sweetie" and saying "love you" numerous times. On February 5, 2010, he had signed off with "top of the morning to you!" On February 11, he had asked, "Hey, Sweetie, what up?" and on February 13, Mundt had proclaimed "I love you dearly, my FWJP." Fierce Wild Jungle Puppy.

Later that day he had texted an invitation: "In honor of St. Valentine's Day and my love for you, the pleasure of your company is requested tomorrow night for dinner at 22:00 at Morton's. RSVP."

As he read the text, Mundt enunciated the entire *Répondez s'il vous plaît* in passable French. The next day he wrote, "Shouldn't be long, my darling. Will call when heading back to the FWJP's lair. Grrrs." When Wolff asked what the *grrrs* meant, Mundt explained, "Puppies go *grrr.*"

To drive home the falsehood of Mundt's claim of living in fear of Banis, Wolff brought up something that had happened in December 2009, just weeks after Jamie Carroll's murder. One day, Joey had announced he would be meeting his parents for dinner that night at Le Relais, an elegant French restaurant housed in a brick Art Deco gem at Bowman Field, one of the oldest airports in the country. Jeffrey had telephoned ahead and had arranged to have dessert sent to their table, said Wolff.

Mundt didn't deny this had happened but corrected the attorney by saying, "I believe it was *champagne* and dessert."

In the questions that followed, Wolff continued to paint Mundt as a callous and uncaring individual, a phony who could muster tears at the drop of a hat. Someone who had laughed during police interviews, knowing full well Jamie Carroll lay buried beneath four feet of earth in his cellar. When asked if he had "continually continued to refer to Mr. Carroll as an 'ugly guy,'" Jeffrey Mundt did not deny it. Nor did he deny it when Wolff said, "You don't recall saying that no matter how many drugs were in you, you would not have sex with an ugly person?"

Mundt was a liar, Wolff asserted, pointing out that Mundt had said he knew a lot about firearms, but then claimed he didn't; when first shown the photo of Jamie Carroll and asked if he recognized the face, Mundt had responded that it didn't "even look remotely familiar." The defense for Joey Banis also produced video of Mundt's initial interview where he slipped up and mentioned Jamie's name before it had been disclosed by detectives.

Wolff also brought into evidence testimony from James Jenkins, who had stayed in the same "dorm" with Mundt during his incarceration. According to Jenkins, the two had shared confidences, and Mundt had revealed many details including his fear that Joey would "blow the cover on everything" and that Mundt blamed Joey for the murder being uncovered, Joey was getting too difficult to keep in check and "had fucked up the whole plan." Jenkins claimed Mundt had also admitted to selling meth at a Chicago gay bar. According to him,

Mundt had harbored some jealousy and didn't find anything wrong with killing Jamie Carroll because he was HIV positive. Mundt had admitted to sexual arousal by the situation and that killing Carroll had been the ultimate high.

"Lies. I did not talk to him about any of that." Mundt tensed his shoulders in response. "He's a known jailhouse snitch."

Jeffrey's purported envy of Joey and Jamie's relationship came up again later, when on redirect, prosecutor Conroy called Detective Middleton back to the stand, where she played video of his interview with Joey the night of the arrest. Aside from the jealousy Jeffrey harbored against Jamie, which provided a motive for Jeffrey to murder his rival, Joey detailed the first night he and Mundt had met and how he had learned about the other's penchant for "weird rubber stuff." Mundt had answered the door in a full-body black rubber suit.

Joey also disclosed in the video that Jeffrey—known by the username of "Gummiklaus," or "Rubber Klaus" in German—had a very active presence on the darknet. When told that Mundt had talked about being terrified of him, Banis replied, "I'm not the one who worked for the NSA. I don't know shit about that stuff." Mundt had worked abroad and spoke German and Russian, as well as some Italian, French, and Czech. When Middleton asked if Banis believed Mundt had worked for a foreign government, he responded in the affirmative, claiming Mundt had showed him articles about bombings he had orchestrated and had told him about murdering his previous associate.

On the stand, Darren Wolff insisted that Mundt had led Banis to believe he had worked as an agent for a foreign government and went into some of the details Mundt had disclosed. "So you would admit to me or this jury that you had said you had a bullet in your head from some work that you did in a foreign country?" When Jeffrey replied he did not recall saying that, the attorney raised his voice. "You don't recall saying to him that you had a bullet in your head from *Bratslavia*?"

Wolff had mispronounced Bratislava, the capital of Slovakia, and Mundt wrinkled his forehead, feigning confusion. "I'm sorry. *Where*?"

"Bratslavia?" Wolff repeated the city, again mispronouncing it. "That sound familiar?"

"*Bratislava?*" corrected Mundt.

"Yes. Thank you. You know where it is, then?"

"Yes, I'm familiar with Eastern Europe." But Mundt claimed it came while role-playing in a sex scene, not to intimidate his partner.

A bone of contention for the Banis defense team—brought up at more than one bench meeting—involved frustration at not having access to laptops seized by the Secret Service in Chicago, and Wolff asked why Mundt had not turned over his password. "Is there something on the computer you don't want them to see?" When Mundt responded in the negative claiming nobody has requested the password from him, Wolff's voice raised in incredulity. "The Secret Service *never* asked you for that password?"

Mundt then amended his statement: "Well, *since* then, nobody has asked me for the password."

Wolff also expressed frustration that the Kershaw knife Mundt had on his belt during the arrest in Chicago had apparently disappeared and could not be examined.

Before finishing his cross-examination, Wolff approached Mundt with one final question. "Is this a fantasy world?" He indicated text message sixty, from February 2010, in which Joey had apologized to Jeffrey for "failing him" before issuing a stern warning: "Jase, I love you, but I hear too many footsteps. Please do not involve any officials. I will inform them of the basement, if you do." Mundt shifted uncomfortably.

"This is Joey threatening to go to the authorities," insisted Wolff. "You didn't respond by saying something like 'What the hell? You killed him, not me.'" This really showed Mundt's complicity, he argued. If Mundt were to have gone to the police about some other issue, Banis was prepared to tell them about the body in the basement.

Before dismissing the witness, the defense attorney reiterated all the lies Mundt had told and insisted that, had Mundt's story been true, he would have used that text to his advantage.

Looking stoically ahead, Jeffrey Mundt replied somewhat smugly with a simple *No*.

"God, it's so obvious that he's lying." A nearby observer whispered loudly and shifted on the bench. Carrie and I exchanged looks and shook our heads.

After 219 pieces of evidence and eighteen witnesses, the Commonwealth rested its case.

When Judge Mitch Perry sent the jury home for the night, he informed them there was a chance of bad weather the next day and to plan accordingly.

# 21

# WITNESS FOR THE DEFENSE

THUNDERSHOWERS RATTLED the windowpanes in the Judicial Center the next day when the defense put on its case for Joseph Banis. Defense attorney Justin Brown first called Kenny Robertson to the stand. The forty-nine-year-old worked for Midwest Construction out of Chicago. In jeans and collared shirt with wide black and red strips on white, the balding man told how real estate agent Chris Eagan had introduced him to Mundt, who needed renovation work completed at 1435 South Fourth Street. "It was pretty rundown, in pretty bad shape," said Robertson of the place, and that he did "about eighteen jobs" for the homeowner. Mundt always seemed to be cheerful, he reported. Robertson never saw him with bruises or injuries.

One of the jobs involved cleaning out the basement, where "furniture, bags of clothes, miscellaneous garbage" from previous tenants cluttered the old cellar with the dirt floor. The last project Mundt had hired Robertson to do was concrete over the earth floors in the basement, which the contractor planned on completing when he returned from a vacation in Texas. He never had the opportunity to finish the job, however, as the news broke about the body in the basement.

Brown next called to the stand Marion Elizabeth Davis, a pleasant Black woman who went by the name Libby. Originally from Indiana, the fifty-five-year-old worked at the University of Louisville for thirteen years as an administrative associate and as assistant to the director of IT communications. On at least two previous occasions in the witness box—once with Ryane Conroy and once with Darren Wolff—Jeffrey Mundt had denied knowing Libby Davis. Or at least he couldn't recall having met her—or so he had claimed—squinting his eyes in an attempt to drum up a distant memory. He had worked with Davis on the main campus—in the same building and in the same department for eight or nine months.

Davis, however, destroyed Mundt's testimony. "He called me Libby." She spoke with him regularly and saw "him practically every day." Davis made his appointments, had to make copies for him, and assisted him "in whatever he needed." Although she only ever saw Joey once, she knew Mundt had a boyfriend because he "often talked about his personal life."

Asked to recall Mundt's demeanor, Davis described her coworker as "jolly," "very sure of himself," and "very assertive." He "really knew what he was doing," she remembered, and came across as "really friendly." According to the administrative assistant, Mundt's demeanor "never, ever changed." He never seemed scared or nervous. Mundt regularly offered to pick up lunch for her and he always carried around a good deal of cash, often fifty- and hundred-dollar bills, usually in his pockets. Davis had noticed the denominations because she had worked as a bank teller for fifteen years.

"Did Mr. Mundt ever invite you to his home?" Justin Brown put a hand in his pocket as he approached her.

"Yes, four or five times." The woman nodded, adding that Mundt had even invited her to a New Year's Eve party at the house.

When the news broke about the murder and who the police had arrested, Libby Davis "got instantly sick" when she saw Jeffrey's mugshot. "Because I knew where those scratches came from. I knew."

One day in late November or early December, Mundt had showed up at work with "fresh scratches on his neck." She had never seen him with injuries or black eyes prior to that. It looked "as though someone had just scratched him really, really hard. I mean they were fresh." When asked about the injuries, Mundt claimed he had fallen off a boat dock into icy waters in South Bend, Indiana. She didn't buy the story, but didn't think much of it—until the news broke.

"At first, I didn't want to be involved, but I knew it was the right thing to do." Davis contacted the Louisville Metro Police anonymous tip line about Jeffrey and spoke with Officer Roy Stalby twice, knowing that the information provided could be used in a murder investigation. She chose not to remain anonymous in the end.

A hush fell over the courtroom as Davis exited the box.

As its third witness, the defense team called to the stand Kevin Schlossberg, the owner of One Stop Knife Shop. The ginger-bearded forty-year-old had left the military in 1994 and in 1998 opened what many considered the best knife and cutlery store in the region. In a white oxford shirt and tie, he confirmed it was his first time testifying in a criminal trial before answering questions about a video showing Jeffrey Mundt with something flat attached to his belt. Schlossberg identified it as a "folding pocketknife," probably a "Kershaw Blur," the most popular seller at his shop. Jeffrey Mundt had used this knife, alleged the defense, to kill Jamie Carroll.

When Ryane Conroy cross-examined Schlossberg, she couldn't do much more than establish that a knife constituted "transferable property" and that one didn't need to "own" a knife in order to be able to use it. In this case, ostensibly, she intimated that Joey could have used Jeffrey's knife to kill Jamie Carroll. She also pointed out that Schlossberg had no qualifications to make determinations about knife wounds. "You are not at all a forensic expert, are you?" she asked.

When she had Schlossberg confirm that he had never earned a college degree, a woman ahead of us whispered under her breath, "God, what a bitch."

The defense then rested its case, after calling just three witness. They announced that Joey Banis would not testify after all. A slight murmur ran through the courtroom and Judge Mitch Perry gaveled the day's proceedings to a close.

The next day would be closing arguments. Then the jury would deliberate the fate of Joey Banis.


Curious observers packed the courtroom the next morning. Outside, news vans had lined up along Jefferson Street in front of the Judicial Center, and reporters stood in front of cameras. Pacing back and forth in a dark pantsuit, Conroy opened the prosecution's closing remarks by highlighting the strength of its evidence and pointing out that Joey Banis had not testified in the end, as promised.

When Darren Wolff delivered the closing argument for the defense, he began with a chuckle and faced the jury. "Wasn't Mr. Mundt the most entertaining witness you ever saw?" He went on to paint Mundt as a "bizarre character," intimating his sexual predilections alone might be reason enough for him to kill Jamie Carroll. Holding up a large color photo of Jeffrey Mundt pretending to cry upon learning police had unearthed a body in his basement, he reminded the jurors that the prosecution's star witness was an accomplished liar. Bringing up the absence of the supposed counterfeit bills, he suggested the prosecution had done something fishy. He pointed out that not a single drop of Jamie Carroll's blood had been found at the crime scene. Joey Banis had no reason to kill Jamie Carroll, someone he cared about, insisted the defense.

Delivering her rebuttal, Conroy shook her head. "I'd love to know why they did it. But this courtroom is not always a place we find out the why. Because people lie." She shrugged. "And . . . the best I can come up with is that I think the evidence supports the idea that these were two desperate people who were sort of living this twisted, dark lifestyle together, and you've got a doctor's son and an IT professional who were used to getting whatever they want whenever they want." Several of the jurors seemed to nod their heads ever so slightly as she continued. "And they get in this meth haze and they get swirled all up together and somebody comes up with this idea—you know, we could just take his drugs from him. Nobody would miss him. And it just snowballs. It just keeps on moving. There's something that's thrilling about it."

Carrie leaned in just then and whispered. "Sounds very Leopold and Loeb, doesn't it?"

I inclined my head. "I was thinking the exact same thing." In May 1924, wealthy University of Chicago students Nathan Freudenthal Leopold Jr. and Richard Albert Loeb committed "the crime of the century" when they kidnapped and murdered fourteen-year-old Bobby Franks. Ostensibly, it demonstrated an intellectual superiority that justified their carrying out the "perfect crime." They were found out, however, and sent to prison.

And now the Commonwealth of Kentucky argued that a jury should send Joseph Banis to prison. "It's twisted. I know it's twisted, but it accomplishes a goal. It happens to a person they knew nobody would care about and it probably was a little thrilling to see if they could get away with it. That's the best I've got." Ryane Conroy turned from the audience and faced the jury. "The best way to say it is they were a deadly combination, Joseph Banis and Jeffrey Mundt."

The prosecution wound down by clarifying a point that had confused many people, namely, which of the suspects had first alerted authorities about the body in the basement. Although the defense suggested Joey Banis had told the police first, Conroy insisted Jeffrey Mundt had beaten him to it the night of the 911 call. She concluded by emphasizing how "strange" it would have been for Banis and Mundt not to act as a "team" for just the several minutes during which Jamie Carroll was killed, while the rest of the time, they had done everything together.

As she walked back to the prosecution's table, more heads nodded in the jury box. The argument and the tone of her voice reminded me of the statements she had made before a jury in another gruesome case the local news had been revisiting in the weeks prior. A former football star at Fern Creek High School, thirty-one-year-old Francois Cunningham, stood accused of a double murder.

Early on an October morning, before the sun had risen, a teenager cutting through Fern Creek Park on his way to school had stumbled across a horrific scene. In a remote parking lot he came across the charred remains of a man, lying in a pool of blood. While waiting for the police, the boy noticed a trash bag, partially obscured by a dumpster. It held a second burned corpse. The bodies belonged to Trevor Alexander and Tykea Sanderson, and the prosecution alleged that Cunningham had murdered them and then set their bodies on fire over a drug deal gone bad. "His crime is not easy to stomach and his appearance today can be deceiving," Conroy had told the court, insisting, "There is a murderer in this courtroom. A murderer who shot two people. A murderer who set them on fire. A murderer who literally let them melt alive."

She had persuaded that jury. Now, would she persuade this jury?

By lunch time, the jury had its instructions and the members had started to deliberate. When they didn't reach a verdict by late that evening, Mitch Perry had them sequestered and sent off to hotel rooms.

# 22

## VERDICT

BY ELEVEN the next morning, the jury had reached a verdict. One of my journalist friends had texted me the news and I quickly drove downtown and parked on Seventh Street. From behind a patchy gray cloud, the sun sent several feeble rays bouncing off the mirrored window of the Judicial Center, where camera crews set up their equipment and reporters preened before going on air. On the sidewalks, crowds had gathered.

In the courtroom, Judge Mitch Perry watched from his pulpit as Bailiff Brown ushered in the defendant and then announced the arrival of the jury. Perry gaveled the proceedings to order and studied the juror's written decisions before reading them aloud.

The jury had found Joey Banis guilty on eight of the ten counts: murder in the first degree, robbery in the first degree, tampering with physical evidence, illegal possession of a controlled substance, illegal possession of drug paraphernalia, and three counts of criminal possession of a forged instrument in the first degree. The prosecution hadn't convinced them of Banis's guilt in the charges of criminal facilitation of murder and criminal facilitation to robbery in the first degree. Judge Mitch Perry dismissed the jury until the following Monday morning for the sentencing phase of the trial, admonishing them to not have any outside contact that could inform them about the proceedings.

Later, after all the records and courtroom videos were made available to the public, it would come out that at the bench, the defense had quickly brought up its intent to move for a mistrial "based on some information found on the internet." Darren Wolff alleged one of the jurors had been in contact with the outside world, while still deliberating. They also requested that Joey be allowed to wear street clothes for the formal sentencing, to which Perry agreed with the stipulation that Joey be "well-behaved." The judge alluded to reports of "behavioral issues" displayed by Banis while in the holding area. Later conversations with attorneys and bailiffs would reveal that Joey had a reputation for flying off the handle and berating his legal counsel outside the courtroom.

The prosecution had suggested that Banis had also been "stirring up problems" because of his access to computers from behind bars. "To my knowledge, Joey Banis is the only person in the history of corrections who has had internet access like that," complained Conroy, requesting that the court revoke his access. Darren Wolff insisted they needed to communicate with their client via internet, however.

When the time came for punishment, the jury didn't need to deliberate because the Commonwealth produced the plea bargain, in which Banis agreed to a life sentence with parole eligibility of twenty years in exchange for his testimony against Jeffrey Mundt.

At the formal sentencing hearing, a fragile Ellen Carroll, who had traveled from eastern Kentucky, needed to be supported on both sides as she talked about how her son's death had impacted the family. "He was the sunshine of my heart." Her voice broke as tears ran down her face.

When a pained Dr. Banis requested through Sally Bean, the victim advocate, that he be allowed to apologize personally on behalf of the family, Ellen Carroll declined. Afterward, she collapsed in the hallway and lay prostrate until paramedics arrived.

Before Bailiff Brown escorted him from the courtroom, Joey Banis embraced his father and mother. "But out of the presence of the jury," Judge Mitch Perry had insisted.

Several days later, Carrie and I sat at a table in Day's Coffee, hunched over a lengthy email that I had printed out. A juror on the Banis trial had reached out, saying, "Please keep this private until after the Mundt trial is over. I don't want anyone to get suspicious or cause any problems for that jury. I am very interested in Mundt's trial and a Google search turned up the Facebook page for your book. I went back and read through the comments during the trial and questions about how we found Banis guilty and why we asked for certain evidence or testimony. I guess I'm at a point where I can answer some of those questions."

I replied with a series of written questions, and the former juror had just sent back the answers.

What are your thoughts now that the trial has ended?

*Why answer questions or talk about the trial after we slipped out the back door and decided as a group not to talk about the trial? To my knowledge, none of us wanted our names made public, our faces in the news, or any publicity at all. It was a scary trial, one that will haunt some fellow jurors for a long time. Some scary people were also involved. There is always a fear of retribution from the parties involved or their acquaintances.*

*The trial was surreal from the very start. I had never been on a murder trial. I listen to the news every day, yet I never heard about this case. It surprised me since it was so bizarre. The jury selection alone was nerve-wracking. We had individual voir dire so each of us took the stand and answered questions. I'm terrible at public speaking and felt like an idiot trying to give an intelligent response to questions from the attorneys. Would the fact the defendant was gay influence me in any way? I think I went into too much detail about a person's guilt or innocence having nothing to do with sexual orientation and that I had many gay friends. Gosh, I was sweating up there and I wasn't even on trial. When I got picked, I was both mad and relieved. Mad because I knew it was going to be a long and difficult trial but relieved because I found some of my potential jurors incompetent. With such an important matter before us—potentially sentencing a person to death—he deserved a competent and interested jury.*

What did you think when the murder and subsequent events were laid out for you?

*As I said, I hadn't heard about the murder at all. We started getting bits and pieces during jury selection. Drugs. Sex. Buried body. Etc. It was surreal. Seeing stories like that on TV cannot prepare you to see and hear a true life event.*

What about the credibility of Banis and Mundt? Did one come off more believable than the other? How do you think the prosecution did in the court room? The defense?

*In regard to the actual murder, I didn't find either credible. It was impossible to find either guilty of the actual crime without the complicity. What I saw through the evidence and testimony was two people doing everything together, from the moment they met, to the night of the 911 call. I didn't believe either was scared of the other. I found both to be very smart. I ignored most of the theatrics of the courtroom, showing the actual tote, the big pictures of Banis and the victim looking happy, etc. Like I said, from day one they did everything together. They hooked up for sex—rough sex to say the least. They were involved in numerous criminal activities together. They were both familiar with guns and knives. Lots of drugs. They were both there. They were both doing drugs. They both cleaned up. They both buried and mutilated the body. They both went on with their lives together. The victim was buried with a sexual device still attached, so that suggested, to me at least, that the murder did happen during sex, not after as Banis stated in the police interview.*

I stopped reading and looked at Carrie. "Let me get this straight. Is this person saying that one of the reasons why they didn't believe Joey was because Jamie still had on a cock ring when he was killed?"

"Kind of looks like it," said Carrie. "Maybe she didn't know that some guys wear them all the time?"

"So, you think it's a woman as well? I was getting that same impression. Now, look at this next bit."

*I thought both attorneys did fairly well in the courtroom. Some of the visuals were hard to see but I think we saw enough. A lot of the props did nothing. All of gardening equipment was unnecessary. Unboxing every gun and ammo box was unnecessary. I was impressed that the defense attorney was never able to break Mundt. He seemed to go after him very hard but never got him to say anything to cast doubt or "catch" him in a lie.*

"Come on. Are you serious?" Carrie gave me a look of incredulity. "Were we even watching the same trial? Never caught Jeffrey in a lie? Never cast doubt?"

"I know. Isn't that crazy? It was obvious that he was lying about knowing Libby Davis, for one."

"It seemed to me that he was caught in lie after lie. Or am I just biased about the whole thing because from the moment he walked in I had a feeling in my gut that he was a sociopath? Didn't they pick up on that? Remember how we almost felt for him before the trial began? Like Joey had pulled him into his seedy den?" Carrie moved her head sadly.

"And then all the stuff about the drugs and the other things he lied about. Come on."

"You know. I just think Jeffrey is a creep. And a sociopath. I don't feel like Joey is a sociopath. Maybe an arrogant self-centered, narcissistic rich kid with a bad temper and a drug problem. But a sociopath? Clearly the combination of the two led them to burying someone in their basement." She shook her head again. "I don't know. I'm all over the place with this."

"Well, it goes to show you how complicated being on the jury can be." I turned to the next page of print. "Remember, the jurors were seeing Mundt for the first time on the stand. We've been privy to a lot of things they were not. This could have colored our perception."

"Apparently so. Well, let's see what else she has to say."

What about the bizarre circumstances surrounding the case? Had you ever heard of such a strange set of circumstances before—a weird love triangle, the drugs, all the kinky details that came out in the courtroom, the counterfeit money and all that? And, did you know the victim was at one time a well-known drag queen in eastern Kentucky and West Virginia?

*Taken together I had never heard of such a case. Individually, they are not so bizarre. There is some weird stuff on the internet! I did not know the victim was a well-known drag queen until a couple of weeks ago. It did bother me that no one filed a missing person's report or that a warrant wasn't issued when Jamie didn't show up for court.*

What do you really think happened that night? How do you think Jamie Carroll really died?

*Based on the evidence, both Banis and Mundt were violent people. It's hard to say what effect the drugs had on them, but I believe it contributed to their violence that night. I believe Jamie was engaged in a sexual act at the time he was attacked based on the naked body and the sexual appliance still worn. I guess that means I believed Mundt's testimony to some extent. Whether Mundt started stabbing him out of sexual fantasy, or they both started stabbing him, and then one shot him to stop him from screaming—I don't know. I found it interesting during testimony they both knew exactly what gun it was. The lime, the clean-up, the laptop password, taking the sim out of the phone—it all points to two people looking to get away with murder. And they would have, if not for the "fight" in June.*

*To give you a little more insight into the deliberations, we immediately went to the back and chose a foreperson. We then started with the lesser charges and worked our way to the most severe. What was bothersome was we couldn't request specific exhibits or testimony. For example, on the charge of possessing fake bills, all of us but one had it in our notes that Detective Lesher took possession of them. After the trial, we asked him, and he actually had them in his backpack. The judge did not allow them to be entered as evidence because they were presented too late.*

"There we go with the counterfeit money again." I narrowed my eyes. "Something is going on with those bills, what with how they kept disappearing and reappearing."

"I know. I thought the Secret Service had them. So bizarre." Carrie continued reading the lengthy response.

*The sequester was interesting. This was the first sequestered jury in almost three years. They called in reserve sheriff officers. The sheriff who drove the bus didn't know how to operate the door, which added a bit of lightheartedness to what was otherwise a stressful evening. I had no change of clothes. There was no clock in the room and I didn't have a watch so I had no idea what time it was. We got to the rooms a little after midnight and I probably looked out the window every half hour to try and figure out what time it was. Our wakeup was at six. We were escorted at all times by three officers, one in front of the line, one in back, and one directing traffic. Suffice it to say, we got a lot of looks and the hotel was packed.*

*Once we got to the murder and robbery charges, we focused on the jury instructions and definition of complicity. We must have read the instructions 50 times and examined how they were written legally. Literally every comma and semi-colon changed the way the instruction applied. Once we were pretty much close to a decision, several people were exhausted, and really didn't feel comfortable sentencing a man to what would likely be the rest of his life in prison. That's when we decided to basically sleep on it. Mind you, no one slept. But it gave everyone a chance to really look within themselves and make sure they were completely comfortable with the decision. We all were.*

*It was difficult from a personal sense. I couldn't talk to my spouse about what was going on. I didn't read any news or watch any TV about the trial. I know we were given strict instructions not to, but I'm still pretty proud of myself for not even googling a name or catching a news report. In the building, it was hard to avoid everyone associated with the trial. In the jury box, I kept my eyes off the public and Banis. Other jurors actually got into a staring match with Banis.*

*We were very surprised Banis didn't testify. In speaking to the attorneys after the verdict, we got some more insight. Apparently, the prosecution had some additional video of Banis that would have been pretty harmful if played. They were only allowed to play it if Banis testified. We asked their impression of him. They said he was very smart. He had a very bad temper. Apparently he yelled at his lawyers a lot? And apparently, he didn't think very highly of women. We asked the defense team why Banis didn't testify. It was purely his decision. We asked why they made a deal. Banis was scared we would recommend the death penalty.*

*No one was looking forward to the penalty phase and the testimony of Banis's family and Jamie's family. Many were upset already and truly just wanted to go home and move on with their lives and never think about this trial again. It was hard on several people. I will never be on another murder trial. I will use the stress and anxiety from this trial as an excuse.*

*They were scary, smart, bad MFers. I hate using any attorney's reference as I don't let people influence my decisions, but Conroy's "both did it" speech pretty much summed up our conclusion as a jury. If Mundt gets off, I would be very, very surprised and upset.*

"This poor juror. It is all clearly eating at her. I would feel the same way." Carrie pushed away the email and pulled close a copy of the *Courier-Journal* lying between us. "Also, the fact that this was the first jury sequestered here in years adds to the drama of the entire case."

After taking a sip of coffee, Carrie looked at me seriously. "So, what do you think about the defense intimating that killing Jamie would have been one of Jeffrey's fantasies? Could he really have done something like that?"

"Hmmm. Lots of people have dark fantasies, but making them happen is another thing." I looked down. "Take this guy, for example." I pointed at a headline in the newspaper. "He had some really bothersome fantasies. And he was the police."

That week, the news had hummed with the trial of Gilberto Valle, the notorious "cannibal cop" in New York City, whose wife had turned him in after discovering some disturbing things on his computer. In chat rooms, he liked to describe his desires to kidnap, torture, rape, kill, and cook women—preferably his own wife. He had also accessed the National Crime Information Center without proper authorization. After twenty-one months in prison, a federal judge overturned his sentence, contending the evidence showed that the policeman had engaged in "fantasy role-play" online only and had never acted upon his fantasies. Hardly surprising, his wife had divorced him and he lost his job on the police force.

Carrie studied a small photograph that showed the man standing in front of a courthouse. "God, what a creep."

"Hey, not to change the subject or anything, but do you want to come to a party with me tonight? On St. James Court. Actually, it's a book signing for Sena's new novel." Sena Jeter Naslund, Old Louisville's resident *New York Times* bestselling author, had just written, appropriately enough, a book titled *The Fountain of St. James Court.*

"Sure, sounds fun, but won't Frances get jealous if you take me instead of her?" Carrie gave me an impish grin.

"I think she'll be okay." I snickered. "And anyway, she had a previous engagement this evening."

"Seriously?" Carrie's smile melted into a deadpan stare of incredulity. "You mean you asked her, before me?"

"Nobody said I couldn't bring more than one person. It's nice to have a third wheel to absorb all the chatter with Frances anyway. She never stops."

A man with frazzled white hair and a neat beard approached the table just then and greeted me. It was Frank, a coffee shop regular with writing interests who often liked to chat about our recent projects. "Hey, Frank. How have you been?" I introduced him to Carrie and he accepted the invitation to join us.

"How's the writing coming along?" He settled in with smile. "What's the latest project?"

"Did you see anything about the trial that just wrapped up? The two guys in Old Louisville accused of murdering and burying a guy in their basement?"

"How could you not know about that trial?" Frank broke into a smile. "I guess if you live under a rock, maybe. It's all the city's been talking about for weeks."

"Well, that's my current obsession." I nodded in Carrie's direction. "Carrie and I were there for every day of the trial."

"Is that so?" Frank took a slow drink of coffee and set his cup down without a sound. "Well, that's funny, because you will never guess who one of my students was at Kentucky Country Day."

"Who?"

He fixed me with a serious gaze before speaking. "Joseph Richard Banis." He took another long drink of coffee, staring off into the distance, and soundlessly returned the cup to its saucer. "One of the strangest students I ever had. But very meticulous and very articulate. And extremely intelligent."

"Wow, small world." I leaned back in my chair. "Were you his English teacher?"

"That I was." Frank spied someone at the door and waved a hello. "You know he had a very privileged upbringing, right? Prominent doctor father who was the plastic surgeon for the Louisville elite. Joey was an odd duck, though. He had a sibling who was kind of a nervous nelly, too."

"Yeah, heard he was a bit off."

"Anyway, I was talking to Joey's former art teacher, Ann Marie Yates, and she reminded me of something very weird he used to do. There was this really pretty girl at school and he was just obsessed with her. He'd yell out 'I love you, Sarah!' every single time he saw her. Of course, it always embarrassed the poor child, but he still did it. Maybe he got off on it or something." Frank squinted his eyes and drained the last of his coffee.

"But that wasn't the strangest thing, by far," he said. "Another colleague was his French teacher—Josette Kearns—and every now and then the family would hire her to babysit when Joey's parents went off on their European vacations. He was the only sibling left at home, I believe. She'd stay at the house and keep an eye on him and make sure she cooked him something to eat three times a day for the two or three weeks he was alone."

Frank leaned back and crossed his arms. "But she said Joey was very particular about certain things, including where and how he would eat dinner every night. You know what he would do?" Frank made sure he had our attention before he continued. "Well, he refused to take his meals in the nice dining room, preferring instead to eat at the small table in the kitchen. My colleague said as soon as he had finished, he would pop up, carry his dirty dishes to the sink, and wash them." Frank turned around to cast a gaze around the crowded interior of the coffee shop. "And then he'd take out a big pail, fill it full with bleach and scalding hot water, and scrub down the entire kitchen. From top to bottom. Walls, ceiling, and all. He was a clean freak."

"Oh my god. That's so strange." Carrie shot me a look and then glanced at Frank. "We were talking about this during the trial. They didn't find a single drop of Jamie's blood in the very room where Joey supposedly murdered him."

"Yeah." I pushed the newspaper aside. "I talked to one of the people from CSU and she said the tiny amount of blood they did find in the room was consistent with what you'd expect to find in any household where two people lived in close quarters. Shaving, minor accidents— stuff like that, where people might bleed a little."

Carrie shuddered. "Poor Jamie Carroll was stabbed numerous times, shot in the head, had gashes on his neck—and there was broken glass cutting people all over the place. Can you imagine all the blood in that room? And in the end, they found just a drop here and there— none of it Jamie's?"

"Remember in the trial how Joey said there was blood gushing all over the place? It was all over the walls, the floor." I lifted my cup to drink, but the coffee had gone cold.

"That's quite a clean-up job." Frank thought again, slowly moving his head up and down. "Who knows? Maybe Joey had been practicing for this murder his entire life." He rose from the table and went to get a refill.


Several hours later I flipped through the channels, looking for the afternoon news on WHAS11. One of the stations ran a feature on Spike, the tortoise at Wayside Christian Mission, and how he had become especially close to a couple of the residents there. They tended to care for the creature and escort him on his daily walks. He loved to eat cucumbers, apple slices, and romaine lettuce, but bananas and green bell peppers most of all, one of them reported.

Eventually, the story I wanted surfaced and I turned up the volume. Several days before, Adam Walser had brought a camera crew to my house for an interview; now the segment, called "The House in Old Louisville Has a Dark History," was airing. In it, Walser detailed the murder of Jamie Carroll and gave a brief rundown of the first trial and my involvement in the case. Then he pointed out a number of strange coincidences with the first season of a popular television series that had earned 1435 South Fourth Street the nickname of "Kentucky's *American Horror Story* House."

Both stories involved a gay couple. There was also kinky sex and an old house that seemingly had the power to drive people to do terrible deeds. Both houses had functioned as sanatoriums and had associations with creepy doctors. Bad things happened in dungeon-like dark rooms. There were basements with dead bodies. There was a nurse. And a guy in a rubber suit.

Walser had interviewed several neighbors, one of whom remarked with a shudder that he "always knew there was something creepy about that house."

Before signing off, Walser announced that, to top things off, another body had recently been found on the premises, and the camera zoomed in on the walkway marking the southern boundary of the property where police had discovered the drug overdose victim. According to the report the house in Old Louisville truly did have some sinister associations.

Within minutes my phone began pinging with notifications from my Facebook page about the book, and soon likes and comments came pouring in. My phone rang several times as well, one of the calls from a production company in New York. They wanted to come to Louisville to interview me about the murder for a true-crime show they would be filming in the next several weeks.

The last time I answered, however, an angry voice boomed from the other end. "I'm going to fucking kill you!"

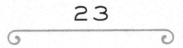

# 23

# PARTY ON ST. JAMES COURT

AT THE book signing that night at John and Kim Crum's house on St. James Court, champagne flutes clinked and applause echoed after Sena gave a brief reading before retreating to a corner desk to autograph books. Piano music lilted softly and a small fire crackled in an ornate marble fireplace flanked by Solomonic columns studded with colorful mosaic tiles. Dr. and Mrs. Crum, Sena's neighbors from a few doors down, lived in the newest house on the court, a spacious red-tiled and stucco Arts and Crafts house built in 1911. One of Louisville's most lauded architects, William J. Dodd, designed it as a wedding present for his wife, Ione Estes, and they had lived there for a time, before relocating to Los Angeles.

Carrie and I stood in a corner near a large leaded-glass window— with Frances Mengel, who had decided to show up after all. "Oh, darlins," she exclaimed when our arrivals coincided at the front door. "That other event was boring and that woman with the dessert truck catered the sweets. It all tasted like sandpaper. Just don't tell my family that I drove all the way down here at night. They would have a fit if they knew." Out in the street, Frances had parked her Lexus with one wheel up on the curb.

"So, do you think you need to worry about him threatening you like that?" Carrie grabbed us glasses of wine from a passing tray while Frances went to greet several familiar faces. "I do kind of feel sorry for him, but still, that's no way to act."

The call had come from one of the hotheads Kelly had complained about on Fourth Street—in this case the father of the drug overdose victim whose body had been found outside of 1435 South Fourth Street—and the story about the house in Old Louisville had made him livid. Even though I had declined to speculate about that detail on camera, the grieving parent accused me of sensationalizing his daughter's death.

"He's not a bad guy, just letting off a little steam," I confided, after a sip of wine. "I'm the one who put him in contact with Adam Walser after all."

"Yes, but only because you thought an investigative reporter could get to the bottom of things. The dad was claiming the EMTs had botched things and you were just trying to help."

"No good deed goes unpunished." I raised my glass and touched it to hers.

Soon, Lucie Blodgett and Louise Cecil emerged from the crowd at the front door and came to greet us. "My, there is always something going on in Old Louisville, isn't there?" Lucie gave me a hug and then winked. "So many scandals, so little time."

That evening, talk buzzed not only about the WHAS11 story, but also about a rash of thefts at Conrad's Castle, the opulent limestone mansion at the north end of St. James Court. Shaded by the canopy of towering, old-growth trees, this residential enclave featured a broad, grassy median with a picturesque fountain featuring a Venus statue at its center. Here and there, tall gas lamps flickered twenty-four hours a day, a trait that made the sidewalks a favorite spot for late-night strolls. Framed on both sides by two blocks of mansions, townhomes, and an elegant multi-family construction or two, St. James Court basked in its status as the most charming spot in the city.

Conrad's Castle counted as one of the largest—and first—mansions built on the court. Its original owner, a Frenchman named Theophile Conrad, had made a fortune in the leather tanning business. He set out to solidify his reputation as one of the most successful men in the city by inhabiting one of its most extravagant homes. For his new residence, he drew on inspiration from his well-to-do family's imposing, moat-surrounded mansion back in Strasbourg, France. The construction of the huge Richardsonian Romanesque structure began in 1893, and two years later, its anchoring towers, abundant Roman arches, and squat columns and pillars dwarfed most other residences in the burgeoning suburb. From high above, whimsical stylized faces reminiscent of hooting owls and roaring lions peered down from the rusticated stones that comprised most of the exterior.

Since the 1980s it had operated as a historic home open for tours, its impressive hardwood floors and Edwardian décor earning it a spot as one of the city's most visited attractions. Recently, cash had gone missing at the Conrad-Caldwell House Museum—as well as a good deal of valuable silver—leaving the director and the board in a dither.

I knew this firsthand, because, in not so many words, it had been intimated that I might have had something to do with it all.

After my first book came out, I became involved in the startup of a small tour business conceived to make money for the neighborhood chamber of commerce. Our most popular evening walk ended with a short lantern-guided viewing of the bottom floor of Conrad's Castle, for which the museum would get a cut of the ticket sales. This meant that I—and the two guides who helped me—had a key and the alarm code that afforded full access to the mansion.

I had no idea about the problems until I was escorting a large group from the Kentucky Library Association into the mansion one night. After unlocking the massive front door, I turned to usher in the visitors, when an angry face suddenly confronted me, demanding to know how I had acquired keys to the museum and with what right was I on the premises.

It was a board member who lived on the court, and when I informed him of the arrangement I'd had for over a year with the selfsame board which he sat on, he became incensed and stormed off.

Red-faced, I let the librarians in and apologized for the scene before finishing up the tour.

The next day I learned from another board member about the thefts. Within a week, I handed over my key, and we cut out the nightly mansion visits. Angelique, one of two other guides, had moved to the West Coast the week before, so she had already turned in her key. Still the thievery continued. That's when suspicions turned to Peter, the last tour guide, who hadn't returned his key because he was also a longtime employee of the museum. They dismissed him and demanded his key, to which he took great umbrage, but things continued to go missing.

Now, Adam Walser of WHAS11 news had been snooping around and people were talking.

"What did he find? Oh, darlins, I know it'll be good." Frances gave us a furtive smile and nibbled at a beaten biscuit with smoked ham. "Did I ever tell you about the time Lucie Blodgett and I had to kick out one of the members of our Antiques Club because we caught her dipping into the coffers? I'm telling you. Where was that now? Out at one of the Herr mansions where the meeting was? You've been out there to give a talk, remember?"

"Yes, I—"

"Goodness gracious!" Frances bugged her eyes out at a tray mounded with chicken salad sandwiches made with silver dollar rolls and held out by Kim, who had emerged into our midst. "Oh, dear! Chicken salad! Did you know about the infamous chicken salad tragedy at the Herr Mansion? I told you about that, darlin', didn't I? The wedding feast in the 1800s that horrified the city?"

On April 15, 1891, Winfred Snook wed Fannie Belle Herr at her father's estate, Magnolia Stock Farm, near Lyndon Station in east Louisville. On the manicured grounds of the Herr Mansion, close to one hundred guests sipped lemonade and bourbon while dining on mushrooms, cake, ice cream, and chicken salad. Within hours most became violently sick, including the bride and groom who had boarded a train for Niagara Falls but had to disembark in Cincinnati due to the illness.

Word spread and newspapers in the region soon began speculating on the cause for the sudden mass illness. At first, most suspected the wild mushrooms as the culprit, but then family members alleged one of the bride's sisters had poisoned the wedding out of jealousy. Fannie's grief-stricken father accused household servants of poisoning the guests with arsenic, claiming a young Black boy had warned other servants not to eat.

And then people began to die. The first victim, the wealthy capitalist and uncle of the bride B. Frank Guthrie, lived near St. James Court, on Third Street. In the first two weeks, six more followed him to their graves. Then the sad news arrived that the groom himself had

expired. In the following months, more would die, bringing the esti-
mated total to as many as thirty. The medical college at the University
of Louisville eventually found the cause to be food poisoning, due to
bacterial contamination of the chicken salad. The chicken had been
cooked two days prior to the wedding and stored in broth at room
temperature for the whole time.

"Well, I sure hope these chicken salad sandwiches aren't tragic,"
Kim, our hostess and fellow writer, said with a laugh. "I made them
myself and I used David's recipe!"

"Ah, that's why they looked so familiar." I bit into a sandwich before
changing the subject. "Well, I hate to say it, but I'm glad the thefts at
the museum continued after I turned in my key. I was really getting
paranoid that somebody thought I had something to do with it."

"It's always good for your public persona to be involved in a little
scandal, isn't it? Even if it is just guilt by association." Jim Segrest, looking dapper in a pastel pink suit and bowtie, had arrived and inserted
himself into the conversation. "But no matter how famous you become,
just try to downplay it, act humble. Here in Louisville the elite want
to prove to you that they're 'just regular folk,' which is just another
form of pretension."

"Jim, you hit the nail on the head," said Lucie Blodgett, while
scratching notes on a pad for a story in the *Voice Tribune*. "And you
know, deep down it's because we want you to relax and enjoy yourself
in Louisville!"

"That's exactly right." Jim smoothed the lapel of his silky suitcoat.
"When Princess Margaret of England visited for the Derby in 1974,
she was hosted by the Binghams, one of the bluest-blooded families in
the state. And what did they serve her for dinner?" He paused for a sip
from the drink in his hand. "Turkey hash!" He cried out in a burst of
laughter. "I mean, it was more than just leftovers from Thanksgiving
dinner—but still!"

"Luce, I remember the pictures you took of her," said Louise Cecil.
"They were just beautiful." Louise raised a hand to her throat. "And
the dresses she would wear—just stunning."

While Kim went off to the kitchen, Segrest placed his empty glass
on a passing tray and grabbed a fresh drink. "Hey, speaking of royalty,
did you know we had our own queen here in Louisville at one time?"

"Do you mean Lucinda?" I said.

Jim laughed. "I should have suspected you'd know about her."

A regular sight on the streets downtown and in Old Louisville during the 1880s, Lucinda cut a somewhat eccentric character. But, as her eccentricity increased, her grasp on reality loosened; somewhere along the line, she proclaimed herself "Queen of America."

The *New York Times* picked up on Lucinda's antics in 1885 and reported the details of her most recent appearance on October 30. "An old lady, with a remarkable appearance and bearing, swept into the Circuit Court this morning with queenly grace. She was under the escort of a couple of policemen, and was given a seat in front of the jury. This was a celebrated crank, Lucinda, Queen of America," it reported. "For several years, she has been a conspicuous character, and she was in the habit of appearing in public places in regal attire. She would go to the Galt House and ask for the king and everywhere she was the same queenly personage."

But Queen Lucinda had some problems in her kingdom. "She feared a plot to assassinate her and usurp the throne . . . The next thing heard . . . Lucinda was in Washington besieging President Arthur" and issuing "long weekly proclamations, sending them to all the newspaper offices."

Back in Louisville, terrified that assassins had found her, the seventy-four-year-old barricaded herself in her rooms on Sixth Street. The authorities hauled her off to a courtroom, where the regent declared that the country enjoyed good governance and the threat of assassination had passed and that "Her son was emperor and Bob Ingersoll was king. Mr. McDonald, of Texas, was president."

"Poor thing." Jim Segrest frowned. "They sent her off to the insane asylum and nobody knows what became of her."

"Well, I love that we had our own queen at one time, but what do you think will become of Jeffrey Mundt when he goes on trial? The plot thickens." Kim had returned with a silver platter holding new hors d'oeuvres: bacon and benedictine canapés. "Do you really think they acted together like the prosecutor claims?"

"Oh, I think he was the one behind it all," said Louise. "Just from the one interaction with him, I could tell he had a dark side. And to hear him on the stand—what a fake!"

"And especially with the counterfeiting," added Lucie. "Acting like he had nothing to do with it, but he was the computer guy with all the knowledge."

"What do you think, Kim?" I accepted a canapé.

She finished passing the tray around and smiled mysteriously. "I think John and I have been considering buying that old house and turning it into a bed and breakfast or maybe a writer's retreat."

"Seriously?" Lucie and Louise both said it in unison.

"You wouldn't be bothered?" said Jim Segrest. "A lot of people would be bothered by what happened there."

"Not really, and it's just a house anyway." Kim turned toward the next cluster of guests.

"I'm not so sure about that." Eyes narrowing suspiciously, Segrest watched her move away. "I've heard some things about that house."

# 24

## DERBY

SPIRITS WERE high the night before the Kentucky Derby when I went to meet my friend Richard Burchard on the front patio at Chill Bar. I had parked several blocks away, on the same street where mystery writer Sue Grafton had grown up. Her neighbor, Hunter S. Thompson, the Louisville writer who would earn fame for his embodiment of gonzo journalism, was a few years ahead of her at Atherton High School. "Oh, he was such a pain," she once said, "always riding up behind me on his bike and running his front tire into the back of my shoes."

Richard was sitting at the bar. "Hey, what's up? Happy Derby Eve!" He had ordered me a bourbon, neat, and the tumbler waited for me on the counter. "No Pappy Van Winkle twenty-three-year-old, but they did have the ten. Cheers!"

"Nice." I raised my glass and touched it to his.

"Where's Ramon?"

"He's got the night shift at the hospital today and tomorrow. He'll try to make a couple of parties, though, and we'll go to the track for a bit."

"Probably see you at Churchill Downs then." At the next stool, Richard's friend Ricky was talking to a guy in a red Coke T-shirt who knew about my book project.

"Hang on a sec." The guy in the T-shirt waved over a burly dark-haired man and they came to me. "There's someone you need to meet."

He introduced me to Casey, a former manager at Starbase Q, the bar where Joey Banis had worked.

"That is, before he stole half of our stuff and opened Fuzion in Butchertown," said Casey. "Joey made a good drink, I'll give him that. And with his blue mohawk and colorful tattoos and body paint, he was very popular with the patrons. Many followed him to Fuzion, which really hurt Q."

According to Casey, Joey had been part of the first group to work at Q and acted as a "self-proclaimed" manager. "They were all into drugs and Joey always had that metallic smell. He was forever going to his 'office' in the back of the bar, but it was just a little room where he kept his crack pipe." While working, Joey kept meticulous notes and carried around a notebook where he sketched plans for his future bar.

Joey had told Casey he had grown up in New York but the Browns had convinced his father to move to Louisville to do their plastic surgery when Joey was twelve. Casey wasn't sure how much to believe. He did believe him when he said he had attended Kentucky Country Day, however. "Most of the time, you never knew, though. He was a pathological liar and always getting into trouble but his daddy bailed him out every time. Stole my passport one day at the bar. I'm glad he's out of commission for a while."

Just then the crowd outside began hooting and cheering as bright flashes and colorful sparkles began dancing around the patio. Out on Bardstown Road, a white pickup truck slowly rolled by, pulling a trailer. On the platform rested an enormous glitter ball and it threw back the light from the streetlamps. Onlookers in seersucker and pastel-colored suits clapped and whistled as it disappeared from view, the driver waving goodbye from his window.

"Did you see that? It was huge," I said.

"Oh, that's one of the big ones you can rent for parties." Richard drained his drink, raised the empty glass to his nose, and smiled after inhaling. "Hey. Let's you and me have a party and rent one of those big-ass glitter balls. What do you think?"

"Sounds good to me. But when? There are already so many established parties and events leading up to the big race."

Richard grunted. "That's right. Louisville, the only place they party two weeks for a two-minute race."

"And where would we hang it?"

Richard took another sniff and wrinkled his brow. "Hmm. Good question. Let's think on that."

The next day azaleas and dogwood blossoms were in full bloom and wherever you turned, splashes of purple, pink, soft yellow, and ivory met the eye. Spring grass had taken root and yards and gardens had that fresh, clean look.

In Cherokee Triangle, another of Louisville's historic preservation districts, women in tight dresses and extravagant hats waited politely as men in bowties and colorful suits opened car doors for them. It was the first Saturday in May and revelers were heading off to attend the famous races at Churchill Downs, most likely stopping off for brunch or early mint juleps beforehand.

Smaller than Old Louisville, this district also had a reputation for its grand houses and Victorian architecture. While this part of town enjoyed its fair share of eccentrics and scandals, they had already gone through many of the growing pains Old Louisville still experienced. The many restaurants on Bardstown Road and the huge Olmsted-designed park nearby made it attractive and like most of the neighborhoods in the Highlands, Cherokee Triangle didn't have the same rough patches and seediness that blemished Old Louisville.

Ramon and I made our way up the front walk to a brick house with large arched windows and an enormous tower. From inside, soft strains of bluegrass music wafted out to the sidewalk. The university colleague who had invited us greeted us at the door with two mint juleps in silver cups. "Cheers." He handed one to each of us. It wasn't even noon yet. "Come on in and make yourselves at home. Food's in the dining room."

Next to an overflowing cheese board rested a butcher's block with smoked trout and salmon arranged around mounds of chopped onion and capers. Large silver platters held slices of beef tenderloin with small porcelain tureens of Henry Bain sauce and baskets of yeast rolls on the side. A crystal punch bowl cradled piles of chilled shrimp layered with lemon slices.

"Hey, Mr. Author Man!" Someone squealed from the buffet and waved a pink napkin.

"Yes, how you been, Mr. Writer Friend? Look at you in your pretty blue suit." Another shriek cut through the din of conversation, and the two drag queens I had met at Dale and Bill's party beelined for me, stiletto heels clip-clopping the hardwood floors. They both sported lavish hats and wore tight silk dresses; again, one had a pink theme and it was green for the other. I wondered if Book Man and his seersucker suit would make an appearance as well.

Ramon shook his head and hid behind a sweets table laden with dishes of pulled candy, pecan pies, and lemon bars.

"Saw you interviewed on the news the other day. Can't wait to read the book."

"Yeah, hope we're in it!" The one with fuchsia marabou at her neck sipped from a gold chalice and slapped me playfully on the arm. "And I don't know if you've heard, but the CIA has been snooping around the Derby City. Ask Miss Thing over here."

"Gurl, we got a visit last week from two men in black—seriously, they looked just like in the movies—two *men in black* who wanted to ask questions about little Jamie's murder. Well, let me tell you, there is more going on than meets the eye. It's not just about drugs and kinky sex—and, guurrl, I loves me some drugs and kinky sex." Moving a shiny green leather handbag from one arm to the next, she reached for a piece of cheese and pointed it at her companion.

"Somehow, they found out Miss Thang in Pank over here got us our party favors from little Jamie. They talked to her as well."

"It's all so exciting." Miss Thang in Pank took out a Gucci tube of Millicent Rose lipstick and hurriedly applied a touch-up coat. "But they weren't interested in the drugs at all. Whew, that was a relief!" She paused and dramatically wiped a make-believe layer of sweat from her forehead. "They had lots of questions about Miss Jeffrey Mundt, though, that's for sure. They even wanted to know if we had slept together. Ew. I didn't even know that freak."

"I know, so strange," said her friend. "They asked me if I ever delivered packages for him or if we had ever gone to any secret clubs together." She had laid her cheese on a cracker and took a bite. "Nasty. I love me some secret clubs, but not with Miss Jeffrey Mundt."

The other turned over her wrist and studied the delicate gold watch there. Before even giving me a chance to speak, she grabbed her friend by the arm and said, "Honey, we have to run. It's showtime!"

Her friend in green squealed and they turned to make their exits. "We're performing in the tent out back." She batted her eyes coquettishly. "Come and see us!" Still prattling, they blew kisses and hurried for the door. As they retreated, a figure in a pastel yellow suit and bowtie emerged from the crowd.

"I see you're making the rounds." Jim Segrest lifted a champagne flute in greeting.

"Hey, good to see you again. Got any good gossip over in Butchertown?"

"Well, not too much at the moment. Old Louisville seems to be getting all the attention again."

"I know. Well, at least we're halfway through the trials."

"Say, I was meaning to tell you this the other night at the party, but you skedaddled before I had the chance." He raised his finger and shook it in mock consternation. "I knew the woman who lived in that house on Fourth Street before the two guys moved in."

"Oh, really, the one who was a nurse?"

"Yes, it's been so long, but if I recall, her name was Paulette or something like that. She was there from the '60s on. But you know, I remember that house from before then as well. I grew up in Old Louisville and I knew all the places. It's a shame so many have been torn down here and there. I always had a thing for old houses."

"What else do you remember?"

"Oh, Lordy, that house always had a creepy vibe. When I was a kid, they talked about it being haunted all the time. It seemed like people could never stay there very long. Within a few years of moving in, tragedy usually befell them." He raised his glass and sipped. "Supposedly, there was a morgue down in that basement at one time."

"A morgue? Seriously?"

"Oh, yes, my grandmother used to tell me about it. One of her relatives worked there when it was a cancer hospital."

"So, there really was a doctor there at one time? They reported it on the news, but I couldn't find any proof of that."

"Oh, he was there. Don't remember the name, but there was a doctor there—with, shall we say, questionable ethics—and I think that's when things started going downhill for that house."

Through the back window, I could see Ramon standing in front of the stage where the drag queens were performing.

"And the woman who lived there, the nurse? She was a real die-hard Catholic, you know. Hung out with the nuns who used to run the place on Park, right across from the Witches' Tree," Jim said.

"You mean that old house with the tall brick wall? I always wondered about that place."

"Yeah, Our Lady's Home for Infants. They built that wall to protect all the unwed mothers who went there to hide their shame." He took another drink from his glass. "I actually have a couple of the old woman's pieces at Linden Hill. Antiques I bought off of her as she declined." His nose twitched as he reached for the silk pocket square near his lapel. "I think she was having a hard time making ends meet."

"Really now? What kinds of things?"

"Oh, I've got some really nice old crucifixes—she had tons of them—and a beautiful chest and an interesting altar set. You should come over some time and see it."

"I'd love that, thanks." I prepared to ask him when, but a scream from the backyard cut the music and lively chatter short. Heads turned in alarm. Footsteps echoed across the floorboards as people began stampeding out of the house.

# 25

# THE SECOND JURY

JEFFREY MUNDT stood trial two months after Joey Banis, in May, right after the Kentucky Derby. Around the city, many still had the shell-shocked look that often came to the faces of the residents once the two weeks of festivities and nonstop parties finally ended and people were forced to return to the mundanity of everyday life.

At the Judicial Center, some expressed a weariness at being involved in a second trial for a case that had been tried once before. In the waiting area on the first day, one observer remarked that "they already had a convicted killer and that should be enough." Another observer complained that "those goddamned gays are always stirring up trouble."

My writer friends Kelly Morris and Julia Blake were in town and they had come along to sit in on the day's proceedings. "It's a shame you two weren't here last week for the Derby. You would have loved the parties," I said. "Especially the one where these two drag queens caught their tent on fire and had the fire department called on them."

"Oh my god, what happened?" Julia squirmed in her seat and turned to face me.

"They were dancing around and lip-syncing and one of them grabbed a lit tiki torch and began twirling it around, but it caught her friend's wig on fire."

Kelly started to laugh but caught herself. "Nobody was hurt, were they?"

"No, but she threw her burning wig on the ground and before you knew it, the tent went up in flames. Fortunately, the host had a fire extinguisher nearby and they got it under control."

"Hair on fire," said Julia. "I bet that smelled terrible."

"Yeah, and they did a real number on the yard out back, running about and punching holes in the grass with their high heels, but it was Derby. Everyone moved back inside and resumed the festivities like nothing had happened."

"Hmm. Louisville." Both Kelly and Julia said it in unison.

The elevator door slid open and Bailiff Brown emerged with several men in suits. He opened the courtroom and got things running for the day.

Once again, Judge Mitch Perry presided in the courtroom, this time for the trial of *Commonwealth v. Jeffrey Mundt*. And familiar figures sat at the table for the prosecution: Ryane Conroy, Josh Schneider, and Jon Lesher. But the defense team had a markedly different makeup—and not just for the new faces, but for its size. Four stood at the ready to defend their client: Steve Romines, Ted Shouse, Annie O'Connell, and Sean Oates. Jeffrey Mundt, wearing a dark sweater vest with a white wing-collared, long-sleeved shirt and khakis, folded his hands and looked forward somberly.

The first matter at hand was the jury selection, and once again, they would have to whittle down an enormous pool of prospective jurors—144 in all. Individual voir dire began on the second day; however, this time counsel had expedited the process by a more extensive polling of the potential jurors in writing beforehand. And the questions about views on capital punishment didn't need to be addressed because the Commonwealth had already dropped that option in exchange for Mundt's testimony. Candidates, therefore, spent much less time on the stand than their counterparts in the Joey Banis case.

As with their counterparts in the previous trial, their views on homosexuality would play a large part in the questioning. And both sides understood the importance of weeding out the homophobes.

In a 2008 publication titled "The Gay Panic Defense," Cynthia Lee of the George Washington School of Law wrote that homophobes generally fell into one of two classes. Category one consisted of the "explicit" homophobes, individuals not ashamed of expressing negative views about homosexuality in public. Category two was comprised of "closet" homophobes, people who knew that it looked "bad to appear biased against gays and lesbians."

Understandably, ferreting out closet homophobes presented a much greater challenge to the courts. Prosecutors, therefore needed to pose questions designed to indirectly gauge a prospective juror's attitudes. Psychologist Drury Sherrod and sociologist Peter Nardi conducted a study to identify potentially homophobic jurors during voir dire, realizing that some might try to hide their true biases to "save face in the courtroom." They came up with a series of proxy questions that could more subtly elicit truthful responses about homosexuality.

The questions asked of the prospective jurors in the Mundt case mirrored those designed by Sherrod and Nardi: *Do you have any close friends who are gay or lesbian? Politically, are you liberal, middle-of-the-road, or conservative? How important are your religious beliefs in guiding your daily decisions? Do you think the world would be a better place if more people followed old-fashioned values? Do you try to attend religious services at your church or temple every week? Are federal and state governments doing enough to make sure industry does not pollute the environment we live in? How thoroughly do you read your local newspaper every day? What is the postal zip code where you live? What is your current marital status? What is your religion? Have you ever served in the U.S. Armed Forces? Do you feel your life is more controlled by fate than by planning? Do you read any magazines on a regular basis? What is your highest level of education?*

In the Mundt trial, while many candidates had already been ferreted out in the initial questionnaire, negative attitudes about homosexuality surfaced quickly. The second candidate, number 875356, likened homosexuality to lying, stealing, and cheating and thought "it shouldn't be happening." He claimed not to have an issue "with the people," though. His "special needs daughter," he explained, rode to work with openly gay guys, and they "treated her better than anyone."

A testy exchange with Judge Perry ensued when lead attorney Steve Romines asked for the man to be stricken. "Judge, in writing he said he can't be impartial," Romines insisted. Perry didn't agree but the prosecution had no problem with removing the candidate, and in the end the man was stricken. This set the precedent for the defense much more vigorously weeding out potential homophobes than in the first trial. And this doggedness would set the tone for the trial to come.

Candidate number 875233, an "Evangelical Christian" and "practicing Catholic" whose wife was on the faculty of Bellarmine University, where he himself went to school with prosecutor Conroy, said of homosexuality, "I don't believe it's greater than any other sin—lying, for example." Prospective juror 875577 believed "homosexuality was not natural."

Prospective juror 875510, candidate number sixty-seven, a white male with glasses and a suit without a tie who lived in Old Louisville, identified himself as gay and having gay friends. When he explained that two guys in early 1990s abducted and murdered a gay friend of his in a hate crime, Steve Romines asked, "Would you feel any sort of pressure—because it's sort of made the gay community look bad—to convict because of it?" The juror replied in the negative and I had to ask myself how many times lawyers asked jury candidates for heterosexual murder trials if they had any qualms about convicting the accused because it would make the straight community look bad.

As with the first jury, another striking aspect in the selection of the second jury was the quantity of potential jurors who seemed proud of their uninformed status and eschewal of media outlets. Already by the twentieth prospective juror, it seemed that many were proud to announce how rarely they watched the news or read newspapers. "I *never* watch the news," said a female candidate smugly, crossing her arms and lifting her chin. Prospective juror 875074, a young white female, whose father was a police officer, said resolutely, "I don't watch the news."

So it was a breath of fresh air when it came up that the occasional individual was particularly well informed. When jury candidate 875453, a middle-aged woman, admitted to knowing "many things" about the case, both the defense and prosecution, "in an abundance of caution," agreed to her dismissal because of excessive knowledge. At this time Steve Romines brought up *Courier-Journal* reporter Jason Riley, lamenting that every article about Joey Banis and Jeffrey Mundt included at least one "and after a night of drug-fueled sex" or some such, which he maintained was prejudicial.

Although Judge Perry agreed to strike the woman, he made it clear he was "not happy with the situation." The situation being the defense's rigorous objection to so many potential jurors. "I absolutely do not agree with you, counsel. I don't like it. I will tell you I don't like it," Perry said sternly. Then he went on to call out attorney Ted Shouse for being too chummy with the candidates: "And by the way, Mr. Shouse, when I said earlier you were too chatty, here's what I know about you already, you, personally: you're Catholic, you read the paper, you're a news junkie, what time your paper is delivered, what time you leave the house, and you love sports and U of L. Please stop that. What we know about you, for this purpose, is never appropriate. Please."

In the middle of jury selection, while the potential candidates were out on break, came the bombshell that Joey Banis had reneged on his deal with the Commonwealth of Kentucky and now refused to testify against Jeffrey Mundt. And Mitch Perry announced that he "just moments ago" had received a request for a new trial on behalf of Banis. "Banis ain't testifying!" said Steve Romines enthusiastically after learning of this development. The prosecution had lost its star witness. But Romines's enthusiasm was tempered when he considered the motives: "This is just another example of Joey Banis trying to manipulate proceedings!"

Darren Wolff had arrived, with Justin Brown and orange-jumpsuit-clad Joey Banis in tow, to claim that his client had not knowingly and voluntarily entered into the agreement and he alleged "prosecutorial misconduct" because Ryane Conroy had knowingly put together an agreement with key witness Mundt without the stipulation of telling the truth. Several times, Banis leaned forward at the witness table to steal not-so-furtive glimpses of his former lover. When Conroy responded that they did not consider Jeffrey Mundt a key witness in the case, half of the courtroom balked. Ryane Conroy confirmed that she had met with Banis, who had indicated he would not testify because the Commonwealth refused to renegotiate his agreement. Now his fate was up in the air again.

Conroy explained that it all had stemmed from Joey's fear of his status of being a snitch and HIV positive getting into the newspapers. She asked the court if Joey Banis was not one of "the most informed, most intelligent" defendants the court had ever seen and explained his change of heart simply as "just buyer's remorse."

Although Mitch Perry did take issue with the lack of a stipulation for telling the truth, he denied the motion for a new trial. General voir dire would resume the next morning, with a pool of fifty-nine candidates, he announced.

On the drive home, I drove past the Connection, the biggest gay bar in town. A cherry picker stood on the corner and from the basket two workers in hard hats hoisted a large glitter ball up past the second-floor balcony. It hung from a protruding beam, sparkling and twirling. A minute later, I saw Mark Anthony Mulligan shuffling down the sidewalk, dangling a piece of posterboard at his side. I had seen him on the news just the day before.

Local filmmakers Gregory Luchini Maddox and Jeffrey Randall with support from producer Gill Holland had started work on a short film about Mulligan, who grew up in the West End in the 1960s. His neighborhood, Rubbertown, teemed with chemical plants, oil refineries, and colorful commercial signage that captivated his young imagination. After dropping out of high school, he began recreating streetscapes while living in homeless shelters and mental health care facilities. He gained a following after Louisville artists Bruce Linn, Al Gorman, and Chuck Swanson took him under their wings and cultivated his talent.

Mark Anthony seemed somewhat out of sorts and far removed from the benches and bus stops he usually frequented, so I pulled the car over and buzzed down a window. "Hey, Mark Anthony! You need a ride somewhere?"

He turned and smiled, then hesitated. "Where you going?"

"I'm headed home but I can drop you off someplace if you like."

He scratched his head and thought for a moment. "How about Wayside? You going that way?"

"Sure, hop in." I opened the door for him.

After buckling himself in, Mark Anthony placed the posterboard on his knees. I gazed down and beheld a vibrant hodgepodge of recognizable buildings, Omega National Products clearly visible among them, interspersed with roads and billboards. One of the streets was identified as "Goatkitten Lane" and another he had labeled "Happy Birthday Highway." He extracted a blue marker from a side pocket and began lettering an empty street sign. "Dis-co-Ball-Drive," he slowly pronounced while scratching out the letters.

"So, how have you been?"

"I'm good." He looked out the window and belted out a tune. "God is good. God is good. God is goo-oo-ood!" Then he returned his attention to the artwork in his lap. "I'm just paintin' what's on my mind. I'm just paintin' what's on my mind. On my mind is somethin' aa-aa-all the time."

"So what's on your mind today?" I asked.

He pointed his marker at a tall green steeple and continued his singing. "They got skeletons in the basement, skeletons in the basement."

I chuckled, realizing that he had included a rendering of an old church known for having the full skeletal remains of two Catholic saints. Off in the distance, the spire of that very church appeared over the rooflines. I pointed. "Ah, you mean St. Martin of Tours?"

Mark Anthony vigorously shook his head but didn't look up. "No, down in Old Louisville. Skeletons in the basement, skeletons in the closet, too."

A slight shudder ran down my spine, but I didn't say anything. Mark Anthony continued to sing his observations and in a few minutes, we arrived at the shelter.

When I announced our arrival, Mark Anthony didn't look up. Engrossed in his drawing, he added an orange outline to a gnarled and twisted tree I hadn't noticed before. A multitude of crosses of varying sizes dangled from the branches. "Is that the Witches' Tree?" I asked.

"Nope, that's the God's Tree. Don't want no witches."

I prepared to ask him more, but he lifted his head at that moment and a smile broke out on his face. He pointed and quickly opened the car door. "Spike!"

Around the corner of the brick building lumbered the large tortoise, his wobbly head swaying back and forth. His usual handler walked slowly behind him.

Calling out a thank you over his shoulder, Mark Anthony Mulligan exited the vehicle and made for his animal friend.

* * *

In the general voir dire the next day, one potential juror was dismissed because of his connection to a very high-profile murder case. On July 17, 1994, University of Kentucky football star Trent DiGiuro was slain in a sniper-style shooting while celebrating his twenty-first birthday on his front porch. An anonymous tip led police to former UK student Shane Ragland, whose ex-girlfriend secretly recorded incriminating conversations with him. DiGiuro had supposedly blackballed Ragland from their fraternity. A jury convicted Ragland of murder and recommended a thirty-year sentence.

The Kentucky Supreme Court overturned the conviction, however, citing concerns over questionable ballistics evidence. Prosecutors offered Ragland a deal and he left court a free man after serving only four years. A Lexington jury awarded the DiGiuro family more than sixty-three million dollars in a record-setting wrongful death lawsuit filed against Ragland, however.

Ragland had just made the news again. Dave Spencer of WLKY in Lexington reported that "the man involved in one of the most notorious murder cases in Lexington is once again in trouble with the law." Ragland, who had moved to Pennsylvania, where it was illegal to garnish wages, had been involved in a hit-and-run with a blood alcohol level of 0.252. After serving time in jail, Ragland had now been cited for driving on a suspended license and harassment. There were no details about what the harassment entailed.

By the end of the next day, they had picked the final fifteen members of the jury, sworn them in, and empaneled the jury. Now, it was Jeffrey Mundt's turn in the courtroom.

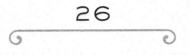

# 26

## OPENING STATEMENTS: ROUND TWO

IT HAD just gone past two in the afternoon when Mitch Perry gaveled the proceedings to order and invited the prosecution to deliver the opening statements in the trial against Jeffrey Mundt. In a gray sweater and white winged collar at the defense table, Mundt coughed once and looked around him, slightly nervous. Most of the time, he appeared ill at ease in the courtroom, in contrast to Joseph Banis, who always came across as relaxed, almost as if he felt at home. A hush fell over the gallery as observers waited for something to happen.

Josh Schneider rose then, walked over to the Rubbermaid container that had been sitting off to the side, and held it up for the jury to see. "Three men enter, two men leave," he said and continued much along the same lines as he had in the opening statements for the first case. Carrie and I exchanged glances but didn't say a word. While referring to the "Rubbermaid casket" the lanky prosecutor brought in Joey's murder conviction and his previous felonies, because "that's the kind of guy Joey Banis" was.

Then he set down the storage bin and approached the jury box. "And who is Jeffrey Mundt? Well, Jeffrey Mundt is an extremely intelligent individual," he said. "He spent most of his professional life as an IT guy with computers, working at pretty prestigious universities. He's well-spoken. He's a bright guy." He also said, "Jeffrey Mundt, for a period of his life, while he was with Joey Banis, was addicted to meth. And, Jeffrey Mundt is a liar. He is an absolute liar, there is no doubt about that." Less than twenty minutes later, the prosecution had finished its opening statements.

Seconds after Josh Schneider concluded his remarks, Steve Romines jumped up and went to the jury. "We'll prove to you before this trial is over that Jeff Mundt is innocent. And we'll prove to you that they know it." Very animated, Romines raised his voice and lifted the folder in his hand, using it to indicate the defense table. "And they have perpetuated this lie for three years! They have had the evidence in their hands and they have either ignored it, they have disregarded it, or they have hid it." Then he pointed directly at Josh Schneider. "What he just told you is a lie and you'll know it!"

Dramatically, Romines went to the Rubbermaid storage bin and rolled it to the side, as if to convey to the jury that he and everybody else recognized it as a cheap gimmick. "We warn our kids about internet predators, but nobody warns the adults. In November of 2009, Jeff Mundt was a thirty-eight-year-old director, consultant, who was working at the IT department down at U of L. He's making about two hundred fifty thousand dollars a year." Again, his voice rising, Romines turned and singled out Josh Schneider with an accusing finger. "He just stood up here and told you that a month later, he robbed a small-time meth dealer of seven hundred dollars and killed him. Now, they know that's bull but that's the story they keep telling."

Romines paused, collecting his thoughts, and his voice returned to a normal volume. "Jeff Mundt's working at U of L; he's got a good job. He's got a nice car. He's got a house he bought down on South Fourth Street in Old Louisville that he's renovating. 'Cuz that's one of the things he loves to do and he's done well at. He renovated about three older homes and done well." The attorney's voice had lost some of its twang. "He's also recently had a fairly bad breakup with a long-time boyfriend of his, in Chicago. And so, he put an ad on a website, looking to meet someone. Well, little did he know, also looking on that website was a psychopath—who had been out of prison at that time for about six weeks. And his name is Joey Banis."

At the prosecution's table, Ryane Conroy muttered something unintelligible. Romines paused for a moment. "Joey Banis at that time had six felonies, he was a meth junkie, he's a drug dealer. He's a monster. And Jeff Mundt was his prey. What you will also hear is that on that same website, about a month before, Joey Banis met another guy who was prey—and that fellow ended up dead in his basement."

"Wow, Matlock is off and running." The voice that mumbled behind us echoed my same thoughts.

Romines focused on the jury once more. "They have for three years perpetuated that longtime lovers Jeff Mundt and Joey Banis killed Jamie Carroll in some twisted kinky sexual threesome, drug-fueled threesome. And . . . only in some domestic disturbance lovers' spat do the police uncover it. That is a lie and they know it." The twang had returned. "Here's what it is: First, at the time Jamie Carroll was killed on December 15 Jeff Mundt had known Joey Banis less than one month. So they're not longtime boyfriends and longtime lovers. They had actually been dating less than three weeks." He paused and then directed his attention back to the jury box, where several of the jurors sat, their eyes wide.

"Secondly, it wasn't some drug-fueled sex party in which Jamie Carroll ended up dead. Jamie Carroll and Joey Banis had a drug deal and Jamie Carroll backed out of the drug deal and Joey Banis killed him. Jeff Mundt doesn't have anything to do with this drug business. His house is just the place that Joey can run the deal." Romines's voice cracked slightly. "The third . . . is this wasn't just some domestic disturbance. On June 17, 2010, Jeff Mundt says to Joey Banis, 'I'm calling the police.' You will hear that Joey Banis had tortured him, held him hostage, and terrorized him since this occurred. Not only will you hear it, you will see it."

Romines adopted a grave tone. "We will show videos of Joey Banis terrorizing. You will hear audio recordings that Joey Banis made. 'Cuz like any psychopath he wants to document what he does. But on June 17, Jeff says, 'I can't take it anymore. I'm telling the police.' What happens? Joey Banis tries to kill him." In the jury box, one of the jurors leaned forward, apparently on the edge of his seat for more information. "And Jeff locks himself in the bedroom and calls 911. While Joey's at the door with a hammer! Trying to beat through the door like Jack Nicholson in *The Shining*." At this Romines lifted his arm and made a striking motion.

"Well, the police arrive before he can get through the door and kill him because it's one of those houses in Old Louisville with a door this thick." He paused to approximate the thickness by measuring the distance with his hands. "And they take him into custody and that's when Joey Banis—again, he's a career criminal with experience manipulating the system his whole life—goes into action, because when the police arrive, Jeff tells 'em, 'he killed a guy and he's buried in the basement.' Three years ago, Jeff Mundt called 911," repeated Romines, "and said, 'he's trying to kill me . . . and he killed a guy.' And so they take Jeff Mundt down to the police station and he tries to tell 'em, 'Man, this guy's been terrorizing me, he's threatened to kill me, here, look at my phone, these are threatening text messages.' And what do they do?"

Romines stopped to stare at the jury with outstretched hands. "They ignore him. Just laugh at him, blow him off. They don't even listen . . . And he's got the proof! You will see the proof that they had in their possession!" Rubbing his forehead, the attorney paused, pacing back and forth. "Thirteen hours later, the police arrested Jeff Mundt for murder—after an exhaustive thirteen-hour homicide investigation. Because they said, 'Joey said you did it.' Of course, if we can't take the word of Joey Banis, who are we going to believe?"

In addition, insisted Romines over the next several minutes, the police ignored evidence showing that Joey Banis had threatened to frame Jeffrey Mundt for the murder he himself had committed. "For three years they've tried to hide the whole truth and told this story about sex, and three men enter and two men leave and all that stuff because that's what sounds good on TV. And they tried to hide the whole truth. That ends today."

At that point Romines grabbed an easel with a large paper pad and maneuvered it noisily in front of jury box so it stood side by side with another easel already there. "So, who are these guys? Because the police say, 'We don't know who to believe. You know, one of you says the other guy killed him and each of you say the other guy killed him and we can't pick so we're just going to charge both of you.'" He positioned himself at the easel and began writing with a black marker. "Joey Banis, in 1994—he's about twenty-two years old—is picking up his first of seven felony convictions. What's Jeff Mundt doing about that time?"

Romines then switched over to the other board. "He's graduating Phi Beta Kapa from IU." A loud scratching noise filled the courtroom as he wrote out the words.

"Later on, in '94, Jeff starts his first job in Washington, D.C., as a consultant with Noblestar Systems. What's Joey do? He's catching a couple more felony convictions. Now, Jeff is moving up—he was born and raised here in Louisville." Romines pointed into the audience. "His father, Bob Mundt, is sitting there on the first row; his brother Mark sitting there beside him. Dad worked out at the GE plant here, Appliance Park. Went to Atherton High School. Was a Governor's Scholar. Went to Indiana University on a scholarship. Wasn't a juvenile delinquent, wasn't getting into trouble then. Never even had a speeding ticket!"

In the row in front of us, a woman leaned into her companion and whispered loud enough so that observers several benches away turned around to stare. "My mother used to carpool my brother to school with Jeffrey and another student. And she said every morning when they picked up Jeffrey at his house, he'd get into the car smelling like bacon and eggs. My mother always felt guilty because we only got cereal at home."

Back at the jury box, Romines zeroed in again on the faces in front of him before speaking. "But on the word of Joey Banis, he's charged with murder." Shaking his head, the lawyer scratched something new on the easel. "In '98, Jeff is promoted to senior manager at KPMG, still working in D.C. What's Joey doing? He's charged with trafficking meth in United States District Court. Now, on that charge, Joey is in some serious trouble." Romines paused to shuffle through a bunch of papers clutched in his hands. "But Joey is already fairly familiar with the system, so what's he do? He cooperates with the government. And instead of getting"—Romines consulted his files—"the fourteen years that he should have gotten, he gets it down to seven."

Romines produced a document and showed it to the jury. "And he also has some information that is provided to the court to reduce his sentence. And it says, 'He has had a lifetime of mistakes, which have landed him here. We have heard of his—quotation marks—stories before but we now believe he's ready to turn the corner. He has discussed verbally and in numerous letters his desire to help children avoid the trouble that he has come into. He finally has remorse for the incredible damage he has wreaked, the severe damage to his siblings through his dishonesty, criminal behavior, and pathological personal interactions.'"

In the jury box, a middle-aged man with glasses shook his head almost imperceptibly. "And who said this about his dishonesty, criminal behavior, and pathological personal interactions?" Romines widened his eyes and looked around the room. "His *father*!" The juror with glasses flinched and leaned back in his seat.

"But it works, because Joey gets out, he gets a lesser sentence. What does he do when he gets out? Well, he gets charged for trafficking in meth again." With a series of loud squeaks, Romines added this to the tally on the Joseph Banis board.

With obvious good reason, Mundt's parents had hired Steven Romines to defend their son. Often described—even by his competitors—as "Louisville's hottest criminal defense attorney," Romines, who grew up on a tobacco farm in southern Kentucky, told more than one jury he used to while away the tedium of hot summer afternoons picking burley by dreaming of becoming a lawyer: "I always envisioned myself standing up in a courtroom defending an innocent man."

Described by adversaries as charismatic and tenacious, the forty-six-year-old had earned his law degree from the University of Louisville in 1993. His pronounced Southern drawl, silvered hair, and folksy demeanor often drew comparisons with famed television defense attorney Ben Matlock. "A lot of lawyers who have a lot of charisma rely solely on that, and a lot of lawyers without charisma try to compensate for that by preparing to death," explained former prosecutor Brian Butler, who dueled with Romines in several high-profile cases. "The thing that makes Steve so tough is that he does both."

Like Banis defense lawyer Darren Wolff, Romines had garnered no small deal of media recognition and he cut a familiar figure on the all the major news outlets. Television shows, such as *Snapped* and *The Montel Williams Show*, had featured him numerous times.

Just a few years before, Romines had achieved notoriety for representing a thirty-eight-year-old Florida man accused of making a hoax phone call that resulted in the sexual assault of a Kentucky girl. Prosecutors charged David Stewart with impersonating a police officer, soliciting sodomy, and soliciting sexual abuse, alleging he had called a nearby McDonald's, claiming to be a police officer, and induced the managers to strip search an eighteen-year-old employee. The victim testified that the caller had accused her of theft and insisted she remove her clothes to prove her innocence. The call lasted almost four hours, during which time the victim was forced to perform sexual acts on the boyfriend of the store's assistant manager.

Although the boyfriend had received a five-year prison sentence for his part and authorities placed the female manager on probation, a jury acquitted Stewart of all charges after not even two hours of deliberation. During the trial, which had dragged on over three weeks, prosecutors produced evidence connecting calling cards found at the suspect's home to similar incidents in Florida, Oklahoma, and Idaho, but they had no de facto witnesses identifying Stewart as the perpetrator. The hoax calls had stopped after his arrest, but he remained a suspect in a multitude of similar incidents stretching back to 1992. The case earned Romines spots on *20/20* and *Dateline* and would go on to inspire an episode of *Law and Order* and the 2012 movie *Compliance*.

In Louisville, many residents still remembered Romines from the case of *Arnold v. Strathmore Village*, in which Maria Arnold confronted a policeman who was interrogating several children playing hide and seek in her yard. The officer took offense and arrested her, charging her with multiple misdemeanor offenses. After being found not guilty, she sued the officer and police department for false arrest and excessive force. The police offered thirty-five thousand dollars to resolve the matter, but Arnold hired Romines and went to trial, where the jury awarded her over a million.

For the next hour, the gallery had a ringside view of Louisville's hottest criminal defense attorney in action, as he continued to illustrate the stark differences in life choices made by his client and Joey Banis. He painted Banis as a career criminal, who upon release from prison in 2009 had a well-thought-out plan to search for a victim and continue his life of crime.

Referring to a checklist found on Joey's computer, Romines enumerated Joey's first priorities as needing "to ensure security and safety, anonymity, audio-video calling, retainer for attorney, escrow account for bail, and a home security system." Animated, Romines turned to the jury and exclaimed, "This guy's planning on having money for bail before he's even been arrested for anything! But they're going to use him to send a man never in his life charged with a crime to the penitentiary."

According to another to-do list, Banis also needed to apply for Social Security and food stamps, look for a car, and go "scouting." The attorney clarified, "now, what we will learn is he's scouting for marks, he's scouting for targets, he's scouting for victims. He's not in the Boy Scouts." Then, noisily moving the easel out of the way, Romines had Sean Oates project an enlarged image on the screen, a shot of another of Joey's immediate objectives, which he proceeded to read out loud: "'Review online profiles of potential marks. Determine city based on likely profiles; try to go after specific targets.' Wonder why they didn't tell you about that. 'Keep in mind to be on the lookout for the next great proxy, mark, coordinator, etc.' Well, you know who the next mark was?" He pointed to the defense table. "Jeff Mundt. 'Plan for latex gloves, leather, rubber hoods, scarves, hats, sunglasses, hair coloring—no trace.' This guy is a monster!"

In the box, several jurors moved their heads back and forth in disbelief. Romines then listed examples of how Joey went on to "woo Jeff" and move himself into the Fourth Street house. Jamie Carroll, he argued, mattered to Banis only because he wanted to take over his drug business while Carroll served his time in prison. "Because as a lifetime snitch, he has a tough time getting back into business. But Jamie's his in, and what's Joey doing right before this? He's on the internet searching for things to take this dope business over."

On the screen, Sean Oates projected several lists of internet searches, which Romines explained. "December 10, machine guns for sale. Page after page, looking for machine guns, looking for Uzis. Submachine guns. This is what Joey's doing right before the meeting with Jamie Carroll. What else is he looking for? What's a drug dealer need besides guns? Scales."

Romines paced slowly by the jury box and then turned an accusing glare at the prosecution. "And this whole 'night of sex'? That's just Jeff's house where Joey is going to make the deal. Jeff's a hapless dupe in this whole thing."

Then the defense played part of the 911 call made by Jeffrey Mundt from 1435 South Fourth Street the night of June 17, 2010:

911:  *911 Operator Walker. Where is your emergency?*

JM:  *I'm at 1435 South Fourth Street. (inaudible) attacking, my ex-boyfriend in my house. Please come immediately.*

911:  *Wait a minute. What is your address?*

JM:  *1435 South Fourth. Please.*

911:  *1-4-3-5 South Fourth Street. Is that a house or apartment?*

JM:  *It's a house. 1-4-3-5.*

911:  *1-4-3-5 South Fourth Street. You said it right, right?*

JM:  *Yes.*

911:  *What's your phone number, dear?*

JM:  *639-2133.*

911:  *What's your name?*

JM:  *Jeffrey Mundt.*

911:  *OK, who is attacking your door?*

JM:  *Joey Banis.*

911:  *Is he the ex-boyfriend?*

JM:  *He's my ex.*

911:  *OK. Are you hiding?*

JM:  *(unintelligible)*

911:  *He's breaking—*

JM:  *He's in the house. (unintelligible) . . . quick to the bedroom.*

911:  *Stay on top of it—*

JM:  *Please. (tearful) Please hurry. (sharp bang on the door)*

911:  *Stay on the phone with me.*

JM:  *I'm trying.*

911:  *What's his name?*

JM:  *Joseph Banis. Please hurry. (crying)*

911:  *Banis? Is he a white male, black male?*

JM:  *White male. (another sharp bang on the door) Please, please hurry. (frantic, unintelligible)*

911:  *Stay on the phone with me. I'm giving the police this information. They're driving.*

JM:  *(unintelligible, crying)*

911: *Is he known to carry any weapons?*
JM: *I don't know.*
911: *Is he known to be intoxicated?*
JM: *I don't know.*
911: *Do you got an EPR against him?*
JM: *I don't know. (unintelligible)*
911: *Stay on the phone with me. Stay on the phone.*
JM: *(sobbing) Please. (bang on the door)*
911: *They're coming. (bang on the door)*
JM: *(sobbing)*
911: *Are you hiding?*
JM: *Yes.*
911: *Where are you at?*
JM: *In the second-floor front bedroom.*
911: *You got the door locked?*
JM: *(unintelligible)*
911: *Stay on the phone. Is the door locked in the bedroom?*
JM: *(unintelligible)*
911: *Is the door locked in the bedroom?*
JM: *(unintelligible) . . . door.*
911: *OK. Stay on the phone with me.*
JM: *(sobbing) Please. (bang on door) (unintelligible)*
911: *OK, honey.*
JM: *(bang on door) (sobbing) (unintelligible) (really loud bang on door) (unintelligible)*
911: *Honey, are you sure that's not an apartment building?*
JM: *I'm sorry? (unintelligible)*
911: *Let me make sure I got it right:1-4-3-5 South Fourth Street.*
JM: *(unintelligible) (sobbing) (unintelligible)*
911: *Stay on the phone with me. Police should be in the area. Police are in the area.*
JM: *(unintelligible) (high-pitched) Please hurry. (crying)*
911: *Wait. Just . . .*
JM: *(crying, unintelligible)*
911: *What, hon?*
JM: *I can't do anything.*

After the loud hammer bangs on the wooden door and Jeffrey Mundt's plaintive, high-pitched cries for help, the silence that followed came as a relief to most in the courtroom. In the jury box, two people who seemed slightly shell-shocked, shifted in their seats.

"Wow." My eyes slid to Carrie. "He really was terrified."

"I know."

We studied Jeffrey Mundt, who sat, resolute, at the defense table.

Romines, after gathering his thoughts, continued his meandering opening statements. His client had lived in fear of Joey Banis, he argued, and Banis had gone to extraordinary measures to intimidate and surveil his client, including rape and torture. He would produce witnesses to demonstrate Joey's psychopathic tendencies and violent temper, he promised. And James Jenkins, the witness the prosecution had to back their allegations against Jeffrey Mundt? He was just another jailhouse snitch who couldn't be trusted.

Romines then picked up a massive file and held it high. "I think if you looked around Louisville to find somebody with more felony convictions than Joey Banis, you would have found him with James Jenkins." He put down file with a thud.

"Let's look at his criminal history. Because they knew this when they made this deal to him. In 1990 he goes into Kmart and steals a microwave. When a manager confronts him, he pulls a fencepost out and smacks him with it. Alright. Now, he tells the judge, 'Judge, I learned my lesson, I'm a new Christian man now, so let me out.' So, they do," said Romines. "Then he steals a car—carjacks it, basically, somebody's getting gas at a gas station and he jumps in and takes off, tries to run over somebody. Then he gets a burglary and grand theft charge, breaks into somebody's house. Then a trafficking in cocaine charge, then an escape—he escapes from prison and they catch him."

At that point Ryane Conroy objected and at the bench she argued the irrelevance of every single crime committed by Jenkins. "This is not proper evidence submitted at a trial, not good faith."

Tending to agree with her, Mitch Perry told Romines to "wrap things up" and make his final remarks. "This opening has been extremely argumentative, long. It should be a forecast," the judge lamented in a grave tone. "The jury's uncomfortable, I'm uncomfortable, this has been way too long." Romines promised to conclude in ten minutes, but it took more than half an hour, and at the objection of the prosecution, Judge Perry called them back to the bench and once again admonished Romines.

After almost two hours, the defense for Jeffrey Mundt finally closed its opening statements.

I leaned over to Carrie. "Well, if Ramon and I ever get caught burying anyone in the basement, I know who we're calling to defend us. Look at the jurors, how many have been nodding their heads in agreement with Romines."

She gave me a knowing look. "I won't be surprised if Mundt gets off."

The next day at the bench, Mitch Perry would admonish the defense, explaining he had struggled overnight whether to address the issue or not. "It was a very curious opening, Mr. Romines, yesterday, in several ways." He brought up the fact that the defense had publicized potential witness Jenkins's multiple felonies and wanted to know Romine's good-faith reason for doing that.

Romines responded that anything was admissible when it came to character. "When you make a deal with a snitch, his entire history becomes relevant."

Ted Shouse added, "This is the third murder trial in which Jenkins has offered testimony."

# 27

## WITNESS FOR THE PROSECUTION: ROUND TWO

**WHEN THE** prosecution called its witnesses, the lineup mirrored that of the Banis trial. Detective Collin King, first on the stand, repeated much of what he said in the previous trial. When asked about Mundt's demeanor when they located him at the neighbors' house, he said, "He was shocked that we were there." When they took him downtown for questioning, "He was very cooperative at the time." However, King said he started to pick up on signs of deception. "Everything was not coming out." Details on some things were specific, on other things, they were cloudy.

At that point Conroy played the video of the interview with Mundt and his initial thoughts on Joey. "He seemed like such an erudite and interesting person, and so forth. And well-spoken on the telephone, very, you know—I'm a sucker for someone who's somewhat educated, very articulate, you know, and a cultural bon mot thrown in."

But, soon, Mundt began to see a different side. Joey was once a quite well-known drug dealer who had sold LSD and followed the Grateful Dead around. He had robbed at least one bank in town. "It was a US Bank, I believe, on Bardstown Road near Impellizzeri's." According to Mundt, Joey's own parents had confided in Jeffrey, telling him about their son's "problem" and expressing hopes that he would "go straight." Since the "Chicago incident," Joey hadn't spoken with them.

"In fact, his father called me, right before I called you this evening, because he was so worried I might have been hurt by his son. He was going to call the police because he hadn't heard from me," Mundt told King. When the detective replied that Banis Sr. sounded "like a real good guy," Jeffrey concurred: "His dad is a real sweet guy. Hard to believe how far the apple fell from the tree."

Despite his economic circumstances, Joey always maintained his "expensive tastes." His former lover insisted Joey had to have "the best of the best." Clothing, electronics, cologne, toiletries, soaps, linens. "My house was broken into and his clothing was stolen and he wanted me to go and buy him a goddamn five-hundred-dollar pair of jeans." Complaining, Jeffrey described Joey as "entitled" and "ungrateful" and bitter that Jeffrey had ruined *his* life. He displayed psychopathic tendencies that involved lots of made-up stories and revenge fantasies. He had a grudge against the police and had vowed to shoot them if ever arrested again.

"All the times he has been locked up, he never did anything when he had the chance," said King. "Sounds like a coward, talks a big game."

Jeffrey claimed that Joey obsessively plotted to murder the individual or individuals he held responsible for the loss of his livelihood. "He wanted retribution for the people in Louisville he felt stole his club from him," said Jeffrey, mentioning "some truth" to the part about the club being taken from Banis and a related civil suit being a matter of public record.

King wanted to know more. "Did he ever go into detail? Would he shoot them? Would he stab them? Would he burn them? Would he torture them?"

"He had mentioned the bloodlust he had about getting retribution against these people," said Jeffrey. "For the people in the civil suit, he was talking about shooting them and then cutting their hearts out and eating it."

Soon thereafter, the judge called for a lunch break.


When the prosecution resumed playing the video, which coincided with a bathroom break Jeffrey Mundt had taken in the taped interview, he had no idea where King, who from the beginning had been solicitous and empathetic, was headed when he came back. He had told Jeffrey that he had nothing to worry about and painted him as the actual victim. When King showed Mundt a mugshot of Jamie Carroll and asked if he knew him or had ever seen him before, he shook his head and said, "He doesn't even remotely look familiar."

In reference to returning to the Fourth Street house after a short Thanksgiving break—presumably when Mundt wanted police to believe Carroll was killed in his absence—King asked if Jeffrey recalled "anything different about the house" when he came back, about Joey's demeanor. Jeffrey thought for a moment and said, "Um, the front hallway had been cleaned, and the woodwork waxed . . . He was really good at cleaning."

No too long after that, Jeffrey Mundt, who thought he was in the clear, was arrested and read his rights.

When Mundt protested his innocence, the detective claimed Joey "was telling a totally different story" and had "said, 'Jeff is a cold-blooded killer and there's a body in my basement.'" He concluded with: "If you didn't do it, why is he coming down here and telling us first?"

King wasn't persuaded when Jeffrey produced threatening text messages from Joey. "If you want death and destruction, continue on this path," read one of them. The detective only continued asking Jeffrey why he hadn't come to police earlier. In referring to Jamie Carroll at this point, Jeffrey called him "the guy" or pretended he couldn't remember his name. "What was the guy's name who was getting killed?" he had asked once. Earlier on in the interview he had slipped up and referred to "Jamie" without having been told a name. When confronted, Mundt claimed he must have "seen it on the photograph."

At one point, when asked what he thought should happen to some-one who killed another person, Mundt said: "They should be executed. I believe in the death penalty." Throughout the interview Mundt repeatedly brought up the fear he had of Joey Banis and described a "second hole" in the basement, which Joey insisted was for him if he didn't follow instructions. They had to fill it in, though, Mundt explained, because people were coming to do work down there. At this development, Joey had said, "What a waste of a good hole."

I thought back to my night in that basement and I couldn't recall seeing any area that looked like a filled-in hole. Granted, it was dark and I was preoccupied with Candy but I would have noticed it, especially given how hard-packed the soil was down there. It should have stood out. Also, both Jeffrey and Joey had remarked in previous interviews how tedious and exhausting the multi-day process of digging the grave for Jamie Carroll had been. Had Joey Banis really spent another two or three days of back-breaking work down there?

On cross-examination, Romines said, "Let's start where you say that Jeff Mundt's story was not matching up with the physical, scientific, forensic evidence that was collected. What was that evidence?" King replied that he had none and had just been lying. "But when you obtained that evidence, his story did match up with the 'physical, scientific, forensic evidence,' didn't it?" King replied in the affirmative.

"Would it have been helpful to know Jeff Mundt was making eight thousand three hundred thirty-three dollars every two weeks?" Romines brought up the issue of the robbery, a supposed motive for Jeffrey Mundt, adding, "sixteen thousand dollars a month. And you are accusing him of robbing a drug dealer of a couple hundred dollars?" The defense also went on to establish that people had seen Joey on several occasions with a large hunting knife, the kind used to kill Jamie Carroll—and that King had never bothered to interview Jason Keith Robertson or Katie Richards, associates of Joey's who could have corroborated many of Mundt's allegations. "And even after all your ruses and tomfoolery, Jeff Mundt did not say he killed Jamie Carroll." Romines concluded by arching his bushy gray eyebrows.

On the cross-examination of the second witness, polygraph examiner Detective Mark Bratcher, the defense attorney once again drove home that his client had never admitted to the murder of Jamie Carroll. "Jeff Mundt never confessed to killing Jamie Carroll, did he? To stabbing him? To shooting him? To robbing him?"

The detective answered in the negative; however, he countered that Mundt had confessed to burying the body in the basement. "But he had a gun on him!" Romines quickly retorted, referring to the pistol Banis had, and things became heated when Bratcher refused to concede this point, ending the testimony for the day.

In the hallway outside someone from the gallery commented that she thought the defense had adequately called into question the memory and abilities of the first two witnesses.

The next string of witnesses, including the medical examiner, blood experts, forensic biologists, evidence collectors, and responding patrol officers, repeated much of what they said during the first trial, but things began to heat up when the defense crossed the eleventh witness, Officer Roy Stalby. The patrolman had arrived very early in the morning of June 18 to secure the premises, and Steve Romines had him confirm that his client had never attempted to flee, unlike Joey Banis. When Romines repeated a question, the gum-chewing and clearly annoyed Stalby would say, "I already answered that" or "I don't know why you're making it so confusing."

When the defense criticized Stalby for not following up with potential witnesses such as Libby Davis, implying information she had could have exonerated Jeffrey Mundt, the officer responded tersely. "That's a ridiculous statement on your part."

Without missing a beat, Romines pointed to the jury and said, "That's for them to decide."

Several minutes later, when Stalby bristled at the tone of Romines's questioning, he fixed him with a glare and said, "Are you implying that I'm dumb and don't understand your question?" Things became even testier between the two when the defense implied that the police came to a conclusion and then conducted their investigation accordingly, without exploring all the possible leads. Judge Perry had to gavel the room to order.

Romines got in one last parting shot before he wrapped up his cross-examination, though. "Is it a demotion to go from detective to officer?" He glared at Stalby.

The bald policeman suddenly clenched his jaws before slowly resuming the chewing of his gum. "Absolutely not."

Carrie shot me a devious look. "Oh my, Romines is going for the jugular, isn't he?"

I crossed my arms. "I guess so. I heard Stalby had been demoted but I couldn't find out if it was because of this case or a previous one."

As the prosecution's twelfth witness, Libby Davis, the assistant to the director who interacted with Jeffrey almost every day for the several months he had worked at the University of Louisville, came back to the stand. In a brown floral skirt and pink frilly sleeveless blouse, the woman recounted how she had called the tip line after seeing the news about 1435 South Fourth Street. "I immediately got sick at my stomach because of a conversation we had had." She recalled the day Jeffrey Mundt had stood at her reception desk with a multitude of scratches in the neck area. When asked what had happened, Mundt replied he had fallen off a boat dock into a lake in South Bend, Indiana. "I got sick at my stomach because I knew where those scratches came from. But I waited two days before calling because I really didn't want to be involved." Davis drew in a deep breath. "I have a daughter and that could have been her. I had to do the right thing."

On his cross-examination, Romines established that the police had never consulted her for more information and that the relationship Davis had with Jeffrey Mundt wasn't such that he would have told her he was being beaten by his boyfriend. On her redirect, Conroy established that Davis's relationship with Mundt was also such that he wouldn't have told her he had participated in a homicide and that Davis had provided all the information that she had to the police.

When Conroy pointed out that Davis had once mentioned not being able to imagine Jeffrey Mundt doing something like this, that "he was such a nice guy," Davis shook her head sadly. "Originally, yes. I don't feel the same way now." At the defense table, Jeffrey Mundt slowly cast his gaze down at his folded hands.

The next four witnesses didn't add much to the information presented previously. They included the firearm and toolmark examiner and the CSU employee who processed Jamie Carroll's truck, which had been towed from in front of 1435 South Fourth Street to make room for street sweepers. Officer Selenica, the cop who had arrested the pair in Chicago, mentioned Joey's colorful mohawk and that Mundt had "some kind of rubber shirt on him." Kenny Robertson confirmed that Jeffrey Mundt had arranged for him to cover the floor in the basement with concrete when the contractor returned from vacation.

The courtroom perked up when Bailiff Brown escorted Joey Banis, in glasses and an orange jumpsuit, to the stand. As Banis passed in front of the defense table, he gave his ex-boyfriend a strange lovesick look and greeted him softly. "Hi, Jeffrey."

Mundt, in turn, cast his gaze down, visibly shaken.

"Oh my god. Did you see that weird stare?" Carried nudged me. I nodded.

When questioned by the judge, Joey confirmed his intent not to honor the agreement entered into with the Commonwealth. At the defense table, Steve Romines whispered something loudly and the word "manipulation" echoed in the gallery.

Not long after, Judge Mitch Perry called for an early end to the day and he gaveled the proceedings to a close.

The next morning, jailhouse snitch James Jenkins took the stand. Housed at the Kentucky State Reformatory in La Grange, the prisoner had been in custody for three years and it was not his first time. In September 2010, while he was in jail with Jeffrey Mundt, he struck up a conversation after hearing that Mundt had attended Louisville Collegiate School, like his wife.

"My personal opinion meeting him? I think he's kind of an elitist. I think he believes he's smarter than anyone else in the room." Jenkins recalled the murder coming up after his third or fourth time talking to Mundt and that Mundt had expressed the most concern about what the Chicago newspapers and the academic community at Northwestern were saying about him. People had accused Mundt of necrophilia and that especially bothered him. When prodded for more information, Jenkins said, "He had told me about Jamie Carroll driving a little pickup truck. Said he'd bring antiques and stuff over—under that pretense, but actually it was mostly meth that they were dealing with."

At the defense table, Ted Shouse and Steve Romines did little to hide their disdain. "He's just making shit up," one of them whispered loudly.

Undeterred, Jenkins continued, saying that Joey's relationship with Jamie had hurt Mundt, and made him jealous. "He had mentioned that they had discussed the fact that if Joey was murdered he wouldn't be missed because he had a court date that was in the next day or two or so and when he didn't show up for court people would just think he was on the run."

At that, Jenkins turned to glance at Jeffrey. "So if something happened to him, he wouldn't be missed. And it was at that point I realized, I thought, man, this was planned, they talked about it, they planned it, they plotted it all the way to the callous end." Jenkins went into details about Mundt's revelations about the drugs and counterfeit money, and then claimed that "Jeffrey was worried about him spilling the beans about the murder" and "after that Joey was really hard to control, running his mouth." The guys "wanted to teach Jamie Carroll a lesson."

Several minutes later Steve Romines rolled his eyes and exaggeratedly rubbed his face when Jenkins said, "I didn't really care for him a lot, you know, very arrogant. No remorse at all" and "it seemed like he had an infinite capacity for self-rationalization." The Commonwealth objected to the theatrics again, and at the bench Josh Schneider said, "Judge, I think communication to the jury includes these two just sitting here laughing and carrying on and stuff. It's getting to the point where it's almost getting distracting."

Romines scoffed. "He is making things up on the witness stand. I mean, just flat out making them up."

"Well, then let's be professional." Ryane Conroy, trying to keep her voice measured, turned to the judge. "I just don't know that it's acceptable that we're laughing out loud and in the middle of—if you think it's ridiculous, then show the jury. But there should be professionalism. I don't think it's an unreasonable request." Mitch Perry instructed the defense to use decorum and told the prosecution to control their witness by asking direct questions.

But Steve Romines didn't sound very reassuring. "I will try not to laugh."

Back with her witness, Ryane Conroy had Jenkins confirm that he approached them with the offer of information and that the Commonwealth hadn't sought it out. And in discussing the agreement reached with Jenkins, she mentioned Jenkins's attorney's name: Scott Drabenstadt. Down the bench, a man from the local LGBTQ newspaper I had talked with earlier let out a groan.

Many in the Louisville gay community despised Scott Drabenstadt. Many outside the gay community despised him as well. He had defended accused killer Joshua Cottrell in the infamous "Suitcase Murder" case just several years before.

On June 25, 2003, two Kentucky fishermen had pulled a suitcase out of Rough River Lake, unzipped it, and discovered a body inside.

Personal items and a Kentucky Wildcats tattoo on the shoulder identified the corpse as that of Guin "Richie" Phillips, a thirty-six-year-old gay man who had disappeared the month before. His mother had told people she feared harm had come to him because of his homosexuality.

Witnesses had last seen the victim on June 17, 2003, having lunch at a local restaurant with an acquaintance, twenty-one-year-old Joshua Cottrell. Several days later, authorities found the truck and other items belonging to Phillips abandoned in southern Indiana. A witness reported seeing Phillips and Cottrell together in the truck the very same day. On June 27, 2003, police arrested Cottrell and charged him with murder. Prosecutors announced that they would seek the death penalty.

A canceled check showed that Cottrell had purchased the suitcase six days before the killing, and blood and DNA samples solidly connected him to the crime. At the trial, family members testified that Cottrell had confessed to the murder and that he had announced his intentions to kill Phillips beforehand—because he was gay. "He's gone. He's dead," he had told a cousin after disposing of the body.

As Cottrell's attorney, Scott Drabenstadt employed the "gay panic" defense, painting Phillips as the aggressor and arguing that Phillips's actions had led to a chain of events that caused his death. Cottrell, he argued, was within his rights under Kentucky law to fight back to protect himself from rape and sodomy, including use of deadly force if necessary.

According to prosecuting attorney Chris Shaw, the evidence showed, however, that Cottrell had lured Phillips into his hotel room where he encouraged a sexual advance and then beat and strangled the man. Then he attempted to cover it up in a calculated manner. The prosecution pointed out the irrelevance of Phillips's sexual orientation, citing Cottrell's "steaming anger" toward gays as the only connection.

The jury had the option of finding Cottrell guilty of murder, reckless homicide, or manslaughter. After deliberating for nine hours, they found Cottrell guilty only of second-degree manslaughter, as well as theft and tampering with physical evidence. "I think they were looking at my brother being a homosexual when they made their decision to pick the lesser charge," said Greg Phillips in an interview with *The*

*Advocate.* Cottrell received a maximum of twenty years—but less than three years after conviction, he was eligible for parole.

This hearkened back to another infamous murder trial for a slain Kentuckian in which the killers of the innocent gay man also received a lesser charge of manslaughter and a much more lenient sentence. And as with Cottrell, the defense had successfully employed "gay panic" as a defense. In this instance, however, many, such as Graham Brunk of *Erie Gay News,* considered it the very case that gave rise to the gay panic defense.

In 1951, William Simpson moved to Miami from Louisville for his career as a flight attendant with Eastern Airlines—and most likely because of the more active scene there. The homosexual community in Miami lived mostly in obscurity, but a lot of gay men lived in the area.

According to his landlord, who was the last to see him alive, the twenty-seven-year-old Simpson left his apartment on the evening of August 2, 1954. On the way to a rendezvous on a secluded lovers' lane, he was approached by Charles Lawrence, a young thug notorious for "rolling" gay men—as local media referred to it—by luring them to a secluded spot where an accomplice, Lewis Killen, waited to help rob the victim. They usually didn't kill their target, but Simpson didn't cooperate like other victims and Lawrence shot him. According to the police report, the attackers made off with twenty-five dollars and acted surprised to learn that Simpson had died.

A police investigation uncovered a much larger gay presence in the vicinity than anticipated—as many as five hundred as opposed to a prior estimate of just thirty men—and rather than report on the crime itself, one reporter, Milt Sosin, focused solely on Simpson's homosexuality, something rarely mentioned in mainstream media at the time. His front-page story in the *Miami Daily News* ran with the headline "Pervert Colony Uncovered in Simpson Slaying Probe." He accused Simpson of mixing with the wrong crowd and suggested "gay drama" might have been the motive behind his murder. One investigator even hinted that Simpson was looking to become "queen" of the colony and that had led to the killing.

Although both criminals admitted to their part at trial, they used the gay panic defense, testifying that, while they did like to "roll" gay men, Simpson provoked the situation and made them feel unsafe. Swayed, the jury went only with a conviction of manslaughter.

In the aftermath, Christian groups called for raids of known gay bars and hangouts. In the mid-1960s, a local station aired a documentary warning of the dangers of gay people and all the major newspapers in the area ran article after article advising readers to be aware of their surroundings and who among their neighbors might be gay.

The Florida Legislative Investigation Committee, commonly known as the Johns Committee, distributed literature warning citizens of homosexual activity and stripped suspected gay teachers of their credentials. In the 1970s, singer and orange juice spokeswoman Anita Bryant showed that gay panic was still alive and well when she launched her now infamous "Save Our Children" campaign against the LGBTQ community.

On the stand, James Jenkins shook his head when talking about his reasons for coming forward. "I am tired, I'm tired of it all. I'm getting old. I have a long criminal history." And revealing he had stage three liver cancer, he said, "I can't change the past, but I can change today and start the future."

Those declarations provoked more noise from the defense table. Ryane Conroy objected once again and asked to approach the bench. With a pronounced pause before each of her last three words, she said, "I guess my objection is going to be the continuing inappropriate communications."

When Romines complained that the witness had "just lied under oath again," Judge Perry fixed him with a stern gaze. "You will calm down. You will become not responsive at all." When the judge then announced they would take a lunch break at the Commonwealth's conclusion of its questioning, Steve Romine almost comically begged for "just ten minutes with him" before they took a break. The judge refused with another stern warning: "Consider this a sanction for your conduct. I'm having to avert my eyes because you're distracting me. Please. Please. You know how to behave. I'm asking you to comport."

However, Romines kept getting into trouble and the defense raised their own issues so often that for the next several hours it seemed they spent more time at the bench than in front of the jury. "I am still concerned about your conduct during trial. Next time it will be admonishment directly to you in front of the jury," Perry told Romines. And: "Counsel, you're trying my patience."

In the end, Romines did manage to chip away at the credibility of the jailhouse snitch and it came as a relief when Jenkins finally left the stand.

# 28

# SEX, LIES, AND VIDEOTAPE

FOR WITNESS number eighteen, Ryane Conroy called Jon Lesher to the stand. After going through much of the same information as in the first trial, she played what came to be known as the "suicide tape" found on Joey's laptop. The prosecution would have played it in the first trial had Joey taken the stand in his defense. But, because Joey never took the stand, only a few in the courtroom had an inkling of what the recording contained.

In the video, Joey appeared to sit at a desk, and behind him lay Jeffrey Mundt on a bed, presumably unconscious. Joey began to read from a prepared script:

> *This is to any concerned persons regarding my death. My name is Joseph Richard Banis. Most know me as Joey. I am recording my death for the purpose of informing all informed—or all concerned— of my own willful suicide and the complete non-involvement and culpability of anyone else. Specifically my boyfriend, lover, life-partner, and friend, Jeffrey Steven Mundt. Notice that he is sitting, or lying on the bed near me, and it's only because I have a gun pointed at him. (holds up gun) The gun is right here. And he is right there. (camera pans to Jeffrey Mundt lying prone on bed, then the pistol is raised so it can be seen pointing at Jeffrey) I have threatened him to the point of breaking. (clears throat, sighs) I'm scared that he will try to intercede because I know that he loves me. (sighs) And I don't want to be [loud cough from audience interrupts . . .] found,*

*for this to be stopped. (inaudible sentence) I'm also here to state that any animal property belonging to myself as well as any funds forwarded to my estate or through my part in the lawsuit involving the club go to Jase. I specifically name him. I am in love with him and consider him my lifelong partner and it is my will that he be the beneficiary. I am holding him hostage because I have failed him and hurt him and done terrible things which I can never recover him from. This includes killing (long pause) someone who (long pause) . . . This includes killing someone. I apologize to everyone I've hurt, most especially my family. I have no one to blame for my incapability to cope with the world and my failure except myself. I was so afraid (long pause) to face my life (long pause) that I often blamed others for my own faults. Both through this video or for everything from now to my death—and I will leave quietly. I am sorry for any pain that this causes.*

In the gallery several confused faces turned and looked at their neighbors, as if to say, *What the hell?* Carrie leaned in for a whisper. "I don't get how that was supposed to help the prosecution's case. Joey just confessed to the murder and exonerated Jeffrey."

"I know. Maybe it's because they know the defense has this tape and will play it anyway. Maybe they wanted to beat them to the punch. But still."

Conroy continued to work her way through the evidence in Jon Lesher's possession and she played another video. In this tape, music blared in the background. And Jeffrey could be heard berating Joey, who responded by saying, "You're the super spy guy. How many people have you killed, Jase?"

Then, over the objection of the defense, who argued the prosecution only wanted to play it to inflame the straight men on the jury, Conroy played the infamous sex tape. Ears reddening, Jeffrey Mundt looked straight ahead for the entire length of the clip as the jury and everyone else in the courtroom watched Joey and Jeffrey have sex on the screen.

Amid a good deal of groaning and profanities, Jeffrey, in the dominant role, could be heard over and over denigrating Joey, his "bitch boy" and stating that he didn't mind having sex with him despite his HIV status. Made after the murder of Jamie Carroll, this tape demonstrated that Jeffrey had not lived in fear of Joey Banis and had been the aggressor in many circumstances, argued the prosecution.

Following that, Conroy played the "counterfeit" video, taken by Joey, which showed the "paper cleansing site" and other parts of the fake money operation presumably set up in the house at 1435 South Fourth Street. As she prepared to show the next video, a tape made in the Chicago hotel room, the defense objected again, but at the bench Conroy promised the judge she would "stop before the blowjob." She also took this opportunity to mention that Lesher, her witness, was feeling uncomfortable because Jeffrey Mundt had been staring directly at him the entire time the sex tapes played.

Steve Romines explained that he had instructed his client to look off in the general direction of the witness stand during the uncomfortable moments and that Mundt wasn't staring at the detective. During his cross-examination, Romines hammered Lesher for a number of derelictions including not documenting wounds on Jeffrey Mundt or the various threatening text messages from Joey. After Lesher said of the suicide video, "If we had that here then, we would not be in court today," Romines moved for a mistrial, which the judge denied.

Before concluding his questioning for the afternoon, the defense attorney drove home several times that, while in custody, Joey Banis had continuously tried to get a deal out of the police, whereas his client, Jeffrey Mundt, had attempted no such thing.

The next morning Mitch Perry announced that Joey Banis had changed his mind and wanted to testify for the Commonwealth after all. Ted Shouse objected vociferously, citing Joey's cunning and manipulation of the court. "He's engineered this whole thing! He's manipulated this court from Jump Street, if I may say so!" The defense attorney then brought up the fact that Joey had "managed to get a computer in jail," which no one had "ever heard of before" and "he had manipulated the court into getting him internet access."

Carrie leaned in after giving me a grave look. "So, he did have internet access. I bet he was the one putting all that crazy stuff on the Facebook page. "Bizarre Love Triangle" and "Die in Your Arms."

The judge denied the request to honor the agreement because Joey's denials had constituted "a moment of such finality" that it counted as "final and binding" and the court would not allow him to change his mind: "He may not be presented at this time." Perry's ruling threw a huge wrench in the prosecution's case.

Back with Detective Lesher on the stand, Romines continued impugning the detective's thoroughness, criticizing him for not doing more to access the information at his disposal and not taking more seriously witnesses such as Katie Richards, a young woman whom Joey had taken under his wing and gotten addicted to crystal meth. "The two of them were very weird," she had said, adding that Joey Banis had talked about wanting to kill someone. "He was an evil and manipulative person." Romines also found it curious that the detective hadn't taken much note of a Zoomback GPS tracker Joey had purchased and used to monitor Jeffrey's movements.

Romines frequently objected when the prosecution attempted to enter evidence such as Jeffrey's Adam4Adam profile photo—which showed him in a rubber suit—because it painted his client "as a freaky guy." Ryane Conroy, however, countered that it proved Jeffrey wasn't an innocent victim. He cruised hookup sites, knowing exactly what he wanted, kinks and all.

Romines had no qualms about trying to make Joey Banis look like a freaky guy, however. When he asked Lesher what Joey's password for a particular website was, the detective responded somewhat sheepishly, "myasslovescock." Nearby, a now-familiar groan rumbled quietly from an unseen observer.

Before the day closed, things would be upended once again when Judge Tom Wine, Ryane Conroy's boss, appeared in the courtroom, at the prosecution table, to ask Mitch Perry to reconsider his decision in disallowing Joey Banis's testimony for the Commonwealth.

Perry agreed to reverse his decision and allow him to testify, explaining there could be exculpatory information to help the defense's client. Steve Romines moved for a mistrial because of prosecutorial misconduct, but the judge denied it. The following day Joey Banis would take the stand after all.

\* \* \*

It was going on eleven the next morning, when the prosecution called Joseph Banis. Things started to heat up right away, particularly when the defense clamorously objected to a laptop in the courtroom, which they claimed Joey had tampered with. The judge urged Steve Romines: "Slow down and calm down! Lower your voice!"

When asked about his origins, Joey Banis, now forty-one, said he was born in Falls Church, Virginia, near D.C., and then had lived in Hawaii and California before spending a considerable portion of his life in Louisville. He had met Jeffrey on Adam4Adam, most likely Halloween night October 2009. Jeffrey was into a number of things, including PNP, chat room lingo for party and play or having sex while doing drugs. Banis recalled with some trepidation the distant Halloween night when he went to 1435 South Fourth Street to meet Jeffrey, who came to the front door in a black latex suit.

About a half hour into his testimony, Joey said, "I wanted to get away from that creepy house." Jeffrey, he insisted, "scared the piss out of me," which elicited a rebuke from the judge because of its salty language.

Jamie Carroll liked him a lot, Joey claimed, and that made Jeffrey jealous. The night of the murder, Joey had "heard a noise and turned around and blood was flying." At first, "I thought it was a case of robbery; now I believe it was jealousy," he said. That night Jeffrey had spent two thousand dollars on four eight balls of crystal meth. While Joey cleaned the room after the murder, Jeffrey removed the SIM card from Jamie Carroll's phone and got rid of all devices that could be traced.

The night of June 17, 2010, Banis claimed to have been asleep when alarms went off and he exited the room thinking someone had attempted a burglary. That's when police arrested him, and conveniently found the brand-new drug paraphernalia. Jeffrey had made it all up, Joey insisted, because he wanted to prevent Joey from going on the run. Mundt had threatened to make Joey the scapegoat before and getting him arrested would make it easier to retrieve the twenty thousand dollars in bond money paid after the arrest in Chicago. After handcuffing Banis, the police draped a backpack with drug paraphernalia over his shoulder and took a picture—presumably to frame him.

On cross-examination, Romines alleged the only job Joey ever had was as a drug dealer, to which Joey responded he had worked in fine dining restaurants and as a professional ski instructor, and once had his own night club. The attorney then went on to paint Joey Banis as a dangerous and violent individual, someone who witnesses would testify had attempted to assault people. In prison, Romines claimed, Joey had been "running the walk," and along with an inmate by the name of Michael Woodham, he was harassing and bullying fellow inmates.

"No," said Joey. "He was a white supremacist, straight, and liked to make fun of people." Woodham was under psychiatric treatment, was a nutcase. When the defense brought up that another inmate had claimed Joey had tried to throw blood in his face to infect him with HIV, Joey responded that "he was a child molester, a nine-time rapist, an ignorant homophobe from Texas."

"Ah, just another example of another conspiracy against you," concluded Romines, also alleging that Joey had waited to two weeks before revealing his HIV status to Jeffrey. Joey scoffed at this, pointing out that Jeffrey had "actively stated he did not mind HIV" on the many internet hookup sites he frequented.

# 29

# WITNESSES FOR THE DEFENSE

THE COMMONWEALTH closed its opening arguments the following Tuesday after a long weekend for Memorial Day. Ted Shouse rose and asked the judge for a directed verdict, that he make a decision as to Jeffrey Mundt's guilt on the spot with no need of continuing the trial, presumably because the preponderance of the evidence pointed at his client's innocence. There was no proof of robbery. No proof or murder. No reasonable juror, the defense argued, could find for the Commonwealth given their own contradictory evidence. Tampering with physical evidence? If Jeffrey did so, it was only under duress. Mitch Perry denied the request and invited the defense to put on its case.

As the first witness for the defense Ted Shouse called Linda Krauth, a project manager at the University of Louisville, who had met Jeffrey Mundt at a conference in Anaheim. Mundt made a good impression and earned a lot of money as a consultant. "We hit it off right away," she said. "He went to the same high school I went to. We grew up like six blocks apart." She and Mundt had lunch together almost every day, often at the Cottage Inn or the Third Avenue Café, and Jeffrey always paid by credit card.

Krauth recounted that when she had health issues in fall 2009 and had to go into the hospital, Jeffrey had come to visit her, even though her boss had told people not to visit. She knew Jeffrey to be lonely and was glad when he found somebody. But after meeting Joey, Jeffrey started coming in late, leaving early, and was always on the phone. Joey would drop him off and pick him up. She had asked to meet him, but "Joey refused to meet" her.

Krauth had noticed the scratches on Jeffrey, but didn't really suspect anything.

On January 11, when Jeffrey did not show up to work, she sent people to check on him and they called police when they got no answer. The next day, Mundt showed up at work with severe burns on his hands and fingers and he appeared to be in pain. "Jeff just couldn't focus," she said. The defense argued these burns came about as punishment from Joey, who had poured lye in a bowl and submerged Jeffrey's hands into it.

The prosecution countered the burns most likely arose as a result of Jeffrey's clumsy attempts at bleaching smaller denomination bills in their counterfeiting endeavors. Mundt lost his job at the end of February, ostensibly due to his poor performance and absences because of his drug use.

Next, Ted Shouse called to the stand Antonio Robinson, a dreadlocked Black man in an orange prison jumpsuit. According to Conroy, who had previously prosecuted him on two counts of murder, he was doing time for manslaughter in the second degree and criminal syndication. When asked to introduce himself, Robinson shook his head. A hushed rumble ran through the courtroom when he responded. "Man, I would like to plead the fifth."

Shouse did a double-take and then took a step in the direction of his witness. "You don't want to be here, do you?"

Robinson said, "No, sir." When prodded several times more for information, Robinson only repeated, "I would like to plead the fifth."

At the bench, Ted Shouse apologized to the judge. "Sorry, I had no idea he was going to do this." Bailiff Brown led away the witness without testifying. It was widely assumed that somebody, probably Joey Banis, had managed to intimidate Robinson into keeping his silence.

Steve Romines took over for the third witness, Jason Keith Roberts from Cartersville, Georgia. Also in orange prison garb, he had been held in the Jefferson County Jail for the previous three weeks. "In the past week have you received a threat from someone?" asked Romines.

"Yes sir," said Roberts, a certified glazier. "A guy walked up to me and told me if I knew what was good for me, to keep my mouth shut."

"Did he say who had said that?"

"Yes, Joey Banis." Apparently, the threat hadn't worked, because Roberts went on to detail his relationship with Banis, including spending time together in prison from 2008 to 2009. Roberts had stayed with Joey and Jeffrey at 1435 South Fourth Street and he described hearing them fighting on occasion, and he would overhear Joey telling Jeffrey to tell Roberts that "everything was okay." Several times he witnessed Joey assaulting Jeffrey, and once, when he tried to intercede, Joey had pulled out his gun and pointed it at him. According to Roberts, Banis had just fired the gun a couple of times in that room, which had prompted him to enter.

Roberts also described several times Joey had taken him along for robberies and a time he pulled a gun on a dealer, in an attempt to take over his business. "If Joey didn't have no dope, you couldn't deal with him," Roberts said. "He had to have it." According to the witness, Joey forbade him from having a cellphone, but he had one anyway, and Jeffrey, recognizing that he "was a good kid," had given him money so he could escape. He bought a Greyhound ticket to Marietta—but under a fake name because he was afraid Joey would trace him—and he got off in Dalton, Georgia, to throw him off the track. He stayed with a brother for a few days, then turned himself in.

"Where would you be if Jeff hadn't given you that money?" asked Romines.

"Honestly, I'd probably be in that basement," said Roberts.

After calling Jon Lesher as a witness, and again questioning the thoroughness of his detective work, the defense called Brian Johnston, who had just flown into Louisville that morning to testify. In 2005, Joey Banis had hired him to work as a manager at Starbase Q, and when Joey left to open his own nightclub, Fuzion, Johnston had followed him there. Annie O'Connell did the questioning this time. "What was it like to work for Joey Banis?"

"Honestly, it was a very bad experience." Johnston described situations in which he had seen Joey use guns and knives to threaten people, for example on opening night, New Year's Eve of 2007. "We had just started the night . . . and all of a sudden there was a ruckus out the front door and I looked over and I saw Little Joe." This was Joey's lover. "Joey always told me he was twenty-one but I heard from other people he was seventeen. He was running down the sidewalk and I saw Joey chasing after him with his big hunting knife, screaming 'I'm going to fucking gut you.'"

Next to the stand came Lieutenant Norman Norris, a sixteen-year employee with Metro Corrections who had worked as a "shift commander" and interacted with Joseph Banis. On one occasion, during a search of the unit that housed Banis, he had noticed that "each cell was stripped clean, except for Mr. Woodham's cell and Mr. Banis's cell, which had about two hundred dollars' worth of commissary."

After interviewing the inmates, the corrections officer determined that Banis with the help of Woodham "was trucking the housing unit." In prison lingo, Romines had explained in his opening statements, this meant "he's got guys acting as muscle for him so he can control what everybody does." And because Norris believed Banis and Woodham had violated the PREA, the Prison Rape Elimination Act, he recommended Banis be classified as a sexual predator. He also recommended Joey be "kept from" a number of other inmates, including James Jenkins and Jeffrey Mundt.

This all hearkened back to another allegation Romines had made: "While Jeff is in another holding cell, Banis has two guys hold him, Jeff, down and a guy took a bread bag and used it as a condom and raped him."

The defense also produced documents to show that after news about the murder aired on local stations, people had called the police to report that Joey Banis had slept with them—and others—on multiple occasions without revealing his HIV status in hopes of infecting them.

Romines then had Latanya Jones on the stand. An advocacy programs administrator for nine years with the Kentucky Domestic Association in Frankfort, she, over the course of the next half hour, established that Jeffrey Mundt displayed all the signs of a typical "battered spouse." When the defense asked the witness to confirm that just because the prosecution had played the sex video showing Jeffrey Mundt in a dominant position, it didn't mean that he couldn't have been abused by or terrified of his abuser, Ryane Conroy objected and the judge admonished the defense and instructed the jury to disregard "that last question and answer."

It came as no surprise that Romines would employ the battered spouse syndrome. It had worked for him before, most notably in the case of *Commonwealth v. Fryman*, which appeared on *Snapped* and *Dateline*. Donna Fryman shot her husband Dan in the million-dollar home they shared in Prospect, an affluent Louisville suburb rated as one of the best places to live in the state. Prosecutors argued that "Donna Fryman could never get over her partner leaving her for another woman and that their business had collapsed." Romines, however, claimed audiotapes and journals kept by the accused documented years of abuse and threats from Dan Fryman—which culminated when he pointed a loaded gun at her and prepared to kill her. She only shot to defend herself. He also impugned the quality of the police investigations at the time, saying detectives ignored crucial evidence in the case. "They misrepresent and they omit and they misstate. And they take Dan Fryman's place in terrorizing her and placing her in the shadow of the penitentiary." After a two-week trial, the jury found his client not guilty.

Several minutes after the objection, when Romines said, "Judge, the defense rests," Mitch Perry seemed a bit surprised. Many had heard that Jeffrey would testify on his own behalf. But, he confirmed he had decided not to testify after all based on his lawyers' recommendations.

When attorney Shouse once again asked for a directed verdict, the judge denied the request and adjourned for the day. The trial would wrap up the next morning.


After court let out, I drove into Old Louisville. I was finally getting around to visit Margie, my friend who lived in the Hillebrand House, a high-rise assisted-living facility that stood across from my old place on Third Street.

In her Hoveround, Margie Cook greeted me at the door of her apartment on one of the topmost floors. She welcomed me in and told me to sit while she prepared tea.

I sank into a comfortable armchair by the sofa. A soft and melodious series of what I assumed to be gongs or wind chimes drifted through the bedroom door while scenes from the local news flashed across a small television set in the corner. WDRB showed a crumpled 18-wheeler wedged under a viaduct near the university, letting its viewers know the infamous "Can Opener," the low underpass at the corner of Third and Winkler, had claimed another victim. An assortment of crystals sparkled on a glass tabletop nearby and the bookshelves held an interesting array of medieval weapons and figurines. The spines of several books flaunted enigmatic titles dealing with spells and magical herbs. Margie Cook was one of the witches who called Old Louisville home.

Her powered wheelchair suddenly buzzed up an octave as she zoomed back into the living room and deposited a cup of tea in front of me. "Cheers!" The large and friendly woman raised a brown ceramic mug and grinned eagerly. "So, what do you want to know about S&M?"

"You know, I'm not really sure." I hesitated and took a sip of the tea and tasted peppermint. "It surprised me to learn you were a well-known dominatrix at one time."

"Yeah, some called me the Bitch Witch but most called me Witch Mistress." She arched an eyebrow. "Who knows? I might get back into it one day."

"Ah, nice." I started to chuckle but cut it short, in case she hadn't meant for it to be funny.

"It's more than just whips and riding crops, you know. So much more to it." Margie slowly shook her head, as if trying to grasp it all. "There's also chains, ropes, paddles, floggers, canes. Then you got your chastity devices, bar spreaders, padlocks, and pinwheels. Hoods, hand cuffs, leg cuffs." She stopped abruptly and looked at me, then blew the steam from her cup. "Or maybe you want to know about the more serious things? Nipple clamps, cock rings, butt plugs? Ball stretchers?"

I tensed involuntarily and my spine stiffened as something akin to a whimper escaped my lips.

"Penis cage? Penis plug? Glans ring? Urethra stretcher?" Margie took a noisy slurp. "I can tell you about it all."

"Oh, my." My voice shifted to a falsetto.

"Yep." Margie took another sip and settled back with a pensive gaze. "You know, being a dominatrix isn't just about doling out punishment and pain. For some *dommes*, the discipline part is actually secondary to wielding control and humiliating the sub. You need to be confident and adopt the correct language, use the right costume and tools."

"And you did all that, used those . . . *things?*"

A complacent glaze filled her eyes just then, perhaps an indication that she was reliving the good old days. "Yessiree. But it's all about the language: *Lick my feet, slave. Crawl across the floor to me with your head bowed, you little pipsqueak. You're a nasty worm. You're such a dirty little boy. Lie face down spread-eagle and don't move until Big Momma Witch gives you further instructions.* That's the kind of stuff they like to hear."

"Kind of like in the movies," I said. "Interesting."

"Oh, the movies don't show the half of it!" Margie zoomed over to a shelf and produced a small framed photograph of a distinguished-looking local news anchor who had retired not too long before. "See this guy? He used to be my favorite. Always so nice and obedient." Margie paused to make sure I still followed. "Well, his thing was getting spanked with a rubber chicken and then having fried eggs and toast afterward. He wanted breakfast, even if it was midnight."

"I guess getting worked over with a rubber chicken really works up an appetite?" I turned up my palms and shrugged.

"It sure did." She nodded sagely. "And you know what Chicken Boy liked to hear me say?"

"Cluck-cluck-cluck?"

"Close! You're catching on." Margie beamed. "But it was *buck-buck-buck-ba-GAWK!* That's what he wanted to hear."

"Seriously?" I full-out guffawed this time.

"Exactly right. The whole damn time. *Buck-buck-buck-ba-GAWK!* Spank spank spank. *Buck-buck-buck-ba-GAWK!* Rubber chicken, rubber chicken, rubber chicken. *Buck-buck-buck-ba-GAWK!* Spank spank spank." Margie set her cup down and rubbed her hands together. "And then after an hour or so, as things were winding down, I'd have to say, 'And now I'm gonna fry ya up and eat ya!' in a really exaggerated Southern accent."

My laughter hadn't bothered Margie, but I forced myself to quit anyway and adopted a more serious demeanor. "Well, I was kind of curious about the local scene," I said. "I didn't realize how prevalent it was."

"Oh, yes, there were a number of organizations," said Margie. "I was part of one SMBD group that met in the subbasement of the pizzeria downtown on Second Street, Bearno's by the Bridge." She stopped and gave me a conspiratorial wink. "Let me tell you, they were tossing more than just pizzas down there."

I groaned while she grabbed a set of Tibetan prayer beads and began worrying them between her fingers. "Well, let's see. I know of at least five or six places in the city itself, and we also had a playhouse across the river in Indiana. The group that I was involved in was called Paradox, but they don't really exist any longer." Her smile slid away as she set down the beads and reached for her cup. "It morphed into what they're now calling the Louisville Munch."

"You know, I've heard from several sources that there was a secret S&M club in the basement of the house I'm writing the book about, the one over on Fourth Street."

"Oh, yep, know about that one. And a couple of others in Old Louisville." She took a sip of tea and nodded eagerly. "Was only there once, but it was a tiny place. Don't think it had a name, but it had disco balls. It was an interesting group of people, that's for sure." All of a sudden, Margie's smile returned and she pointed to the screen behind me. "Hey, look! They're in front of Conrad's Castle."

On St. James Court, reporter Adam Walser stood in front of the Conrad-Caldwell House Museum, gesturing at the stone mansion as the cameras rolled. "It all started when cash and valuables began to go missing at this, one of the city's most beloved historic homes and a mainstay on St. James Court," said Walser.

Over the next minute or so, he gave a brief rundown of the mansion's architectural significance and then detailed the events leading up to the discovery of the culprit. "And in the last few days, police were able to trace over thirty thousand dollars in missing silver and family heirlooms to a well-known pawnshop."

Up popped a close up of Little John, appraising an item behind a counter at this shop.

Margie cheered and bounced in her Hoveround. "Hey, his commercials are the best, aren't they?"

I mumbled an answer but kept my eyes glued on the story. "With the help of John Tan himself, LMPD detectives were able to link the thefts back to a household on St. James Court." A man's mugshot appeared with a name. "And the suspect has been identified as the son of a board member."

Although I didn't recognize the individual, I did recognize the last name.

It was the son of the selfsame angry board member who had confronted me the night I was escorting the library tour.

For weeks the board member's son had been sneaking in through a back door at night and helping himself to the museum's valuables. He had such easy access because his father had strongarmed the board into renting the troubled individual one of the rooms in the annex behind the museum. Only a door with a simple lock separated the residential annex from the cash register—and the silver safe.

"Goes to show you." Margie lowered the volume. "You never can tell."

"I guess not. But I bet this is going to throw everyone on St. James Court into a frenzy." Shaking my head in disbelief, I got to my feet. "Well, thanks for the information. Fascinating stuff, but I need to head home."

"Get back in touch with any questions you may have." Margie buzzed to an end table, grabbed a red silk bag with embroidered Oriental motifs, and tossed it to me. "Hey, you mind leaving that at the Witches' Tree for me? It's been a while since I left an offering and it's really hard for me to get out nowadays."

"Sure, not a problem," I said.

Then she reached into a drawer and extracted two braided leather bands, each with a chunky crystal dangling in a gold filigree cage. "Here, take these as well. They're protection amulets for you and Ramon. With all that's going on, you could use a little extra help."

"Aw, that's nice."

"You been sleeping well? You look tired."

"Not really." I shook my head. "All this has been getting to me."

"Don't worry. I'll light some candles for you as well."

"Thanks. I'll take any help I can get."

As I walked out, she zoomed along behind. "Be careful. Those two guys—Joey and Jeffrey?—are very dangerous. I didn't know them personally, but word on the street is they were into some very dark things."

I said goodbye, but right before she closed the door, she beckoned with a pudgy hand and whispered impishly. "By the way, I was always a mistress and never a slave!"

During his closing remarks the next day, Steve Romines stood and pointed at the prosecution. "They have wasted enough of your time. Make no mistake, Jeff Mundt is innocent! What they have shown you is nothing. It is suspicion and accusation and prejudice. That's all it is."

The attorney's twang seemed more pronounced than ever. "Some of you might have noticed that I have an accent. I grew up on a tobacco farm in southern Kentucky and I always wanted to be a lawyer. And I know more about this case than anybody in the world." He then mustered a somber gaze for the jurors and pointed to his client. "If I let him go to the penitentiary because I did not do enough? Well, that's not going to happen. Jamie Carroll is dead and Joey Banis is a monster who killed him."

For the next hour, Romines continued, making comparisons with the Salem witch trials and pointing out the lack of evidence connecting his client to the charges levied against him. He hinted again at prosecutorial misconduct and on more than one occasion he drew objections from the prosecution, who wanted him admonished for "talking about facts that were never introduced."

As he prepared to close, Romines compared what the Commonwealth had done to Jeffrey Mundt with slut shaming. "A picture of Jeff Mundt in a rubber shirt? Really?" he bellowed. "Homosexuals are the last group that it is okay to be prejudiced toward in our society today. I was amazed at the number of people in the questionnaires who said, 'I don't like gays.'" Then he added, "I am forty-six years old and Jeff Mundt is the first gay male I have ever hung out with. I am ashamed it was under these circumstances. It has been my greatest privilege to defend Jeff Mundt because he is innocent."

Jeffrey Mundt, in a light blue sweater, looked somberly straight ahead, his arms stretched out in front of him on the table.

Ryane Conroy started her final remarks by replaying the video of Jeffrey Mundt fake-crying when told about the body in the basement, the body he knew about the entire time. "Jeff Mundt is a liar," she said.

"Do not let them convince you that convicting Jeffrey Mundt means that Joey Banis isn't a bad person." She pointed out his lies, his involvement in drugs, and the counterfeiting of money. Referring to the "stupid" defense tactics, she added, "Mundt is an arrogant, cocky person who thought he would get away with it. They were a team. They were a unit."

Several minutes later, Sheriff Brown drew the three alternates and judge sent off the dozen final jurors to deliberate the fate of Jeffrey Mundt.


Not even eight hours later, the jury had its verdict. When the judge asked the defendant to rise, Jeffrey Mundt appeared unsteady on his feet. He took a deep breath as Mitch Perry read the results. Ted Shouse had his hands on the shoulder of Jeffrey Mundt, who cast his gaze down, clearly shaken. They found Jeffrey Mundt not guilty of murder, criminal facilitation to murder, and robbery in the first degree—all of the most serious charges. However, the jury did find him guilty of two minor charges, criminal facilitation to robbery in the first degree and tampering with physical evidence. Ted Shouse hugged his client, who seemingly let out a sigh of relief.

Steve Romines requested a minimum sentence but Ryane Conroy asked the jury for the maximum sentence, explaining Mundt had "about three years of credit" and could be released immediately. "Make him take responsibility," she urged, suggesting a sentence of ten years.

The jury deliberated for about a half hour and then delivered its recommendation: three years for the tampering and five years for the robbery, served consecutively for a total of eight years. The defense tried to have Jeffery released until sentencing, but the judge denied it, saying, "He needs to be taken into custody immediately." During a quick bench meeting, Ted Shouse advised the judge that Mundt's life was in danger and requested he be held in isolation, in Oldham County or Shelby County.

It was almost ten o'clock in the evening when Judge Mitch Perry finally gaveled to a close the trial of Jeffrey Mundt. "Good night to all. We're adjourned."

Outside in the hallway, one of the reporters shook her head and muttered, "Looks like Jeffrey Mundt got away with murder."

Next to her, a colleague's eyes widened in disbelief. "What are you talking about? Obviously, he was innocent." They stared at each other for a second, then burst out laughing.

I was conflicted, but the defense had done an admirable job and there was little evidence pointing at Jeffrey Mundt participating in the murder, at least in my mind. He sounded terrified in the 911 calls and they had Joey confessing to murder on video. And so much evidence painted Joey as the psychotic schemer who already sat in jail for the most heinous of the accused crimes, murder. Any jury would have had a hard time getting past all that.

I had exited the Judicial Center and walked into a cool evening breeze when my phone started to buzz.

It was my friend Ron Harris, who lived in the Bishop's Hat House on Third Street, and his tone was breathless. "Guess who's dead?"

# 30

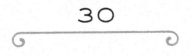

## PIECES OF SILVER

"WHO'S DEAD?" I said. "I have no idea."

Ron had just come from a neighborhood meeting where much of the talk had been of the Adam Walser story and the thefts at the Conrad-Caldwell House. Halfway through the gathering, however, chatter began to die down as word spread about a terrible tragedy on St. James Court. And it had just happened.

Ron told me. I gasped.

Embarrassed by the WHAS11 exposé, the former board member of the Conrad-Caldwell House had taken his son to task and berated him for besmirching the family honor. After a heated discussion at the family's St. James Court residence, the troubled young man grabbed a gun, ran out to the backyard, and killed himself.

Now, the grieving family was looking for people to blame. The father was on the warpath and WHAS11 had become the target of his ire. He threatened to sue the station and had called company headquarters demanding Adam Walser's dismissal.

"Oh, no," I said. "That's terrible. But it's not Adam Walser's fault—or the news station's."

"I know. But the grief must be unbearable. They're looking for someone to blame," said Ron. "But on the bright side, at least they're not blaming you this time."

"Well, there is that," I said. "Cold comfort, though."

"I know. Listen, I need to run. Everybody's in a tizzy." He hung up.

\* \* \*

Back home in the Magic Library, I was doing some work when I heard pounding at the front door. I opened it to find Kelly standing there, in an admiral's bicorn hat.

"Well, if it isn't Horatio Hornblower himself," I said. "Come on in. What's up?"

Taking off the hat, he followed me to several large decanters on a side table, where I doled out bourbon. "Uncle Scratch has found you a bottle of Pappy, that's what's up."

My heart skipped several beats. "Seriously? The twenty-three-year-old?"

"Yep, if you got the moolah, I know someone at the distributor who has a couple bottles set aside."

"Wow, and you're sure it's the twenty-three?"

"Correctamundo." Kelly took his drink and plopped himself down on a sofa. "You hear about that ring of half-wits over at Buffalo Trace?" He took a sip and sighed.

I laughed. "Pappygate?" Police had arrested nine individuals who had purloined upwards of a hundred thousand dollars of Pappy Van Winkle and other whiskies. Much had been nabbed by removing the pins from the rusty storage locker doors.

"Dumbasses." Kelly swirled the bourbon in his glass and drank. "Say, you going to enter the Dainty this year? Now that we're old enough."

"Hmmm. I hadn't thought about it. It looks really hard." The Dainty had started almost fifty years before in the Schnitzelburg neighborhood, arising from a street game of the same name played by German immigrants. It centered around a notoriously difficult competition in which contestants started with a wooden peg—the dainty—with tapered pointed ends. Then they used a larger stick to strike it as it lay on the ground to make it fly into the air. The contestant then hit it again, midair, much like a batter in baseball. Whoever launched their dainty farthest won. The minimum age to enter was forty-five.

"Well, if you want to meet some die-hard Catholics and find out more about the house on Fourth Street, that's your best bet. All the money raised goes to the Little Sisters of Poor."

"Oh, I go every year anyway. Just not sure about entering the contest. I'm too uncoordinated." I rose and refreshed our drinks. "It's always a colorful crowd, that's for certain."

Several weeks later, I was taking my daily stroll around Joe Creason Park when a car slowed to a stop on Newburg Road and a side window buzzed down. "Hey! How have you been?" yelled a cheerful male voice.

I shielded my eyes from the sun and walked in the direction of the idling vehicle. Detective Jon Lesher sat behind the wheel, a big grin on his face.

"I've been okay. How about you?" I was kind of surprised because, despite all the times our paths had crossed in the courtroom, I had never actually spoken with the detective. In fact, after getting into trouble with Ryane Conroy, I had made a concerted effort to avoid coming into contact with anyone from her team.

"How's it coming with the book?" He reached out with a waving arm to indicate the vehicle behind him should pull ahead and pass. "Man, that was a weird set of trials, wasn't it?"

"Yeah, you could say that. I can't believe it's all over, though," I said. "It seems so long ago now, not just a few weeks ago."

"Well, let me tell you, those two were some evil dudes and I'm glad they're still behind bars. Even though Mundt will probably be out on parole soon."

"Really? You think so?"

"Oh, for sure," he said. "He'll be out in another year or so, tops." Just then, Lesher's face turned serious. "Say, you know, now that the trials are over, I can talk about it all."

I started to respond, but then I realized what he was saying and I was dumbstruck. Lesher wanted to talk. I quickly regained my composure. "Oh, I'd love to hear what you have to say."

"Yeah, there's some stuff that didn't come out in the trials," he said, waving another approaching car around him. "Give me a call sometime and let's meet. Or look me up on Facebook. My profile has a photo of me swinging a dead pheasant by its feet."

Dead pheasant?

"Ah, alright, sounds good." I returned the wave as Lesher said goodbye and slowly pulled away.

As the car sped up, Lesher leaned his head out the window and yelled one last thing. "And I'll tell you about that house. There was some weird shit going on in that basement down there."

# PART THREE

# 31

## YOU SHOULD KNOW BETTER THAN THAT

AS I drove down Third Street through Old Louisville, activity buzzed with hundreds of artists and volunteers preparing for the annual St. James Court Art Show. Every year, it attracted some two hundred thousand visitors for the long weekend. Fall had arrived before Lesher and I could finally coincide our schedules, and we agreed to meet for an early breakfast at Wagner's Pharmacy. Popular with trainers and stable hands since 1922, the old brick pharmacy stood alone on an empty block where other businesses had once thrived.

I pulled into the gravel parking lot and in the background loomed Churchill Downs, the stark whiteness of the famous twin spires on the old wooden clubhouse contrasting against blustery gray autumn clouds. A line of horse trailers maneuvered through a gate and disappeared into the backside.

Across the street sat one of the few remaining shops in the immediate vicinity: Little John's. On the sidewalk out front, the pawnbroker himself paced back and forth while chatting on his phone. He sported a neat gold suit.

Wagner's buzzed with chatter. Lesher smiled when he saw me and I joined him in a corner booth. Wagner's had become popular with the breakfast and lunch crowd since gaining fame on the foodie television show *Throw Down! with Bobby Flay*. I ordered my usual, the Pam & Jack's Omelette stuffed with bacon, sausage, cheese, green peppers, tomatoes, and onions—the very item that had enticed the Food Network to come and film here. The detective had egg and cheese biscuits with ham, and we both washed things down with coffee.

"Now that the trials are over, have you been in touch with Joey or Jeffrey?" He studied the plate in front of him and frowned, as if he didn't know which biscuit to start with, then reached for the left one. "Man, those were some evil dudes, and Jeffrey Mundt got away with murder."

"No, nothing yet. Tried several times, several different ways, but zilch. Registered letters, Facebook messages, emails."

Out of the corner of my eye, I saw a hand with rings on every finger flutter in my direction and then a cheerful voice called out: "Hey, there!" I looked up to see Louise Cecil. "Lucie, look who's here!" She waved her companion over and they came to greet me.

"Hey, what brings you both out so early? Especially to this part of town." I made quick introductions and because Lesher looked a bit uncomfortable, I didn't say anything about his job or the reason we had met.

"Oh, we just came for a quick bite," said Louise. "Lucie's meeting Bob Baffert for an interview at the track. You know, with the Breeders' Cup right around the corner, she needs to see all the famous trainers."

"And then we're going dress shopping because someone is getting married." Lucie turned and pointed. "And guess who!"

Louise blushed and then raised her hand shyly.

"Oh, wow," I said. "That's great. Congratulations."

"I know I'm kind of old to get married again, but I'm still excited. You'll have to meet him soon. He's a prince." Louise smiled and then hugged her friend's arm. "I'll bring him to your signing for the new book, how about that? When it's out, that is."

"Sounds great."

"Say, speaking of which." Louise suddenly turned serious. "Did a guy named Malcomb ever call you?" She leaned down and lowered her voice. "Someone came in for costumes last week and he talked the whole time about the Jamie Carroll murder trials. I told him about your book and he just went on and on about the place. He rented a room there something like forty years ago and said it had the strangest assortment of people coming and going. I gave him your number."

"Nothing yet, but I hope he gets in touch."

"Me, too," said Louise. "Well, we need to run. See you soon!" She and Lucie waved and made for the door.

If they recognized Lesher from the trials and the news coverage, it hadn't registered.

"That Lucie Blodgett sure gets around, doesn't she?" He chuckled and returned his attention to our conversation. "So, can't say too much about certain things—gotta be careful for the time being, because I got into hot water after the first trial—but like I said, some weird things went on down in that basement."

"I've heard some interesting rumors myself, like they used to keep bodies down there when it was a sanatorium before the war."

"Yeah, people told me that, too. But that's not the really weird shit; the crazy stuff is what I've heard about that little room, that it was used for rituals and ceremonies at one time."

"Like Catholic stuff, you mean?" I blew steam off my coffee.

"Yeah, and satanic shit, too." He shook his head. "You know we get lots of calls on our tip line, and a lot of them are just plain bull. It's usually some random whack job, right? Like the guy who told me he used the room where they buried Jamie Carroll to get beamed up to the mother ship every Sunday night." He laughed. "But—get this—I spoke to several people who said Joseph Risner had done some weird shit down there. A relative told me she had dropped him off for some kind of initiation ceremony down there once." He bit off a chunk of biscuit but stopped chewing when he saw my blank expression.

"Joseph Risner? Who's that?"

"The Lillelid murders? He was the ringleader."

"Oh." I had heard of the gruesome killings. On April 6, 1997, six young people from Pikeville, in the eastern part of the Kentucky where the famous feud between the Hatfields and the McCoys once raged, started out on a road trip to New Orleans. They ranged in age from fourteen to twenty. Jason Bryant, Natasha Cornett, Dean Mullins, Joseph Risner, Crystal Sturgill, and Karen Howell. As they crossed into Tennessee, they began having car troubles and decided to steal a new set of wheels.

At a rest stop, they carjacked the Lillelids, a family of four returning from a convention for Jehovah's Witnesses. They shot Vidar

Lillelid, originally from Norway; his wife, Delfina; their six-year-old daughter, Tabitha; and two-year-old son, Peter, numerous times—and left the bodies arranged in the shape of an upside-down cross.

Only Peter survived, though he was left with major disabilities, having been shot in the eye like his father. An investigator would refute the allegation of the upside-down cross, but prosecutors brought up rumors that the six were involved with satanism, and the district attorney repeatedly referred to the "occult" angle of the circumstances. Nobody ever presented supporting evidence for these claims, though, and during the sentencing hearing, Natasha Cornett claimed her first attorney had coached her to identify herself as the "Daughter of Satan."

"I thought all the devil-worshipping stuff was just hype, you know, satanic panic."

"When they searched the kids' houses they found stuff they never reported—occult symbols and pentagram bibles—like they all belonged to the same coven or something."

"Hmm. Sounds like lots of rumors and the typical exaggeration."

"Yeah, I know, but friends in the hills over there say otherwise. These were cops with firsthand knowledge."

Still not entirely convinced, I lifted a forkful of omelet to my mouth and thought for a moment. "Is there any truth to Joey's allegations that Jeffrey worked for the CIA? And that they've been snooping around here in town?"

"Well, ask me again next year, after things have died down a bit, and I might have some interesting information for you, but for now all I'll say is the CIA has been involved." He raised his eyebrows at me, and after opening the second biscuit and adding some salt, he took a bite and chewed.

The door opened with a whoosh of fresh fall air. In walked a short man who zigzagged to the counter. Seeing Lesher, he waved. The detective saluted.

"Hey, remember when they found that little Guatemalan boy's body out here? We interviewed that guy. He knows a lot of people who live around the track." After pointing at the guy, Lesher resumed eating.

"I remember." A sanitation worker had discovered the body of four-year-old Ivan Cano in the garbage. Police zeroed in on Cecil New, a registered sex offender living nearby, who had admitted to an acquaintance "that he had raped and killed a child." New failed a lie detector test in what polygraph examiners called the worst failure they had ever seen. He eventually confessed to the murder to escape the death penalty in exchange for a life sentence.

Lesher looked up. "A lot more going on there than what they could prove, as well. They never did get the creep for rape." He waved goodbye to the short man, who was leaving with a to-go bag. "He's a gypsy, you know." Lesher matter-of-factly pointed a coffee spoon at the retreating figure.

"Really? I think they go by the term *Roma* today."

"Well, he used the term *gypsy*. His grandmother had a fortune-telling place here on Central Avenue."

Louisville's forgotten Romani past had always fascinated me and I had amassed tons of old articles about the Travelers in this part of the country.

On July 10, 1938, the *Courier-Journal* proclaimed: "Gypsy Head-quarters Without Any Gypsies." The author, Oressa Teagarden, wrote that Louisville had once been a favorite camping ground for the nomads, "the scene of every Gypsy ceremonial. Conventions, weddings, births, divorces, burials, feast days brought the clans together each summer." Because "conveniently located between the North and the South, Louisville offered ideal camping grounds." Many, on their way north from Mexico or the "Southern States," came together for Easter ceremonies. "Leaving the cold Northern climate after Thanksgiving, they were again in Louisville two or three weeks before continuing their journey to the South." Although police harassment had driven them off, Louisville remained "Gypsy headquarters in legal and business affairs," as they retained two attorneys here to represent them.

I forked up the last of my omelet and swallowed. "Hey, did you ever hear about the famous Roma wedding they were supposed to have here?"

Lesher gave me a blank stare so I filled him in.

In April 1929, the *Atlanta Constitution* reported that hundreds of Roma were converging on Kentucky, where Rosie Stanley, the daughter of William Stanley of Louisville, would marry Frank John, the son of Chief Gregory John of Philadelphia. The wedding would "take place in a three-acre field near the Ohio River" with "pigs, turkeys and chickens . . . being roasted all over town for the feasts" and "an orchestra from Cincinnati . . . engaged to play continuously for the first 24 hours of celebration."

However, two days later, the *New York Times* wrote: "GYPSY WEDDING OFF; LOUISVILLE PUZZLED; Some Say Bride's Father Insisted on $300 More for His Daughter's Hand. OTHERS HINT AT POLICE." But sources corroborated that the bride's father had upped the price at the last minute. When asked whether $3,000 wasn't a lot to pay for a wife, Ruby, the would-be bridegroom's sister, replied: "Not for a good woman. My husband's father, he pay $4,000 for me. For my wedding they rent a hall in New York. There was maybe 400 people there. Everybody get drunk and the police arrest forty-three. The next day they fine everybody $1, whether they just drunk or kill somebody."

"Man, you sure know a lot of useless information, don't you?" Lesher grinned and pushed his empty plate to the side. "But Louisville's a funky town, isn't it?"

"Hey," I said, pointing at the detective's face. "I notice you're not wearing glasses anymore. Did you get contacts or Lasik?"

"Naw, I don't even wear glasses. I just use those on the stand to look smarter."

I froze, cup midair, and stared. "Seriously?" I finished taking my sip.

"Yep. Eyesight's fine, but you have to put on a show up there. Trials are a play. The jury is our audience. We're playing a part, they're playing a part." He shrugged his shoulders.


A half hour later, after agreeing to stay in touch, I headed to the small coffee shop at the corner of Fourth and Crazy, where I had arranged to meet four ladies for a private driving tour of the area. In Old Louisville, many of the streets had been blocked off and hundreds of artists and craftspeople sat in small white tents that lined the sidewalks. As I navigated the congestion and drove down Sixth Street, a number flashed on the console. My brother Mike was calling.

"Paul's driving me crazy," he said as soon as I picked up. "I can't take it anymore."

I took a deep breath. We had had this conversation several times already. "Mike, if he's not paying rent after all this time and making your life miserable, tell him he's got to leave. He'll find someone else to mooch off."

"Why do I always have to deal with him?"

I sighed. "The rest of us have washed our hands of him, Mike. You keep taking him back." The previous year, Paul had returned to the Midwest, where he had joined our youngest brother in his farmhouse in the Iowa countryside. I had heard through the grapevine that things hadn't worked out with Paul's girlfriend in Louisiana. "Nobody will begrudge you doing what's best for you. We've all done it before."

"OK, man. It's just that chaos follows wherever he goes."

We said goodbye and I parked. A squad car blocked the intersection of Fourth and Crazy, where a crowd of people milled about. On the sidewalk, a white sheet lay draped over a supine figure.

Inside the coffee shop, Lee, the owner, was fighting with a customer, angry that he couldn't use the bathroom on the premises. Like the Soup Nazi on *Seinfeld*, Lee had very strict protocols—in her case, about who could use the facilities and when—and at least once a week, this produced shouting matches that scared away more than one potential client. I waited politely for the confrontation to deescalate, and it did several minutes later when the angry man stormed out of the shop, vowing to leave a business-ending review on *Yelp*.

When my turn came, I stepped forward and ordered an americano.

Lee, her voice cheerful, brushed back a strand of blond hair and pounded espresso into a filter. "So, how's it going?"

"Fine, but what's going on out on the corner?"

Lee slammed the filter into the machine and rolled her eyes. "Some crack whore OD'ed and the body's been lying there for over an hour. Really great for the neighborhood."

"That's terrible." Unfortunately, it wasn't the first time something like this had happened. I craned my neck to see out the window, where EMTs had lifted the body onto a gurney. One of them was my bartender friend. He raised his eyebrows in greeting when he saw me. "Well, I'm glad they came before my tour people arrived. It's four ladies from New York with a hired driver and they sounded kind of snooty."

"Fuck 'em if they don't like the neighborhood!" Startled, I turned to find Debra Richards standing behind me. "If they're from New York, they've seen worse, trust me."

"Well, still . . ."

"And notice how all the cop cars and the ambulance haven't turned off their damn engines? They've been idling there the whole time. Really good for the environment, not to mention historic buildings." She scowled as the drivers got inside their vehicles and drove away one by one. As each one sailed by, she flipped them off.

Several seconds later, a loud honk startled us as a large black sedan pulled up. "I bet that's my tour people. See you later!" I grabbed my coffee, waved goodbye, and left.

I hopped into the front seat next to the driver, a short woman with a dark ponytail in a black suit and hat. "Welcome to Old Louisville!" I turned around to greet the other ladies.

"Before we get started, I'm going to need to see your ID please." A vaguely familiar voice came from the driver's seat.

When I turned around, I groaned inwardly. Officer Janet held out her hand expectantly and her face wore the same annoying, deadpan look. "You have got to be kidding." I said it softly, but as if a period followed each word. Then, seeing her out of uniform, I whispered, "I bet you got fired from the police force, didn't you?"

At that, she flinched ever so slightly, but then she doubled down and made a *gimme-gimme* motion with her hand. "Come on."

I had my wallet in my back pocket, but my spine stiffened as I resolved to stand my ground this time.

From the back seat came a short bark of laughter. "Don't be silly. I've talked to this man several times on the phone and know him from seeing him on television." The lady who had organized the tour scoffed. "And anyway, you're not required by law to carry an ID out on the streets."

Ex-Officer Janet started to protest, but the organizer cut her off.

"Drive on. I'm a lawyer," said the lady. "You should know better than that."

# 32

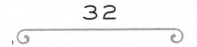

# OLD SKELETONS

A FULL moon, soft and yellow, filled the sky as I parked the car in front of a bank of brightly painted red doors set under lancet arches and headed for the side entrance of St. Martin of Tours. A bell had just tolled midnight and the streets were bare. Surrounded by crenulated stone, a milky green steeple pointed up into the inky sky like an accusing finger. Inside, Kelly Atkins waited for me. He had just texted me to come meet him.

St. Martin of Tours was founded in 1853, in one of the oldest parishes in the archdiocese, for German immigrants on what was then the east side of the city. One of the few remaining antebellum buildings in the downtown area, this was a focal point in the infamous Bloody Monday Riots of August 6, 1855, when hysterical members of the anti-immigrant Know-Nothing Party intended to burn the Cathedral of the Assumption and St. Martin of Tours to the ground because they suspected the German Catholics of arming themselves against the government. However, Bishop Martin John Spalding invited the Know-Nothing mayor to inspect the premises and the congregations were exonerated.

Thugs killed over twenty people, and although five were indicted, no convictions followed—and the victims never received any compensation. This triggered an exodus of many German-speaking residents, who fled upriver to friendlier locales such as Cincinnati, and sent a message of warning to would-be immigrants in the River City.

St. Martin of Tours never shut its doors, and the late-night hours attracted a fair share of insomniacs and curiosity seekers in addition to the devoted. I entered and greeted the guard. Four Goth-looking youths near the front altar whispered excitedly while bowed down over a single cellphone. "Look, there it goes again," said a large girl with shaggy red hair and eyes rimmed in kohl. "This place is buzzing with activity!" On the screen, a green glow had changed from orange to bright red, no doubt the indicator of paranormal activity on some ghost-hunting app.

"O, Captain! My Captain!" His voice respectfully in check, Kelly emerged from beneath an arcade and sauntered in my direction. He had on a long cloth coat, buttoned all the way up, and I dreaded what lay beneath. In the crook of one arm nestled some kind of hat. "Fancy meeting you in a place like this."

"Fancy seeing you in a winter coat when it's not winter outside." I clapped him on the shoulder and followed as he turned for the front of the church. "Please don't tell me you're in another Nazi getup."

"OK, I won't tell you then." Sounding very much like W.C. Fields, he twiddled his fingers at the side of his face. "And it's not techni-cally Nazi this time, just a Wehrmacht officer's uniform." He started humming the tune to "Deutschland, Deutschland über Alles."

"Tell that to the next three-hundred-pound football player named Shlomo you piss off," I said. "Still can't believe that last guy didn't beat the crap out of you."

Just two weeks before, Kelly's penchant for wearing the attire of those defeated in World War II in public had almost landed him in the hospital. While enjoying a late-night breakfast at Denny's on Eastern Parkway he had provoked the ire of a huge Cardinal linebacker in the booth next to him. The athletic star attended Adath Israel Brith Sholom, Kentucky's largest and oldest Jewish synagogue.

"Ah, don't worry about it, pal. Sure, he wanted to take me out in the parking lot and knock me around a bit, but I talked my way out of it." Kelly untucked the hat from the crook of his arm and held it out. It was a furry bison hat with polished horns angling out on each side. "And when you wear a goofy hat with it, they know you're not serious, see?"

I recognized that hat. It belonged to a collection he kept behind the basement bar of his house. The box usually came out after several rounds of bourbon, at which time he cranked up the volume to his favorite Andrew Lloyd Webber CD, and doled out the headgear—which signaled the start of an obligatory singalong.

"Hey, sorry, I forgot to bring one in for you. You want I should go out to the car and get one? I got the Viking hat you like so much."

"No, thanks, I'm fine."

"Well, suit yourself then." Kelly stopped in front of a glass case on one side of the altar. "Did I tell you I attended the solemn high mass for these two? In 2012, when the Vatican authenticated their provenance and they were reinterred." He turned and pointed to matching glass-and-filigree cases on the other side. Each held a skeleton. They had been in Louisville since 1901, when Pope Leo XIII gave the Cisterian nuns in Italy permission to donate the relics of two martyrs in their possession to St. Martin of Tours.

On the last day of the year, the complete skeletal remains of St. Magnus, a Roman centurion and martyr, and St. Bonosa, a Roman virgin and martyr, arrived at the Louisville customs office. Both had been put to death by Emperor Diocletian in the third century AD. More than a millennium and a half later, they found new homes in glass reliquaries beneath the north and south transept altars.

"Hey, it seems like we're always running into stiffs that keep getting dug up and reburied, doesn't it?" Kelly leaned down to inspect the collection of bones in front of him. Hollow eye sockets stared out from a skull nestled in an intricate lace collar at the neck of a red velvet robe. "Just like poor old Frank McHarry the ferryboat operator they buried standing upright and poor old Jamie Carroll in his Tupperware container."

"Ew. Tupperware is for heating up leftovers. Rubbermaid," I corrected him. "Does Tupperware even make something big enough for a human body?"

On the pews nearby, one of the Goth kids stifled a squeal. "Did you see that one? That was a ten!" said a short boy in a black kilt and jackboots. "I bet that's from one of the old skeletons up front."

"Who you calling an old skeleton?" Kelly faced the group and wagged a finger at them. "I may not be a spring chicken, see, but I'm hardly dead yet."

Startled, the kid in the kilt looked up, not quite sure if he should act ashamed for what he said or bothered that an intruder interrupted his ghost hunting. His companions stared at him, then at Kelly. The kid shook his head sheepishly and pointed. "Not you. I meant one of the bodies in the cases up there."

"Ha. Got you. I was just kidding." Kelly clapped his hands together before returning his attention to the skeletal remains of Saint Magnus.

Nodding his head uncertainly, the Goth guy resumed his observations on the would-be supernatural activity in his midst. "Yeah, it's from one of those relics, I'm sure, or maybe from some other dead body underneath us. I'm positive there's a crypt with tombs below the church." His voice dropped to a whisper.

"So, mein Herr, this is why I summoned you here. I think you will find this of interest." Kelly turned over the bison hat and extracted a manila envelope from inside. "Here, take a look."

I accepted the envelope and noticed a stamp from the archdiocese of Louisville on the outside. "What's this?" I removed a thin sheath of documents paper-clipped together. The top of the very first page bore a letterhead with what appeared to be a seal from the Vatican.

"From *il Vaticano* itself." Kelly triumphally tapped the stamp with an index finger and beamed. "See, Uncle K.J. ain't so crazy after all, is he?"

"Well, that has yet to be seen, but this is interesting." I quickly shuffled through the pages, apparently copies of originals, and pieced together what I could. Though many of the identifying bits of information had been blocked out with thick black lines, in several locations they had missed the address: 1435 South Fourth Street, Louisville, KY. All the dates were solidly obscured, however, but the text seemed outdated, as if drafted on a typewriter.

It appeared to be the details of an exorcism carried out in Louisville. "Seriously?" I looked at Kelly in disbelief.

"Told you, chief! See how they missed the street address in a spot or two? It's the selfsame infamous Murder House on Fourth Street, dangnabbit."

"Yeah, I see that, but why would they redact it like this? It's not the CIA."

"Not sure, brother, but that's the only way they'd let me have a copy. I thought I knew some higher-ups in the church, but apparently not that high up." He put the hat on and crossed his arms. "And see how they mention a 'private family chapel' being used? I'm sure that was the creepy-ass room where Jamie Carroll ended up in the ground."

"But that was supposedly the first family's wine cellar, the Robinsons. It doesn't make sense they'd have a chapel there. Other rooms down there had nice concrete floors, so why pick the most primitive room, one with hard-packed dirt?"

"Mysterious are the ways of the Universe, brother," he said. "How am I to know? Nothing says you can't set up an altar in a disused wine cellar and call it a chapel."

"Well . . ." I stopped to consider. "I guess not."

"Maybe they wanted it to look like a secret Roman cave like the ones where Magnus and Bonosa hid out. And those documents are legit, I'm telling you. I have something similar from an exorcism they carried out in the basement of St. John's. That was way before my time, so I didn't actually witness anything, but I've heard about it from a priestly friend or two."

"St. John's? Isn't that the place that's a men's homeless shelter now? What's so spooky about that place, other than being old?"

"Brother, I got ins over there, too! I need to take you sometime. They have a subbasement that will give you the willies for sure. You know the story. Hans Schmidt, the Killer Priest, and poor little Alma Kellner?"

"That's where they found her body?" I did know the story of Hans Schmidt.

In 1908 Schmidt immigrated from Germany to the United States, where he worked at St. John's Parish in Louisville. But he immediately aroused consternation, altering the prayers and rituals to suit his eccentricities and professing his belief in "free love." He conducted haphazard masses rife with scriptural error. Notoriously difficult, Schmidt eventually had to leave and ended up at a church in New York City. Whispers of mental problems and misdeeds followed him as he bounced from one parish to another, but—as a forerunner of the priest sex scandals a century later—the church only transferred Schmidt. They never confronted him.

In New York, he seduced Anna Aumüller, a beautiful rectory housekeeper and recent German-speaking émigré. Despite being transferred, once again, to a church far uptown, Schmidt continued his romance with Aumüller. In a covert ceremony that he performed himself at a makeshift altar, he took Anna as his bride.

But on the night of September 2, 1913, the cleric snuck into their secret Manhattan apartment and cut her throat with a twelve-inch butcher knife. Schmidt dismembered the body with surgical precision, bagging the parts separately before disposing of them one by one during seven macabre late-night crossings on the Fort Lee ferry. Furtively, he would drop one chunk per trip off the stern. Anna wasn't the only victim, however: Schmidt also killed their unborn child, the motive behind the gruesome murder.

On September 5, 1913, neatly bound bundles of body parts began washing up on the New Jersey shore of the Hudson River, and over several days, authorities pieced together six fragments to form the almost-complete body of a woman. They only lacked the head, which never surfaced.

A maker's label on a pillowcase used to package the upper torso led police to a shop, which in turn pointed detectives to Schmidt's secret apartment. There, they found a woman's trousseau in a steamer trunk, as well as a butcher knife, a handsaw, and a trove of letters addressed to the raven-haired beauty. When they confronted the priest, he blurted out in a guttural accent, "I killed her because I loved her. I am guilty and ready to pay the penalty."

Police in Schmidt's hometown of Aschaffenberg strongly suspected him in a murder committed there before he left for the United States. But a U.S. jury sent him to death before German authorities had the chance to question him. Hans Schmidt bid *"auf Wiedersehen"* to his "dear old mother" and went to the electric chair, the first and only priest ever executed for murder in the United States.

Back in Louisville, his first American parish, the handsome cleric remained a suspect in a crime that had rocked the city a few years before, the gruesome murder of an eight-year-old girl that had all the hallmarks of the murder that sent the killer priest to Old Sparky.

Sister Mary Genevieve described Alma Katherine Kellner, a third-grader at St. Mary's Academy, as a model student and a "child of great promise" with an amiable and loving disposition. "Alma would often steal away from the other children and go to the chapel to spend a moment in prayer." But on December 8, 1909, Alma disappeared, last seen on her way to morning mass. Because she had a well-to-do grandfather, many thought kidnappers were holding her for ransom. However, no ransom demands ever came.

On May 30, 1910, barely six months after she disappeared, someone discovered the child's body in the cellar of the church. A monster had dismembered her and burned parts of the body, then dropped the pieces through a small trapdoor in the sacristy. Quicklime had been used to disintegrate the flesh and every bone in the body had been crushed.

Schmidt was in Louisville at the time of the murder and knew the layout of St. John's very well. Although he denied involvement in the little girl's murder up to the last moments of his life, many believed Alma's gruesome murder to be nothing more than a forerunner to the gruesome fate of Anna Aumüller.

"And that poor little wretch's spirit is still active down there, I tell you." Kelly removed the hat and smoothed back his hair. "Every time I take a picture down there, there's a bright blue orb, a big one, that appears over the spot where they found her remains."

I hugged myself for warmth. "Let me know when you can smuggle me in. You know how much I love creeping around old basements. And subbasements are always a plus."

"Will do, Herr Professor." He tucked the bison hat under his arm and gave me a salute. "So, now I bid you adieu for the eventide. I've got a date with a certain broad in the East End, and it's already past her bedtime."

I laughed. "So how old is she?"

"Well, let's just say she remembers Glenn Miller and Count Basie very well. Grew up listening to them as a child." He mustered a sly grin and then bolted for the door. "See you around."

"Hey, come on over soon and we'll break open that bottle of Pappy."

"I'll be there." A cool draft rushed through the sanctuary as he opened the door and went out into the night.

The Goth kids squealed at something new registering on their ghost app and I paused for a moment to study the intricate tracings on the arches framing the altar before I left.

In my car, I checked Facebook before I drove away and I discovered a short message from Jon Lesher. It said, "Hey, did you hear what happened with Mundt?"

# 33

## EXPLORING NEW TERRITORY

JEFFREY MUNDT had made parole a year after his trial, having served just four years of his eight-year sentence. He was remanded to a halfway house, but authorities arrested him soon after his release and transported him to Illinois for another trial.

"It's obvious they're trying to keep him in jail as long as they can," Lesher had said over the phone when we spoke several days after his Facebook message. "Like I said, there's a lot more going on there than meets the eye. And most of what came out of his mouth was all lies. Go sit in on that trial, and you might find out what this is all about."

In Louisville, Jeffrey's release and arrest had barely made a blip on the radar. All my calls ended up at dead ends and it wasn't until my friend Vito in Chicago sent me a link to a story that had just run on the local ABC affiliate that I was able to pin down a court date. Chuck Goudie, the reporter who interviewed me during the first trial, had done another investigative piece, this time about Mundt's acquittal. He described it as a real "How to Get away with Murder" case.

"From the ivory tower of Northwestern University to a bloody basement in Louisville, Jeffrey Mundt lived a double life. He was a top official at Northwestern, leading its technology overhaul, but he also nursed a voracious appetite for violent sex and crystal meth," said the silver-haired Goudie, wearing a dark suit with a red tie. "During a weekend binge of sex and drugs, Jeffrey Mundt and his lover killed a man. Mundt admitted to mangling the body with a sledgehammer to fit it into a storage container and admitted to burying the pieces in his basement" during "a weekend of perversion."

I found it strange that the report claimed Jeffrey had taken part in the killing although he had been acquitted of that crime, and I wondered if his lawyers would get after the station for its inaccurate reporting. And what "pieces" had Mundt buried in the basement? Jamie's body—though bones had been smashed—remained intact.

The camera cut to Jon Lesher in a pink tie. "He lets friends and coworkers know that he has an alternative lifestyle, that he is a gay male, but what happens behind his closed doors, it's a nightmare," said the detective.

The camera showed the exterior of the dilapidated house, where Goudie and Lesher sat on a bench out front, this time joined by Josh Schneider, who sported a green bowtie. "Both of them, Mundt and Banis, were the two most diabolical, intelligent individuals I have ever met," said the assistant prosecutor.

Ryane Conroy also made an appearance, explaining that Mundt "was living this secret life, this life where he was doing drugs, he was counterfeiting money, he was participating in the killing of another individual. As sick as it sounds, I think he was thrilled and loved every minute of that crazy ride."

The report wrapped up with Lesher, Conroy, and Schneider confirming their sentiments that Jeffrey Mundt had indeed gotten away with murder, but not before an angry Steve Romines responded. "They're wrong and they need to get out of this business if that's what they say. The jury found him not guilty of murder, and if they believe he got away with murder they should do their jobs better."

Now I stood in front of the Cook County Courthouse, in Chicago, where they had slated Mundt's next trial. An overcast sky shrouded the imposing structure in a steel-gray pallor. But getting here had been a wild goose chase. I had spent hours on the phone in Louisville trying to get the exact time and location of the trial, but it wasn't until an especially helpful clerk spent an hour calling around and asking questions that I finally had the number of the courtroom. "There's something weird about this one. They keep moving it around and assigning new judges. Double-check the day of the trial to make sure nothing else changes," the woman said before hanging up.

I had double-checked, but when I made my way through security that morning and located the specified chambers, I found no indication of a trial scheduled for Jeffrey Mundt. The docket outside the door didn't have him listed, nor did any of the other dockets in the courthouse. When I inquired at the information desk, they found no record of his name in the system.

A former colleague of Jeffrey Mundt's had contacted me and agreed to a brief meeting in the Deering Library at Northwestern University. By the time I arrived, the clouds had broken a bit and pale shafts of sunlight fell on the stained glass windows running around the sides of the stone Gothic structure. Inside, coffered ceilings and massive carved beams soared as I followed the man to a small meeting room.

"Louisville. That's an interesting city," he said, sitting down at a large wooden table. "Did you know Anne Braden? She recently died. She was a dear friend of mine."

"Oh, I think everybody in Louisville knew Anne Braden," I said. "She was kind of an icon. And she taught at the University of Louisville when I used to teach there."

In 1954, journalists and activists Anne and Carl Braden purchased a home in the Shively suburb of Louisville and transferred the deed to Andrew and Charlotte Wade, a Black couple who, because of Jim Crow housing practices, had failed in attempts to buy a house of their own in that part of town. They took up residence just two days before the U.S. Supreme Court struck down the nation's racist segregation policy in the *Brown v. Board of Education, Topeka, Kansas.*

Upon discovering that a Black family had moved in, white neighbors burned a cross in the Wades' front yard and shot out windows. Across Louisville, tensions flared, and six weeks later, somebody dynamited the Wades' new house. However, instead of going after the actual perpetrators, investigators made the Bradens and their associates the scapegoats, alleging they belonged to the Communist Party and had engineered the bombing to provide a cause célèbre and fund-raising opportunity.

After a sensationalized trial, Carl Braden—the perceived ring-leader—received fifteen years in prison. He was only released after the Supreme Court invalidated state sedition laws and charges were dropped. Although the actual bombers were never held accountable, it steeled the resolve of the Bradens, who went on to become recognized white allies in the movement for civil rights. The Wades sold their property at a loss and moved to a Black neighborhood.

"So, thanks for getting in touch with me. What can you tell me about Jeffrey Mundt? Did you know him very well?"

"Well, it was mostly a working relationship, but we did hang out socially on several occasions. A very smart individual, but often very condescending to people 'beneath' him." The man steepled his fingers before continuing. "I remember attending a conference with him once and how he berated the parking attendant for messing up his change. It embarrassed the rest of us in the car."

"Were you surprised when you heard about the body in his basement?"

"Oh, good lord, yes. He was strange, but not that strange. Or so we thought." He raised his eyebrows and then seemed to shake off an unpleasant thought. "But after the news broke, that's when people who knew him started talking, saying that he always had kind of a dark side. From what I gather, he was pretty well known in the underground sex scene."

"And what about the counterfeiting and all that?"

"Well, that stuff would have been right up his alley. He had all the tech savvy to pull something like that off." The man leaned forward on his elbows and lowered his voice, even though the room appeared soundproof. "I followed the trials pretty thoroughly, and I doubt that putz Joseph Banis had the know-how to do it all."

"Yeah, you're not the first to make that observation." I flipped through the pages of the little notebook in front of me and jotted down a line. "And what did you think about Joey's claims that Jeffrey had worked for the CIA?"

The man across from me laughed softly. "You know, it's funny you bring that up, because every now and then Jeffrey would get these mysterious visits from men in black—seriously, just like in the movies—and it always set people to talking. Or else he'd get random calls from Russia and eastern Europe, and what that had to do with our technology overhaul here, I'll never know."

We moved the discussion outside, where the man had offered to take me on a brief walking tour of the Lakeshore Historic District in Evanston, the area where Jeffrey Mundt had restored an old mansion. The choppy steel-blue waters of Lake Michigan visible in the distance, we strolled through tidy tree-lined streets dotted with sprawling homes and impressive mansions. The preferred architectural styles included Tudor, Italianate, Queen Anne, and Georgian Revival.

I felt a call vibrate my cellphone in my pocket, but I ignored it. We came to stop in front of an austere brick house with large windows. "That's where Jeffrey used to live."

I studied the impeccable façade with its neatly painted window frames and doorjambs, realizing it presented a stark contrast with the crumbling visage of Jeffrey's most recent residence. Back in Old Louisville, the elements continued to take their toll on 1435 South Fourth Street and the front porch had acquired a dramatic sag.

A little girl on a blue tricycle came speeding down the driveway just then, her laughter trailing in the air behind as an older girl struggled to catch up with her. In my pocket, my phone vibrated again, insistent, but instead of ignoring it as I had the previous time, I excused myself and checked to see who was calling.

My father's face popped up on the screen. He never called. My heart sank. I hesitated, then answered.

"David," he said. "I've got some bad news. It's your brother Paul."

ABOVE: The Richard Robinson House in 2010. RIGHT: The grand staircase in the foyer of the Richard Robinson House typifies the elegance and craftsmanship so typical of Old Louisville mansions.

ABOVE: In the early morning hours of June 18, 2010, police dug a storage container out of the dirt floor of an old wine cellar at 1435 South Fourth Street. In it was the body of Jamie Carroll. BELOW: This dirt floor served as the temporary grave for Jamie Carroll for almost seven months.

ABOVE: Jamie Carroll came from eastern Kentucky. *Photo courtesy of WHAS News.* BELOW: Police arrested Jeffrey Mundt and Joey Banis for the murder of Jamie Carroll. Here, they pose for a photo in the house, not too long after burying Carroll in the room below them.

ABOVE: The child of a prominent Louisville family, Joey Banis enjoyed his own singular style. BELOW LEFT: On the local club scene, Joey Banis cut a colorful figure when he tended bar. BELOW RIGHT: Joey Banis, dressed for a night out.

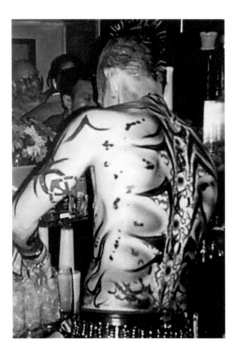

ABOVE LEFT: Jeffrey Mundt, as shown in an online dating profile. ABOVE RIGHT: Jeffrey Mundt, from an online dating profile. BELOW: As Ronica Reed the Pageant Queen, Jamie Carroll enjoyed a faithful following in West Virginia and Kentucky.

ABOVE: Louisville media dubbed the case surrounding Jamie Carroll, Jeffrey Mundt, and Joey Banis the "Pink Triangle Murder." *Photo courtesy of WLKY News.* BELOW TOP LEFT: Judge Mitch Perry presided over both trials for the murder of Jamie Carroll. BELOW TOP RIGHT: The team for the prosecution: Detective Jon Lesher (left), Ryane Conroy (center), Josh Schneider (right). BELOW BOTTOM LEFT: Joey Banis (center) was defended by Justin Brown (left) and Darren Wolff (right). BELOW BOTTOM RIGHT: Jeffrey Mundt sits surrounded by his defense team of Steve Romines (left), Ted Shouse (center right), and Annie O'Connell (right).

ABOVE: Dr. Stanley Bandeen operated a sanatorium at 1435 South Fourth Street in the 1920s and 1930s. BELOW: The Bush-Bandeen Sanatorium in 1933. *Photos courtesy of Marilyn Bandeen-Bradley.*

A post on Joey Banis's Tumblr page shows that he is actively seeking pen pals today.

Hello, my name is Joey. I am a lonely, gay man who is seeking pen pals and true friends. I am 6' tall, 160 pounds with several interesting tattoos which comprise a cohesive aesthetic image. I have a swimmer's build and I am 45 years old, although I look at least 10 years younger!

None of the above necessarily matters but describing myself seems to be a good way to start.

I am currently incarcerated for a crime which I did not commit and my case is under appeal at this time.

My interests vary widely: I enjoy fine wines, philosophy,

# 34

# DOORS TO NOWHERE

I HAD been feeling glum all day, plagued by memories of my brother and dejected that I seemed to be spinning my wheels when it came to finding out more about the motives behind the Jamie Carroll murder. I wanted to learn exactly what happened the night of the infamous 911 call, but neither Jeffrey nor Joey would agree to talk to me. Aside from that, some criticized me for dredging up too much dirt and it was taking a toll. I tossed and turned at night, and when I did manage to sleep, it was accompanied by terrible teeth grinding. My jaws ached constantly and I had several cracked molars. I was exhausted.

To lift my spirits, I took an afternoon off and visited my favorite spots in the city. I strolled through Cave Hill Cemetery and then drove through Cherokee Triangle and Cherokee Park. After that, I stopped at the Heigold House. Better said, I stopped at the façade of the Heigold House, which stood in the middle of Frankfort Avenue at River Road in Butchertown.

The ornately embellished front was all that remained of a two-story house that had originally occupied a site nearby, in an area near the river known as the Point. In the early 1800s, this was home to French-man's Row, a collection of elegant mansions built for wealthy residents moving upriver from New Orleans, but by the middle of the century, large numbers of immigrants from Ireland and Germany began moving in. One of them was a German stone carver named Christian Heigold, who arrived in Louisville at a time of great political unrest.

The anti-immigrant Know-Nothing Party was attacking those they felt didn't belong. Heigold witnessed this firsthand during the infamous Bloody Monday atrocities of 1855. To prove his patriotism and loyalty, Heigold spent his free hours adorning his façade with carvings and inscriptions, in essence using his residence to make a political statement. He decorated it with hewn leaves, wreaths, ribbons, banners, eagles, allegorical figures, and five-pointed stars that highlighted the busts of notable Americans such as then-president James Buchanan and George and Martha Washington.

The big flood of 1937 destroyed most of the area, but the façade of the Heigold House was saved. Eventually the city moved it to the current location on a roundabout that served as a kind of gateway between neighborhoods. Because only sky and clouds awaited those who passed through the main entrance, locals called it the Door to Nowhere.

After that, I stopped for a drink in the lobby of the Brown Hotel and then I headed over to Whiskey Row. When I parked downtown the sun was just setting, streaking the clouds with tendrils of pink and orange as a damp breeze wended its way up from the river. Overhead, a low-flying UPS plane descended and sailed over the Second Street Bridge, where, in the 1981 movie *Stripes*, Bill Murray had stopped his car and hurled his keys into the water below.

Legend had it that, hundreds of years before Christopher Columbus, Welsh adventurer Prince Madoc journeyed to Kentucky, constructing a stone fortress on the Devil's Backbone, a craggy strip of land jutting into the Ohio River. Early settlers claimed to have discovered ancient suits of armor with Welsh inscriptions and that blue-eyed, blond Indians in the vicinity were the result of intermarriage. When they built the Art Deco bridge in the 1920s, construction workers supposedly found remnants of ancient stone fortifications. Recently, a Welsh film crew had come to the bridge to document these claims.

A young Cassius Clay had famously committed an act of protest on this bridge in 1960—at least according to another story. Fresh off his triumphant return from the Rome Olympics, the young boxer had arrived back in Louisville only to be refused service at a "whites-only" restaurant. The enraged champion made his way onto the Second Street Bridge, tore off the gold medal from around his neck, and flung it into the Ohio River. Although the racial abuse most likely happened, many attributed the jettisoning of the medal to legend.

Just several weeks before, I had stood at a river in another state, gazing at a different bridge spanning the water. The Centennial Bridge in Davenport, Iowa. It was a soft summer evening and we had gathered at the banks of the Mississippi for my brother Paul's memorial service. One by one, attendees came to the river's edge and tossed white carnations into the slow current and we watched them bob and float. Sparkles of light, reflected from the bridge, danced on the water's surface, encircling each bloom with a glittery escort as it drifted away.

The crowd at the riverside wasn't what I had anticipated. Blood relations were far outnumbered by street people or volunteers trying to help those in the local homeless community. They had become Paul's family.

After my brother Mike kicked him out, Paul became homeless, living on the streets in Davenport. He had been involved in a hit-and-run accident, and though he could walk short distances, he relied on a wheelchair to get around. This, buoyed by his affable nature, made him a recognizable fixture in the city.

And in all that time, I hadn't heard from him—nor had I bothered to contact him. Talking to several eyewitnesses, I discovered what had happened.

Recent flooding had destroyed a homeless encampment where Paul had been living and he slowly spiraled into a state of despondency. He saw no way out. One afternoon, he rolled his wheelchair to the edge of the water, stood up, removed his clothes, swallowed a mouthful of pills, and swam out into the Mississippi. He never returned.

When my father called to inform me, a boater had just discovered my brother's body floating in the water. The coroner suspected it had been there about two weeks.

Pangs of guilt still tormented me.


Passing traffic hummed faintly as I crossed at the corner of Second and Main, where, behind Whiskey Row, the bridge rose on the Kentucky side. In its shadows hulked a stately ashlar building from 1877. In front, a historical marker gave information about the famous Galt House that had occupied the site from 1835 until 1865. Destroyed by a fire, it had earned praise from Charles Dickens during his visit to Louisville and hosted many other notables, including General Ulysses S. Grant, who met General Sherman there in March 1864 to plan his notorious "March to the Sea."

Rumors abounded that victims of the fire haunted the pizzeria that occupied the location today and that a maze of underground bootlegger tunnels riddled the basement. One summer night years before, I had encountered a real-life, self-professed hobo by the name of Norman who offered to take me on a midnight tour of the subterranean passages. I had politely declined because it was just the two of us and he seemed a bit shifty.

This night, however, I wasn't as hesitant. Dawne Gee, a reporter friend, had asked me to come on air and talk about the history of Whiskey Row. I met her and a cameraman at Doc Crowe's restaurant and the interview went by quickly. Then we got down to the real business of why I was so eager to join her: because she had access to the section of the basement where contractors had been completing renovations. She had invited me to explore the remnants of the long-forgotten S&M club while they shot footage for an upcoming story. I had jumped at the opportunity.

We went down to the Washington Street side of the buildings, where a dilapidated door stood wide open. I followed them into a dank corridor that emptied into a large bricked room used as a storage cellar at one time. From there, we passed through a space with whitewashed stone walls that caught the glare from a single bare bulb in a wall sconce and we passed through a low doorway with wooden stairs leading down. At the bottom of the steps, an eerie blackness beckoned. The door, it seemed, went nowhere.

We descended anyway, and when we arrived at the bottom landing, we entered a large space painted in black and dark green. On one wall, a crudely rendered illustration showed two individuals engaged in a sex act. In a corner stood an enormous cask on its end; nearby, an arched entryway gave onto a separate room. When I peeked inside, I saw a huge pile of glass bottles in varying hues of opaque and milky white that rose toward the ceiling, presumably empty bourbon bottles. Many of them looked very old. From there, another long corridor stretched down for at least a hundred yards, with wooden doors facing each other at even intervals. Off in the shadows, I discerned the faint outline of an individual that emerged into the light but then quickly disappeared.

"Are we the only ones down here?" I asked.

"Workers have been coming and going, but I haven't seen anyone lately." Dawne motioned to the cameraman and they went off on their own to do some filming, leaving me to explore by myself. I followed the dim passageway to the next open door, where I found a bare room with a long wooden bedframe at its center. When I spied a pair of black steel manacles mounted at each end, I realized it was a torture rack.

Just then a shadowy figure emerged from the darkness and startled me. "Psst. What's she doing down here?"

I jumped back and studied the silhouetted form in the corner. "Excuse me? Who—?" But I stopped midsentence when I recognized the face that slowly approached me. "Candy," I sighed. "Once again, you scared the bejesus out of me. What are you doing down here?"

"What are you doing down here, Nancy Boy?" She pointed an accusing finger at me. "I was here first."

I rolled my eyes. "WAVE3 just interviewed me about Whiskey Row and now they're filming a segment about the secret sex club down here. It's all anybody's been talking about lately. People like kinky stuff."

"Well, you're preaching to the choir, doll, when you're talking kinky, but I wasn't expecting to find Dawne Gee down here snooping around. The workers all left. I thought I was the only person."

"Well, think again, Nancy Girl. You're not alone." I raised my eyebrows in a challenge.

Candy narrowed her eyes at me. "Oh, I see what you're doing, Nellie Oleson. Reverse psychology." She took out a cigarette and lit it. "Ain't you clever?"

I shrugged. Then I took the opportunity to study Candy's attire. She wore shiny charcoal stilettos and a tight black leather sleeveless dress that stopped mid-thigh. Her curly wig was a shocking shade of red and studded straps encircled each of her biceps. "Now, that's an outfit I haven't seen before," I said, gesturing in her direction.

"Oh, do you like it?" Suddenly flattered, Candy smiled and executed a graceful curtsy that afforded the opportunity for further praise.

"Yes, very nice. I guess your wife had a more varied wardrobe than I gave her credit for."

"Oh, this old thing?" She paused to smooth a hand down the front. "I gave it to her for Christmas one year, but she only wore it once. Her loss."

"Say, speaking of which, isn't it a bit early for you to be out? I usually run into you after midnight."

Candy took a drag on her cigarette and cradled her elbow in her free hand. "The old banshee's been taking melatonin every night and going to bed early. Snores like a Nazi and she never wakes up. It's been real easy to sneak out."

"Hey, do you smell cigarette smoke down here?" Several rooms down, Dawne poked her head out into the hallway and sniffed loudly.

"No, I don't smell anything," I lied, as Candy lifted a finger to her lips and retreated into a dark corner.

"Strange, I could swear I just got a good whiff of cigarette smoke," Dawne yelled back. "Maybe it's a ghost." She and the cameraman headed down the corridor in the opposite direction.

Candy emerged when the coast was clear and ground the cigarette out with the toe of her shoe. "Gotta keep this side of my life on the down low, you know. Can't be appearing on film." She took out another cigarette and lit it. "If my wife's family found out, we'd never hear the end of it. They're part of the banshee clan that lives out in the East End. Snobby bunch of bitches."

"I think you're safe."

Candy raised her head but then took on a serious air. "And you promise not to disclose my identity in your new book, right?"

I nodded solemnly. "I swear. And like I said, there's not much to disclose because I know very little about you other than the fact that you're a night owl like me."

"Well, thanks, doll. I appreciate it." She exhaled a stream of smoke and coughed. "I got to be careful about protecting the anonymity of the urbex club I belong to as well."

"Urbex? You're part of an urban explorer group? I didn't know that."

"Seriously, Nancy Boy?" She gave me a deadpan stare. "Why do you think I love being out late at night creeping around abandoned places?" She leaned in for a whisper. "Find me an abandoned building and I'm going in sooner or later. But I only dress like this when I'm on my own."

"I see."

"When I was younger, the group would sneak into the old TB hospital all the time, but now it's impossible with all the security they got up there." Waverly Hills, a tuberculosis sanitorium built in the 1920s, had long enjoyed a reputation as one of the most haunted buildings in the country. Estimates placed the death toll during the epidemic as high as sixty thousand.

I stuck my head out into the hallway to make sure the coast was clear, then I motioned for Candy to follow. "So, has the place changed much?" I gestured to the space in front of us.

Candy took a furious last drag on her cigarette before tossing the still-lit remnants into the corner. Somewhat unsteady on her feet, she tottered after me and smiled. "Well, doll, it's a lot brighter than it usually was, but, yeah, it looks the same." She stopped in front of an archway that had been bricked in, and frowned. "It looks like the ass wipes closed off some areas. There used to be a shower and locker rooms on the other side."

"And what about this room down here?" I pointed to the next doorway.

Candy stuck her head inside and squealed softly. "Well, whores in hot pants, this was my favorite room." Clutching her hands under her chin, she leaned back against the wall and closed her eyes, presumably lost in the reverie of bygone pleasures.

I poked my head inside and my eyes adjusted to the darkness. Against a far wall rested a huge wooden wheel with metal spokes and manacles. "They used to strap me to that thing and roll me up and down the hallway." She sighed and languidly opened her eyes. "Up and down, up and down."

"Didn't it make you dizzy?"

"Of course it did, doll. That was the best part." She pushed herself away from the wall and returned to the corridor. On the opposite side, a bank of wooden doors painted green extended down to a brick wall. Outside each door hung a red wooden light post. "When the red lights were on, you couldn't go in those little chambers." She walked to one of the doors and softly knocked the wood twice. "That's where the real hanky panky went on."

"So, is this the first time you've been back since they discovered this all down here?"

"Yes, it's been years, Johnny Bravo. I snuck in right before you arrived."

"Goodness, you're just all over the place with the names tonight, aren't you?"

"Like I said, Nancy Boy, you need to shake things up every now and then." Candy returned her gaze to the passageway and sighed at her surroundings. "It'll never be the same and that's a shame. Good times were had down here. The only bad thing is they didn't have any disco balls like the place on Fourth." She turned back to face me then, her tone changing. "Hey, you been to the house lately? I heard a couple from Indianapolis wants to buy it from the bank and rent it to students."

"I've been once and snooped around. Doesn't look like anybody's been there in ages. The place is looking pretty sad."

"You been able to talk to either of those murderous freaks yet?"

I shook my head. "I thought with the trials being over they'd want to put their spins on the outcome, but still no luck. I'll keep trying, though." We slowly walked to the end of the passage and, in a hidden alcove, we found a huge red pentagram painted over a slick black expanse of brick wall.

Candy gasped. "Doll, I sure as hell don't remember this little area back here. Freaky deaky." She tilted her head and studied the image for a moment. Then she lifted a hand and pointed. "See that?"

"See wha—?" But I stopped when I saw what she was talking about. When you shifted a bit, the dim light highlighted a subtler, more matted tone of black on the shiny surface. Subjacent to the pentacle, somebody had stenciled an enormous, goatlike face of Satan. "Yep, I see it." I turned to head back in the direction we had come. "Well, that's as good a sign as any for me to leave, I guess. Dawne told me to see myself out, but I don't want to get stuck down here."

Candy struggled to keep up with me. "I heard it from a few more people that some devil-worshipping shit was going on in Jeffrey Mundt's place. Supposedly church groups have gotten permission to go inside and bless the house. Cleanse it, I guess. I was walking down the street one night around two or three in the morning and I saw a whole procession of priests in cassocks come out the side door."

"Really? I'd love to see a bunch of priests parading around Old Louisville in the middle of the night." I slowed my gait. "You know, I've had people tell me about the satanic stuff down there as well—and about the Catholic altar—but so far, there's not a lot of proof."

"Poor old house. Nobody wants her just because of a little creepy history. Old Louisville is a fair but fickle mistress indeed." Candy peered into another room and cast a forlorn glance around the empty space. "Did I tell you I heard one of the neighbors is trying to get it condemned and torn down?"

"No way."

"That's what they're saying." Candy took out a cigarette case, but then stowed it away without opening it. "Naw, I should cut down. I'll walk out with you. I've had enough." Hoisting the strap of a leather purse onto her shoulder, she held back until we confirmed that the reporter and her cameraman had already left. "You know, I don't usually come down this way, always stay in Old Louisville, but did you ever notice the historical marker across the street?"

"About the slave pens? Yeah, I've seen it." It marked the site of the Garrison Slave Pens, one of four slave-trading establishments in the city.

"I never even knew that Louisville is where the term *sold downriver* originated!" Candy laughed softly. "Glitter Ball City has all kinds of secrets!" She stopped and grabbed my arm.

"Oh, by the way, I've got something for you, Nancy Boy. Come to the Witches' Tree some night after midnight and I'll make sure I have it with me. I've been going there on my nightly strolls a lot lately."

"Oh, thanks. Is it something about the murder trials or the house?"

"No, but I think you'll like it. I found it on eBay the other day and I thought of—"

Before Candy could finish her sentence, a sudden movement cast a silhouette over the dirty floor and a dark form came barreling out of the shadows. With an angry roar, something large tackled her from behind.

## 35

# THREE DEGREES OF
# SEPARATION

IT WAS a beautiful Friday morning as I walked into my living room, where sunlight streamed through the enormous picture window. I chuckled at the thought of Candy several nights before, lying spread-eagle on the basement floor. A worker coming back for his tools recognized Candy and had bowled her over by way of a surprise greeting. Candy beamed when she saw the burly man and gave him a bear hug after wiping the dirt and dust from her leather dress. He had also been a regular at Latex, where the two spent many an enjoyable evening together in the gritty brick chambers below Whiskey Row.

I walked to my favorite piece of furniture, a large cherry wardrobe from the south of France. The antiques dealer said it dated to 1792, the year Kentucky had become a state, and because of that I had always loved it. I admired the rustic hand-carved vines, birds, and stars before opening the doors. Recently, I had converted it into a liquor cabinet, and now I stood before it, smiling at my latest acquisition.

There, in the center of a marble countertop, stood a pristine bottle of Pappy Van Winkle bourbon, the coveted twenty-three-year-old variety. Kelly's connection had come through and I had received it just two days before.

I had thought about holding on to it, but with my brother's recent death had come a shift in my priorities. Time was too precious, and who knew what could happen? Why wait to enjoy it? Later that evening, Kelly and some friends would come over and we'd crack it open amid much fanfare. I'd bake some bread and put together a nice charcuterie spread. I'd pull out a block of twenty-five-year-old cheddar from Wisconsin I had been saving. There'd be toasts to our friendship and lots of reminiscing.

But before all that, I had things to do.

A friend in Old Louisville had been in touch and he had some information to share about the house at 1435 South Fourth Street. Given the perfect weather, we decided to meet in front of the Pink Palace on St. James Court and go for a stroll. We had planned on meeting at the Mag Bar, a popular neighborhood dive, but a car had just plowed into the front door and they were closed for repairs. It seemed that every month, a car lost control and barreled into the Mag Bar.

The Pink Palace was another of the city's iconic buildings, known as much for its rosy hues as for its colorful history. Now a single-family residence, it wasn't always such. Built around 1890 with a soaring western tower and Châteauesque gables facing the court, the red-brick structure began life as something known as the St. James Court Gentlemen's Club and Casino. Residents of the burgeoning enclave heard that this would be a place for men to gather for a snifter of bourbon, to smoke a locally rolled cigar, to play a hand of poker—and maybe, rumor had it, to do other things if they went to the upper floors, where ladies waited to entertain them in gentlemanly fashion.

Local historians, such as David Williams, the friend who was waiting for me, doubted that this had actually ever happened. Why would they build a bordello in a ritzy subdivision where they hoped to attract wealthy homeowners? Early records did indicate that some kind of men's establishment had been conceived for the premises, but the brothel part was probably thrown in later as the stories surrounding the place grew. In any case, whatever started off there didn't last long, and a family moved in and converted it into a home.

After that family vacated the premises, the Women's Christian Temperance Union eventually acquired it to use as headquarters for their Kentucky chapter. The WCTU was famously against drinking and counted as one of the driving forces behind Prohibition in this country. But alcohol wasn't the only vice they were against. They also frowned upon smoking, gambling, and prostitution. According to lore, when they discovered the original intent for the property, the ladies were so scandalized, they had the red-brick structure painted pink—all in an attempt to wipe away its sordid past and to give the building a new lease on life. It had remained some shade of pink ever since.

I found David Williams in front of the Pink Palace and he waved as I approached. "Hey, how have you been?"

"Everything okay so far." We began strolling around the court. An affable man with longish graying hair, Williams had lived on Second Street for years and locals often went to him for information because of his meticulous researching skills when it came to Old Louisville. He had also earned a name as a founder of the Nichols Archives at the University of Louisville, an extensive collection of LGBTQ documents and materials amassed over several decades.

"So, I've got a pretty good idea of who's lived in that house and some of the things that went on there over the years," he said. "But first off, guess who owned the plot of land where the house was built?"

"No idea. Who?"

"John Atherton." Seeing the blank look on my face, Williams explained. "He's the one Atherton High School was named for."

"Ah, where, Jeffrey Mundt went to school, right?"

"Correct. He was also the head of J.M. Atherton Distillers and had his place of business down on Whiskey Row." He snorted. "Everyone talks about six degrees of separation, but in Louisville it's more like three degrees of separation."

"Ain't that the truth."

"The house at 1435 has seen its share of tragedy," he said, referring to a small stack of papers in hand. "As you already knew, a hardware merchant by the name of Richard Robinson was the first occupant and he lived there for more than twenty years."

"I heard his wife had died and he was pretty distraught when he left."

"Well, he did leave as a widower, so it's likely his wife died at home, rather than at the hospital. That's how it was back then." David shuffled through the papers as we made our way through Belgravia Court. "The people who bought the house from him didn't stay very long and in the 1920s and '30s it was used as a sanitorium."

"Ah, so there is truth to all the sanitorium rumors then. Did you find out anything about a shady doctor?"

"Well, Evelyn Bush, a practitioner of the controversial new branch of medicine called osteopathy, teamed up with Stanley G. Bandeen, and they relocated here. The Bush-Bandeen Sanatorium appears to have done well at first, but after the Wall Street crash of 1929 they ran into financial difficulties and within several years the sanatorium went bankrupt." Williams paused to examine his notes as we exited the gate on Fourth Street. "Bush went on to become nationally recognized, but Bandeen's career came to a halt in the 1950s after the State Board of Health accused him of engaging in questionable medical practices."

"Does it say exactly what questionable practices?"

"Just that it was 'quackery.'" He shook his head and continued reading. "The house experienced a turbulent period of ownership not unlike many others in the neighborhood and numerous boarders took up residence there—until 1961 when Pauline Boren purchased it following a bed and breakfast divorce. The house would remain in the hands of her family for forty-seven years."

"Bed and breakfast divorce?"

"It was a legal separation from her husband but not a real divorce because they were strict Roman Catholics," said Williams.

"Hmmm, I heard she was a diehard."

"In the early 1980s, she moved to the bottom floor and started renting out rooms. All kinds of people came and went."

We passed a modest three-story red-brick house, where all eyes of the city had turned in 1901. Miss Patti Ellison married Sir Charles Henry Augustus Lockhart Ross here, the ninth Baronet of Balnagown, Scotland. They settled on an understated affair in Louisville because Ross had been married once already. Lady Ross, as Patti became known, took up residence part of the year in the family's ancient ancestral castle, which ended up in the hands of wealthy Egyptian businessman Mohammed Al-Fayed in 1972. He was the owner of Harrod's Department Store in London and the father of Dodi Fayed, the romantic partner of Princess Diana who died with her in a Paris automobile accident in 1997.

Opposite the Lady Ross House stood 1435 South Fourth Street. A pair of squirrels scampered across the roofline and hurled themselves into the branches of a nearby tree. On the third floor, movement at a window caught my eye and I startled to see a dim form looking down. "Hey, do you see that?"

"See what?"

"Up on the top floor, it looked like someone was standing at the window, but they're gone now."

"Oh, no, didn't notice anything. I was staring at the front door. Maybe a prospective buyer's inside, taking a look-see." Williams's tone changed as he returned his attention to the typed pages in front of him. "Now this is interesting. Pauline Boren was the longest resident, it seems, but one night in 1992 one of her renters went berserk and savagely attacked her. They moved her to Treyton Oak Towers a few blocks down the road to recuperate, but she never did. She died there."

"Oh, wow. Another rumor with some truth behind it. What about the little room downstairs—anything to that?"

"You know, I didn't find anything out about an S&M club, but I talked to Pauline's daughter, who said her mother was a very trusting soul. As she got older she'd let anyone rent space. In the end, the place became too much to maintain and she couldn't keep an eye on things, so who knows what went on in that basement?"

"Did she mention anything about the Catholic stuff?"

Williams gave a short laugh. "No, but I did talk to a neighbor or two and they had some interesting things to say." He pointed at the large brick apartment complex to the south of the mansion. "Somebody had a thing for nuns, it appears. In the basement and out in the carriage house, they found boxes and boxes of lesbian nun porn and pulp fiction. Whether it belonged to Pauline or a tenant remains to be seen, though."

"Yeah, Ramon and I saw some of that ourselves when we looked at the place." I let my eyes roam over the façade and studied the sad state of the mansion. A gutter had torn away from the roofline and jutted out at a dramatic angle, and rot had done its dirty work in the wooden dentils.

I turned to Williams with a quizzical look. "So, what do you think happened here the night Jamie Carroll was killed? Some kind of sexual escapade gone wrong or something more to it? I still can't wrap my head around it all."

"I'm not sure, but it surely wasn't the first gay murder or scandal here in Old Louisville." Williams shook his head and we started walking down Fourth Street. "There have been isolated incidents separated by many years, but they have given Louisvillians the impression that the neighborhood is some place to be avoided."

We entered Central Park as Williams told me about a number of unsolved killings of gay men in the immediate vicinity, most involving situations where the men had picked up strangers and brought them home. Often, it seemed, the police weren't overly preoccupied with finding the culprits. From the 1930s into the 1980s, the park was a heavy cruising area and in the 1950s neighbors complained about the "wine drinkers, vagrants and homosexuals" there.

"Why Central Park?" I asked.

"Until the 1950s, nearly the entire population of Louisville was concentrated in the area bounded by the present expressway system. Old Louisville had fallen on hard times. The rest of the city was forgetting it was there and gay men and lesbians felt safer because there wouldn't be as many prying eyes." We strolled under the sparse shade of a coffee tree and Williams gestured to a clearing. "In 1982, police arrested an actor for trying to pick up a trick here. The whole affair was hush-hush in the *Courier-Journal*, but rumors flew around the lavender underground. When I found the arrest report I figured out it was an actor who gained fame on a sitcom in the 1990s. He recently died."

"I guess it didn't hurt his career then, but who was it?"

"Remember the sitcom *Wings*?"

"Yeah, I loved that show."

"His name was David Schramm, a Louisville native. He played Roy Biggins, the cantankerous owner of a rival airline."

"No way," I said, laughing. "I had no idea he was from Louisville."

"He was, and I will back you up on it if you use this, because I did the research."


My next order of business included a visit to Omega National Products. Just steps away from the main gate for Cave Hill Cemetery, I found Yolanda Baker in the back part of an inconspicuous building. Her blond hair was done up in a ponytail, and she wore white long sleeves under a black short-sleeved tee stamped with the company's name and a large glitter ball. The sixty-something had agreed to meet me and tell me a little more about her job. When I asked her official job title, she responded, "mirror ball maker" and offered to give me a brief tour. Soon, she'd be reaching her fifty-year job anniversary.

She had just started on a large ball on order from a sheik in the Middle East and she quickly outlined the production process. First, a cloth backing needed to be placed on one side of a mirror, which was run through a special machine that cut glass into strips of mirrored squares. After that the edges had to be sanded and polished. Then, the strips needed to be laid on a layer of glue covering an aluminum core.

"It's kind of like putting a puzzle together," she explained. "And then comes my favorite part—seeing all the bling." She held up a strip of mirrors so it could catch the light and she slowly moved it back and forth, sending bright squares of light dancing around the room.

Yolanda Baker was the last professional mirror ball maker left in the country. Back in their heyday, Omega National Products used to have twenty-five female employees, each one cranking out twenty-five of the glittery spheres per day. "We always had music going and we all got along. It was a fun time." In the 1970s and '80s, while folks were getting down to the Bee Gees on the dance floor, Omega National Products often sold thousands of glitter balls each week. China soon began offering stiff competition, though, selling their products at a fraction of the price. Nowadays, Yolanda might make six or seven per week, when the demand was high. But she still loved her job.

When asked about the quality of the competition's glitter balls, she rolled her eyes. "Theirs don't give off the light like ours do. They're cheap and don't last for long." She scoffed, pausing for a moment to examine her handiwork. "They don't sand the glass properly so there are rough edges. The tiles often have sloppy gaps, and they use a cheaper core, often foam." Her voice dripped with contempt. "And Studio 54 didn't have Chinese disco balls hanging over the dance floors, did they?"

"I guess not." Chuckling, I followed her back to her work space.

"It was a Kentuckian—back in 1917, I believe—who first got credit for inventing something known as a *myriad reflector*. Louis Bernard Woeste of Newport. His wasn't the first mirrored ball ever, but Woeste claimed it with an official patent." She slathered some glue on the aluminum orb in front of her and picked up a strip of mirrored squares. "But I will tell you one thing. In Louisville, they are proud of their glitter balls."

I smiled, watching her lay several of the strips with ease. Seeing her dexterity, it became apparent how she could finish a smaller project in half an hour. "Here, want to try?" She held out a length of the mirrors for me to take.

"Sure." I hesitated. "But I don't want to mess up your work."

"Don't worry about it. Just give it a try."

I took the mirrors and tentatively laid them in a row, picking up where Yolanda had left off. I had to make an adjustment here and there, but there was a satisfying feeling as the small tiles settled into the adhesive and found their places, joining the ranks of hundreds before them. And thousands and so many millions before them. And hopefully, the billions and trillions yet to come. Around and around, they went, sparkling, glittering, turning, and making light.

"Nice." Yolanda smiled and patted me on the back. "Now I know who to call if I ever get fired."

"Ha, I think your job is pretty safe. They don't call you the Reigning Queen of Disco Balls for nothing."

She completed the project she was working on and I thanked her and left.

A text pinged on my phone as I walked to the car. It was Carrie.

"Are we going to be dainty tomorrow?" she wanted to know. I answered yes, of course, we would be dainty and I offered to pick her up. "Thank you," she responded. "That's very dainty of you. I'll just meet you there."

Before I headed home, I drove through Cave Hill Cemetery to enjoy the summer foliage. A reporter friend stood with a camera crew in front of the rather modest grave of Colonel Harlan Sanders. She waved me over and we chatted for a bit. They were working on a documentary about the faces behind well-known food brands across the country. Unlike Betty Crocker and Dr. Pepper, the founder of Kentucky Fried Chicken was a real person, as was Kentuckian and pioneering restaurant reviewer Duncan Hines, most famous for his cake mixes.

"So how's the book coming along?" She unclipped the lavalier microphone from her lapel and handed it to her cameraman.

"Slow going," I said. We began walking in the direction of her news van. "It's hard when the accused won't talk to you. I've heard a lot *about* them, but nothing *from* them. I want their sides of the story now that the trials have concluded."

"You know, I've been in contact with Joey Banis. He still hasn't changed his story and seems so earnest and believable when you talk to him." She opened the passenger side door and grabbed her handbag. "Mundt won't talk. After ABC in Chicago did that story about him getting away with murder, some of us went back and looked at things. Something fishy is going on."

"You think so?"

"Definitely. Lots of missing files and documents and the FBI has things they won't let anyone see."

"Yeah, I heard about that."

"And then our station manager all of a sudden killed the story two days before it was set to air. It was a bombshell. We interviewed an acquaintance of Mundt's who said he knew for a fact Mundt had worked for the CIA."

"Seriously?"

"Yep, and then the guy drops off the face of the planet. No idea what's going on with him."

The cameraman suddenly slammed the back door and rushed to the driver's side. "Hey, there's a fire on Whiskey Row. We need to get down there," he yelled as he hopped in started the engine.

"Gotta go. Talk to you later." She jumped into her seat and waved as the van pulled away.


On the way out of the cemetery, I passed a grave that hearkened back to the story of Lady Ross, just one among a substantial number of Louisvillians to achieve regal status through marriage. Two of whom now resided in Cave Hill.

In 1912, the *New York Times* reported that the heirs had settled the six-million-dollar estate of the late Baroness von Zedtwitz, "formerly Miss Mary Elizabeth Caldwell of Louisville," whose sister, Mary

Gwendolyn, the Marquis Monstiers-Merinville, had also prospered in the marriage market. When they died, their bodies were brought back for internment at Cave Hill Cemetery, where they lay entombed in a regal mausoleum adorned with a sculpture of two women in flowing Grecian-style tunics holding hands.

After admiring their tomb, I ran several errands and picked up some items for the gathering planned for that evening. Before long, I was giddily rushing up the front steps with my purchases, looking forward to seeing my friends and enjoying the elusive bourbon hiding out in my liquor cabinet. Juggling the keys and the mail, I unlocked the front door and let myself in.

In the foyer, I puzzled at a spray of white flakes on the Oriental rug, but I became distracted by the sound of the loud bathroom fans whirring away upstairs. Peering up the stairwell, I saw that all the lights were on. I was sure they had been off when I left earlier that morning.

When I walked through the dining room and into the kitchen I found drawers pulled out. Had Ramon come back from work while I was out?

That's when I realized that something wasn't quite right.

I hastily put down the groceries. On the other side of the foyer, I found part of the jamb from the front door lying on the Oriental carpet in the living room. When I looked back and saw the missing wood from the doorframe, I understood why the white flakes lay on the rug.

Someone had kicked in the front door.

As the realization sank in, panic rose in my throat, and I rushed from room to room. A cold brick of nausea settled in the pit of my stomach.

The entire house had been ransacked.

# 36

## IT'S A DAINTY THING

HAUCK'S HANDY Store stood at the corner of Goss and Hoertz avenues at the edge of the working-class Schnitzelburg neighborhood. At the front of the two-story frame building, no less than three different signs proudly validated the store's existence "since 1912" while the most dramatic of the signs, a huge red, white, and blue neon affair, also hawked "cold beer and lunch meat to go."

Over the street arched a fat snake of red, white, and blue balloons, under which a large cloth banner welcomed visitors to the "World Championship Dainty Contest," though most people in the world had no clue what a dainty contest was. Actually, most people in Louisville had no clue what a dainty contest was. But since 1971, it had been a Schnitzelburg tradition.

At the intersection, excited attendees buzzed around and greeted friends, many of them with cigarettes dangling from their bottom lips and almost all of them clutching cans of cheap beer. In front of the store, in a folding chair, sat old Mr. Hauck, who had started the festival as a way of making money for the Little Sisters of the Poor. Every now and then, he would tip his WWII veteran's hat at a passerby and call out a greeting.

Two lines of people had formed near the entrance of the store, one for those waiting to buy tickets from the Kentucky Lottery truck parked on the street, the other for those anxious to get a "dainty meal" before they ran out. Although something of an obscure neighborhood festival, "the Dainty" had gained in popularity with attendance increasing dramatically over the past few years. Therefore, dainty meals—consisting of a thick-cut baloney sandwich on white bread with a bag of chips and a huge dill pickle on the side, all for just one dollar—tended to go fast.

I had texted Carrie that I would pick up her dainty meal—and a Bud—and meet her near the historical marker at the side of the store. Bluegrass music lilting from a radio in the store's window, I maneuvered around an old man in lederhosen holding a pinwheel and found Carrie hemmed in by the crowd at the sidelines. The mayor had just arrived and the opening ceremonies had commenced. At five o'clock, local politicians would compete and then a half hour later the official world championships would begin. They expected about two hundred competitors this year, a city dignitary remarked over a crackling loudspeaker.

Carrie waved when she saw me laboriously working my way up stream, cutting between a pair of wizened old nuns and a family dressed as hillbillies. "Thank you," she said, when I handed her the beer and sandwich. "That was so dainty of you." Smiling, she cracked open the can and took a sip. She wore a straw hat and a floral print sundress.

"You're so welcome. My, don't you look dainty today."

"Why, thank you. I feel dainty."

We both started to laugh then. Meeting at the Dainty Festival had become an annual tradition for us, and each year we found ourselves trying to incorporate the word *dainty* more and more into our conversation.

Suddenly her look changed to one of earnestness. "OK, but seriously, let's drop the dainty stuff for a bit," she said. "What happened yesterday? Did they find out who broke in?"

"Nothing so far." I shrugged my shoulders and opened my beer.

"Oh my god, that's so scary. What happened?" She bit into her baloney sandwich and looked at me expectantly.

"As soon as I realized that someone had been in the house, I called the police and they told me to immediately vacate the premises in case the criminals were still on site and to wait out on the street." Two officers had arrived within minutes and, guns drawn, they established that the house was empty. A plainclothes detective soon followed and they asked what had been stolen. If they weren't looking for money and valuables, he informed me, they were probably looking for drugs or guns.

"But as far as I could tell, nothing was missing." I sipped my beer and shrugged my shoulders.

"Seriously?" Carrie widened her eyes. "That's totally crazy."

"And the crooks went through the entire house." In the upstairs bedrooms, they had dumped out dresser drawers and the night tables, leaving valuable watches behind. They had been in the cabinets and medicine chests in the bathrooms as well, where there were prescription drugs, including two full bottles of hydrocodone that I never used after a recent surgery, but they didn't take any of that, either. In the Magic Library, a stack of cash rested on a bookshelf because I had forgotten to deposit it that morning. Open laptops and iPads still lay out in plain sight as well.

"Strange. I don't see anything missing." I had scratched my head as I reported back to the detective.

"Are you sure?" The gray-haired man narrowed his eyes. "It looks like they've been through the whole house. Did you check everything?"

"Yes, I looked all over—" But I stopped short when my gaze drifted across the living room, coming to land on the large antique wardrobe. The massive front was closed so I hadn't even thought to look inside.

In my ears, my pulse began to race frantically. Without a word, I walked over and took a deep breath before I opened the creaky doors to take stock of the contents of my liquor cabinet. When I beheld the bare marble countertop, my heart sank.

I groaned.

"What is it?" The detective, walking up behind me, peered inside.

I closed my eyes and heaved an enormous sigh. "You have got to be kidding me." In a world-weary tone, I punctuated each syllable as I spoke.

"Something missing after all?"

All the wine bottles were still in their places, as were all the other bourbons—except for one. "Yes. My bottle of Pappy." I opened my eyes and rubbed my forehead.

"Ouch." The detective jotted down a quick note on a small pad of paper. Suddenly, he jerked his head up. "Wait. Which one?"

At that, the patrolman standing nearby rushed over and examined the liquor cabinet. His partner joined him and they both turned to look at me. "Pappy?" one of them said. "You didn't have a bottle of the—?"

Without a word, I winced and nodded my head once, ever so slowly.

"Not the twenty-three-year-old." The other officer gasped.

"Man, you better sit down," the detective said. "You look like you're going to faint."

Carrie guffawed when I finished the story, but then she caught herself. "Sorry, but it is kind of hysterical. That is so Kentucky, isn't it?"

"Yeah, tell me about it." I gave a half-hearted laugh. "You know, it really is funny because the only other time I ever had a break-in was at the old house on Third Street—and guess what they took?"

"Seriously? A bottle of bourbon?"

"My friend Wendy had just left a huge bottle of Maker's Mark on the kitchen table. While we were around the corner for a poetry reading by Ron Whitehead at the Rudyard Kipling, some crackhead got in the back door and stole her bourbon. Fortunately, the perpetrator was thoughtful enough to shut the back door as he left, to make sure our dogs didn't get out."

"Well, that was very dainty of him, wasn't it?" Carrie polished off the last of sandwich and started in on the pickle. "But you don't really think they burgled your house just for a bottle of bourbon, do you?"

"It wasn't just any bottle of bourbon, though. It was the Pappy Van Winkle twenty-three-year-old."

"Yeah, but how did they know? You hadn't really advertised it or anything."

"No, except for a few friends nobody knew. Maybe the burglars were just your average street thugs with a discerning whiskey palate."

"Maybe, but it seems a bit fishy to me."

"Well . . ." I hesitated and took a sip of beer. "I stopped over at Bob and Eva Wessels for a bourbon on the way here—you know them, the owners of the Inn at Central Park on Fourth Street—and Bob, who's a former cop, said the same thing. Suspicious. He told me to have the place swept for bugs."

"Are you kidding me?" Carrie stopped gnawing on the dill to stare.

"It seems like everybody's getting skittish about the CIA, maybe that's why." I popped a potato chip into my mouth and chased it with a gulp of beer. "I think I'll call Jon Lesher and see if he knows anything."

Just then a roar went up from the crowd. The starting contestant had missed his dainty on the first try but on the second try, the bobbin was launched an admirable distance. As with baseball, dainty allowed for three strikes before moving on to the next hitter. At the end of the competition, the person who hit it the farthest down George Hauck Way would win a trophy and a prize; the person with the shortest distance would get a basket of lemons.

"So, did you say your friend Kelly the Courtly Gentleman was going to show up?" Carrie turned her head and scanned the crowd. Across the way, in lawn chairs, sat the beneficiaries of the event, two rows of ancient nuns in blindingly white habits.

"He tried to convince me to compete this year, but I haven't heard anything from him. I thought he might still try."

"I hope he doesn't show up in Nazi attire if he does." Carrie laughed and ate a potato chip.

I cringed and shook my head. "So, you said you had found out something about Dr. Stanley Bandeen, the guy who had the sanitorium at 1435?"

"Yeah, he actually joined Dr. Evelyn Bush there, and she was quite a pioneer in the field. She became an osteopath to help her son, which she did. But Bandeen kind of sullied her good name and was probably the reason they went bankrupt and parted ways. Let's say he didn't have very good bedside manners."

"Why? What happened?"

"Well, there were rumors about him before, but when he went on and started practicing on his own, they started noticing significant numbers of people dying under his care. He had been promising to cure people of cancer and other ailments with this miracle drug called glyoxylide, but it was just snake oil and most of the people coming to him weren't cured at all." Carrie paused for a sip of beer. "They were suffering and dying. And the thing is, it sounds like he had no empathy at all for his patients. He was kind of sadistic and relished telling people they were going to die."

"Did he kill anyone outright like the rumors say?"

"Well, I didn't find any proof of that, but there were lots of complaints against him and allegations that he had killed at least two people. In the end, he was brought up on ethics charges and ruined, largely because he was grossly overcharging his patients."

"In any case, it sounds like a lot of people could have died in that house. No wonder it acquired such a creepy reputation."

A friend, Catherine Kiely, made her way through the sea of people and joined us. "Hey, how's it going?" she said, giving us each a hug.

"Well, you don't look very dainty." I chastised her. "Where's your dainty meal?"

"I haven't had a chance to get one yet." She laughed and turned her head as another roar went up from the crowd. The fifteenth contestant had hit her dainty and taken an impressive lead.

"Well, hang tight," I said, breaking away from them. "We need more beers anyway, so I'll grab you one."

I wended through the throng, greeting friends and acquaintances as I passed, and finally made it to the line when another huge roar went up from the crowd. Someone must have taken over the lead. Another wave of noise surged through the crowd; that's when a man with a mullet and a sleeveless black T-shirt materialized in front of me. An angry scowl painted on his face, he seemed to zero in on me, but I assumed his wrath was directed at someone behind me.

That was, until he shouldered me roughly in passing and disappeared into the mass of people. But before the crowd swallowed him up, he hissed something. "Joey sent you a message yesterday, dickhead, so knock it off if you don't want things to get worse."

# 37

# THE WITCHES' TREE

PLEASE & Thank You, in the trendy NuLu part of Louisville, claimed to have the "best chocolate chip cookie" ever. Their egg sandwiches weren't bad either, so I ordered one of each and nursed a large americano while I waited near the front window of the hipster record and coffee shop. At a table outside, Mark Anthony Mulligan hunched over a piece of posterboard, squiggling a large black marker across a kaleidoscope of vibrant shapes as he hummed. I couldn't see very well, but it looked like he was drawing a tree.

Across the street sat a collection of brick and limestone row buildings that housed an assortment of bars, restaurants, and specialty shops. This was East Market Street, which silent film legend D.W. Griffith had once called home. Born in 1875 in La Grange, Griffith had moved into town to help his family operate a boarding house and he spent his early years working at a bookstore across the street at 805 East Market. In 1907, Griffith moved to California to pursue a movie career, becoming best known for his 1915 film *Birth of a Nation*, one of the most controversial motion pictures ever because of its sympathetic portrayal of the Ku Klux Klan.

At my table, I leafed through a recent edition of the *Courier-Journal* and found the KKK mentioned several times. A Tennessee man had been convicted of a cross-burning, and alleged ties to white supremacists were causing problems for a state senator. In northern Kentucky, a racist U.S. Senate candidate had admitted to putting up signs telling voters "With Jews You Lose."

On a different page, a photographic retrospective examined different periods in Louisville's history. One photo showed a stylishly dressed Black couple walking down the sidewalk, looking uneasy as two berobed men passed them. The caption read: "In June of 1967, Ku Klux Klan members from Indianapolis made their presence known on Fourth Street in downtown Louisville." At that time, Fourth Street was the thriving commercial corridor and theater district of the city.

I finished the last of my sandwich and checked my watch. Detective Lesher was running late, so I grabbed another newspaper. One article examined the history of exclusionary housing in the city, referring to a well-known book by George C. Wright—*Life Behind a Veil: Blacks in Louisville, Kentucky, 1865–1930*. Wright explored the complex history of race relations in the Derby City, where though "spared the lynchings of other cities in the deep south," Blacks still suffered.

In the 1880s, Moses Fleetwood Walker, the only Black player on a visiting Ohio team, created an uproar when Louisville fans protested the presence of a "Negro" on the all-white pitch. Enraged home-team fans hurled items from their perches and continuous threats distracted the otherwise talented player.

Then there was the notorious Lieutenant Kinnarny, a rogue policeman known for shooting Black Louisvillians first and asking questions later. Confronted as to why, he would simply explain that they were "acting suspicious."

John Lesher came walking down the sidewalk and he stopped to talk to Mark Anthony, who gestured animatedly at his current project. A minute later, the detective materialized in the doorway and waved. While he ordered at the counter, I endeavored to finish the article, which gave an interesting overview of *Buchanan v. Warley*, the Supreme Court case that would codify racist housing policies in America after Louisville passed an ordinance preventing Blacks from moving onto any predominantly white city block in 1914.

Lesher joined me, setting down his hot drink. I folded the paper and made room.

"That Mark Anthony Mulligan is something else," he said. "He just made up a song for me and told me about all the picture he's drawing. He's got talent."

"Was he drawing a tree?"

"Yeah. Said it was a 'god tree' or something like that. To scare bad things away." Lesher took a drink and then smiled. "So, what's up, man?" he said.

"Not much. I see you got your glasses on today."

He laughed. "Yeah, I've got to be on the stand in two hours, so I put them on to make sure I don't forget." He had several cookies and he took a bite out of one. Using the cookie, he pointed at the large color mugshot on the front page of the paper I had just set aside.

"Oh, that jackass is a real charmer, isn't he? I guess he literally wanted to have his girlfriend for dinner," said Lesher. "Geesh, and I thought we had all the freaks over on this side of the river."

Across the river in Jeffersonville, Indiana, police had arrested Joseph Oberhansley for murdering his girlfriend, Tammy Jo Blanton. Her body had blunt force trauma and at least twenty-five sharp force injuries and parts had been cannibalized. Evidence clearly pinpointed him as the perpetrator but the suspect insisted that "two black guys" had done it.

"So thanks for meeting me again," I said. "I assume there's no word on my Pappy?"

"Sorry, man. I'd say it's probably sold or drunk already." Jon Lesher shook his head and chuckled. "I'm from back east, you know, and I've never seen anyone as obsessed with whiskey as they are here in Louisville."

"Well, this is Kentucky after all." I let a beat pass while he finished another cookie. "So, do you think there's anything to that numbskull's threat?"

Lesher looked up as a serious look washed over. "Dude, now there could be something to that." After a sip from his drink, he quickly resumed. "That bastard Joey is a real prick behind bars. He has some influence in the outside world so he could very well have sent someone to give you a message. He had Jeffrey roughed up a couple times." Lesher shook his head. "Or else, he might just be trying to take credit for it—that's the kind of jerk he is. Did anyone know about the break-in?"

"Yeah, I posted about it on Facebook. I didn't mention the bourbon, though."

Lesher grunted. "Well, if Joey somehow saw that, he might just be acting like he had it done to intimidate you. You know, just taking credit for it. I told you, those were some evil dudes. And Banis takes the cake." The detective took a moment to answer a text but then got back on topic. "I told you this before, but we get lots of calls, right? And the amount of calls we got about Joey? It's insane. All the guys who said he tried to infect them with HIV. And people he coerced into smuggling drugs into the prison for him. It's like he's Charles Manson and has this hypnotic control over some people."

"Yeah, I've heard some crazy stories about him."

"And you know his own father warned his friends to stay away from him because he was evil? When your own parents think you're evil, man, you've got to be pretty shitty." He stopped and pointed his last cookie at me. "And you know he was a neat freak? Like really germophobic. Loved to clean."

"You know, I've been going back and reviewing the trial tapes. Am I understanding correctly that they didn't find much blood evidence at the murder site?"

"Case in point!" crowed Lesher. "Jamie Carroll was stabbed numerous times, shot point-blank in the back of the head, and then there was all this broken glass, and comparatively speaking, they found none of his blood. Joey had to do some good scrubbing."

I sipped on my coffee. "You still think both of them did it?"

"Yep. They were a team." Lesher swallowed, sat back in his chair, and crossed his arms. "They talk to you yet?"

"Nope. I still keep trying, though. There's so much about the case that doesn't make sense to me."

"Who knows why people do what they do? When it comes to criminals, they're usually not wired right." The detective shrugged. "You know, the other freak's out now. Parole's up and he is a free man. Only did half his time. That sociopath is out there walking amongst us."

"Jeffrey's out?"

"Jeffrey Stephen Mundt. The one and the same. Word on the street is he's changing his name and moving to Europe." Lesher raised his eyebrows at me. "Who knows what trouble that freak will get into over there. We'll probably see him on the news somewhere down the road. Probably in a rubber suit." The detective snorted. "Maybe he's in Germany. You know one of his kinky handles on the interwebs was 'Gummiklaus.' 'Rubber Klaus' in German. Jesus."

"That's another thing. Weren't there supposedly all these texts found on Jeffrey's phone, like hundreds of them in German and Russian that they never had translated or something?"

"I can't say anything about that." The detective paused to give me a knowing look. "But, let's meet again in a couple of weeks. I might have some interesting information regarding the CIA stuff." He wiped his hands together to rid them of cookie crumbs and arched an eyebrow.

Later that evening, while driving back from a party in Old Louisville, I discovered Margie Cook's red silk pouch in the glove box. I had forgotten about her gift for the Witches' Tree, which was just a few blocks away, so I headed to the corner of Sixth and Park.

A bit of early fall chill hung in the air as several bright stars twinkled overhead. I left the car across the street, next to a high brick wall. It enclosed part of the property belonging to a large house on the corner, which for years had served as a Catholic-run home for unwed mothers. Most recently, a day care had operated there. Creepy nuns, creepy kids. Stories abounded about that place.

Heralding the midnight hour, a perfect full moon sat high in the sky over the craggy canopy of the Witches' Tree. According to legend, witches used to meet at a lovely maple tree on this corner but things began to run afoul when locals decided to fell the beautiful tree. May Day was fast approaching and they wanted it for a May pole. Against the witches' warnings, they chopped the tree down and proceeded with their festivities, but not before the crones fled the area, leaving a curse in their wake. "Beware eleventh month!" warned the head witch as she screeched out of sight.

The curse came to fruition exactly eleven months later—in the form of the "storm demon," a massive tornado that destroyed much of Louisville on March 27, 1890, and killed more than one hundred people. When the twister arrived at the empty corner, a bolt of lightning shot out and hit the old stump and a huge explosion resounded. A new tree sprang up in a shower of smoke, flame, and sparks. The gnarled and twisted replacement that arose embodied the dark side of human nature. The witches returned and resumed their nightly rituals, and visitors began to leave offerings at the tree as a way of appeasing the witches.

I crossed and examined the assortment of beads and charms hanging from the lowest branches. On the tortured trunk, people had embedded old coins and trinkets in the crevices, and at its base mounded pumpkins, gourds, and colorful flower bouquets. Random voodoo dolls and chicken bone ornaments dangled here and there as well, a testament to an overlooked voodoo presence in the Bluegrass.

This tree was a supposed hangout of one of Louisiana's most famous voodoo personalities, Doc Beauregard. In his book *Voodoo in New Orleans*, Robert Tallant wrote that "Doctor Beauregard came to New Orleans from Kentucky in the year 1869. He was one of the only foreign Voodoos that came to the city. He was the most amazing in appearance of all the witch doctors because he had long hair that went all the way down to his knees. He also put the hair into a number of strange knots." In this cape of hair, "he carried all of his gris gris, bottles of oil, dried reptiles, small bones, and a hoot owl's head. After scaring some ladies on the street one night, he was arrested for throwing the hoot owl's head at the police and putting curses upon them." After they released him, he most likely returned to Kentucky "looking for new fields."

I opened the silk pouch from Margie and smiled. A golden glitter ball hung from a silver chain. I lifted my head and looked up. Thieves were always taking things off the tree, so I bunched the ball and chain together and I tossed it up, hoping it would snag on a branch too high to reach. By some miracle, it worked on my first attempt, and the glitter ball became suspended about two feet above my head. As it spun and settled on the twirling chain, it caught the light of the nearest streetlamp and cast about a scattering of white diamonds.

I was admiring the ornament when a form slid out from the other side of the tree. "Well, hello, doll."

I jumped back. "What the hell, Candy—"

"Well, whores in hot pants, Nancy Boy, you're just a regular scaredy-cat wherever we meet." She leaned back against the twisted tree trunk, crossed her arms, and smiled.

"Not like you just don't jump out of the shadows when I least expect it."

"Oh, pshaw. Where you been hiding, doll? I've been hoping to run into you for weeks now." She uncrossed her arms and came down to the sidewalk, wearing the same outfit as the first time I saw her.

"Just been busy and haven't had much time lately." I stopped and studied her, saw that a large tote bag hung from a shoulder.

A look of alarm spread across her face, but then it relaxed into a smile. "Yeah, doll. It's the same getup as our first meeting. Can't deny it. It's my favorite."

"Like I said, it's a nice ensemble. How've you been?"

"Not too bad," she said. "I went to the neighborhood meeting earlier and that was a mistake." She turned and gestured in the direction of the information center building in the park. "I can't take those damn meetings more than once a year. God, they love to hear themselves talk over there. What a bunch of bores."

"Ha. That's one of the things I do not miss about Old Louisville."

"Herb Fink went on and on about the Park and then tonight there was some piano-playing ninny from over on Ormsby who had a fit and stormed out because of the rehab of that building at the corner of Third and Oak. Leah Stewart brought a cake but nobody could eat it because it was so dry. She fancies herself a gourmet baker." Candy rolled her eyes. "And that new director of the visitors center? What a nattering, neurotic chipmunk." Candy took out her cigarette case, opened it, then stowed it without taking out a smoke. "Debra Richards was on the warpath again as well."

I chuckled. "Well, at least you've done your neighborhoodly duty for the year."

"God, I was ready to shoot myself in the head. So I snuck out early. Went home and waited for the old banshee to take her melatonin. Then I raided her closet to release some stress. Been walking the streets ever since." Candy inhaled and gazed contentedly at the moon.

My eyes joined hers and we watched as a low-flying UPS plane cut across the mottled surface of the enormous moon.

"God, this neighborhood. Bunch of backstabbers and bitches," she sighed, turning to look at me. "But you really love it, don't you?"

"I guess so. Not sure why, though. Probably all the old houses, the interesting people."

Candy scoffed. "People are awful. Why do they do the things they do?"

"Who knows?" I hunched my shoulders and smiled.

"Hey, before I forget. I've been carrying this around forever." Candy removed the tote from her shoulder, reached inside, and handed me a plastic document holder. "This is what I was telling you about. You can have it."

My eyes lit up as I extracted the first item, an old copy of the original 1917 patent for the myriad reflector, number 1,214,863, granted to L.B. Woeste. "Oh, wow, this is great." After examining it, I took out the other item. It appeared to be an old sales prospectus for "the Myriad Reflector, the World's Most Novel Lighting Effect, for Ballrooms-Night Clubs-Dance Pavilions-Skating Rinks." Tattered at the edges, the delicate cover sported an image of an early glitter ball set against vibrant shades of bright yellow and electric blue. On the inside, the merchandising pitch read: "The newest novelty is one that will change a hall into a brilliant fairyland of flashing, changing, living colors—a place of a million colored sparks, darting and dancing, chasing one another into every nook and corner—filling the hall with dancing fireflies of a thousand hues." When I looked up, Margie's little glitter ball turned in the slight breeze and began throwing sparkles, as if to illustrate the description personally.

"Wow, this was so thoughtful of you." I choked back a lump in my throat.

"Thought you'd get a kick out of that, Nancy Boy."

A cool breeze rustled a heap of dead leaves nearby, but a warm feeling washed over me as I returned the items to the plastic cover. "Seriously, thanks. I love it."

Candy returned the tote bag to her shoulder and coughed. "You know, maybe we need a Glitter Ball Tree down here, now that the Witches' Tree is so popular. A landmark where people can come and leave disco balls. Big balls, little balls, balls of all sizes."

"Ha, that last bit sounds like something that would look good on a T-shirt."

"Don't ever say Candy's not a clever girl." She turned and looked pensively off into the park. "You know, maybe a tree with glitter balls isn't the way to go. We've already got a famous tree down here. What about someplace else people can come and leave disco balls? Like those chain-link fences around the tennis courts in the park?" Her eyes lit up. "How's about a Glitter Ball Wall?"

"Sounds like a good idea to me." Off in the distance, the *whock-whock* of volleyed tennis balls punctuated the autumn breezes. "You know, if you build it, they will come. Are you going to be the one to start leaving them there?"

"I just might have to do that, doll." Candy smiled, then yawned. "Whores in hot pants, that meeting really wore me out. I'll be seeing you around soon enough." She started to go, but then turned back. "Hurry up and finish that book, by the way. Can't wait to read it. And remember our little deal, doll."

"Thanks. I'm trying—and don't worry."

Candy waved goodbye and crossed the street, but before she disappeared around the corner, she turned one last time. "Don't forget to check out that club on Sixth. It's right down the street." She raised her hand again and then faded from view, heading in the direction of the tennis courts.

My phone pinged just then and I found a message from Margie. All it said was *Thanks!*

I chuckled and gave Margie's disco ball one final look. I had no intention of going to the S&M club, so I crossed the street and hopped in the car. As I started the engine, a call from someone with an unidentified number came through. Normally, I would have ignored the call, but it was after midnight, and I wondered if it was something important. "Hello?" I said.

"If you want some good information about the Jamie Carroll murder, come to this address. Now."

# 38

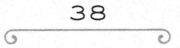

# CABARET OBSCURA

I HELD the phone out in front of me and stared at the screen. After the raspy voice uttered those words, the caller had hung up. Two seconds later, a text message popped up with an address located on Sixth Street.

I pulled away from the curb and drove down Sixth, all the while telling myself not to go to the address. Nonetheless, several minutes later I found myself parked across the street from a three-story Italianate brick house on one of the blocks in the no-man's-land where Old Louisville petered out into the Limerick District and the downtown area. All the windows of the neighboring structures were black and all but one lone streetlight at the end of the block had gone dark. However, at the house number indicated, a strobe light flashed through cracks in a pair of wooden shutters drawn over a large window next to the front door.

"Don't do it," I mumbled again under my breath.

Just then, another text popped up, this time from Ramon, wondering where I was.

*Interviewing someone for the book*, I texted back.

I waited for his response, keeping my eye on the house, but a minute passed, and then another without a reply. Finally, the phone chirped. *Biggest hobo ever*, he concluded.

Across the street, a dark form emerged from the shadows in the narrow space between the Italianate house and its neighbor. Zipping up his coat, a tall man put his head down against the wind and started walking back into Old Louisville.

"Don't do it." I said it out loud this time, but before I knew it, I had exited the car and was approaching the front of the house.

I knocked softly at the main door, but nobody opened it; from the walkway, the faint pounding of a bass beat vibrated the soles of my feet.

At the side of the structure where the man had emerged, a dim light beckoned, so I followed it around to a narrow wooden door near the back of the building. The entrance had been painted black and had exaggerated, medieval-looking hinges and a small window at the top. As soon as I stopped, a panel slid to the side and a large white face with severe eyebrows and Goth bangs peered out at me. How did they know I was there? That's when I saw the camera peering down at me from a mount on the second floor.

"Password?" asked the face in the door.

"Password?" I repeated. The speaker's disconcertingly white eyes had distracted me.

"Yes, password."

My brow knit in confusion. "Like a passcode or something?"

"Call it whatever you want, but you need the magic phrase to get in."

I was confused. Magic phrase? "Uh . . ."

The attendant snarled and eyed me with disdain.

But all of a sudden, realization set in. How had I been so dense? I lurched forward and whispered. "Whores in hotpants?"

The little window slid shut and the big door swung inward with a creak.

The door remained open, concealing the attendant behind it. I entered. The only way to proceed was down a long hallway that emptied into a large room with a violent strobe light. The flashes revealed walls taken down to the studs and two boarded-up windows over a bank of metal lockers. An accordion gate prevented me from taking the stairs up, so the only way to continue was down a set of steps, where the thrumming bass seemed to be getting louder. The wooden stairs and the entire passage had been painted black and at the bottom a red light bulb glowed in a wall sconce next to a huge gold crucifix. A rhythmic slashing sound—that I prayed was not coming from a whip—echoed somewhere in the distance.

Gingerly, I made my way down and stepped onto a floor made of hard-packed earth. In a corner clustered a gaggle of leather-clad individuals occupied with something I couldn't—and probably didn't want to—see.

I immediately sensed I wasn't dressed for the occasion with my jeans, tennis shoes, and windbreaker. A wagon wheel chandelier with lit candles hung from the ceiling and against the far wall stood a crudely constructed bar, behind which stood a male bartender in leather chaps and a harness. He smiled and held up a bottle of bourbon by way of greeting and waved me over. When I saw it wasn't Pappy Van Winkle I timidly waved back and headed for the nearest door.

The next room had hardly any light but I discerned the vague form of somebody blindfolded and tied to a wooden bedframe. Two motionless leather-clad males in director's chairs stared at her and didn't say a word. But then they started groaning in unison, though they remained stock still, and then the woman on the bed began barking, so I decided to leave through the other door, a brick archway with a fuzzy green light on the other side.

But as I approached that doorway, a somewhat familiar voice cut through the moaning behind me. "So exquisite. Yes, simply exquisite, my darlings." I cocked my head and listened. It was coming from the green fuzzy light room. "So exquisite. Yes, simply exquisite, my darlings."

I was kind of afraid to find out what was so exquisite, but that was the only way out, so I held my breath and entered the next space. I was immediately comforted by the sight of a large glitter ball hanging at one end of the room but I stopped dead in my tracks when I saw where the proclamations of exquisiteness came from.

A man encased in a leather cocoon had been hoisted up and hung from a ceiling joist in the corner. Two large drag queens—one in a tight pink leather unitard, the other in green—attended to the man, alternately poking and stroking him with riding crops. Every time they prodded him, he'd exclaim, "So exquisite. Yes, simply exquisite, my darlings." It was the seersucker man with the book from Dale and Bill's gala fundraiser on Third Street. And he was with the two chatty drag queens.

Just then, the one in pink turned and saw me. "Hey, Mr. Writer Friend!" she trilled. "So nice to see you! Come on over here and give us a hand, would you?"

"Well, toodle to the loo, Mr. Author Man, if it ain't a small world!" The one in green waggled her riding crop at me. "I knew we'd see you here sooner or later."

"Aw, shit," I muttered. "I really gotta get out of here now."

"You know, the quiet ones are always the kinkiest," confided the pink leather drag queen to her friend.

"Hey, you and I should write a book together," said the man in the cocoon.

"You, hush up! Mamma didn't give you permission to speak," scolded the green leather drag queen. "You dirty little pissant." She raised her riding crop in warning.

"So exquisite. Yes, simply exquisite, my darlings." The man in the leather papoose groaned in ecstasy.

I took a few hesitant steps in their direction and lowered my voice. "So, sorry to interrupt, but could you just point me to the easiest way out of here?" I stretched and feigned a yawn. "Kinda late and I'm new here."

The one in pink aimed her riding crop at a metal spiral staircase in the corner. "That's the only way out, honey pot. You gotta make your way up to the attic and then work your way down to get out."

"Oh, you mean there's more?" I tried to hide a crestfallen look.

"Oh, silly pie, the best is yet to come."

"So exquisite. Yes, simply exquisite, my darlings! More, more, more!"

"You mean there are no shortcuts?"

"Why would you want to take a shortcut?" The one in green was about to land a blow on Cocoon Man, but she stopped in midair. "My you're a strange one, aren't you?"

"Mamma?" whimpered the man.

"Silence, you little bitch!" The green drag queen bellowed and aimed her riding crop at the man's crotch. "You want me to report you to the Witch Bitch and have her come and take care of you herself?"

The man in the leather papoose started moaning and howling, his head ecstatically writhing back and forth.

"Thanks, gotta go," I said. "I'll be seeing you around the neighborhood!" I grabbed the railing and started up the spiral staircase.

\* \* \*

A half hour later, I was installed on a stool at the bar in Kelly's basement. Kelly lived at the top of Joe Creason Park; I lived at the bottom of Joe Creason Park. He had poured us both a measure of Pappy Van Winkle fifteen-year-old, saying "Late-night visits call for the good stuff." Andrew Lloyd Webber played in the background and we both wore hats. Viking for me, coonskin for him.

"Man, I'm glad your lights were still on. I had to go somewhere after being in that place."

"Glad you stopped by. You know I'm always up late, brother. I was just catching up on the paranormal news." He turned his laptop in my direction, so I could see an article with a photo of an old iron train trestle. "You hear the Goat Man killed another dumb kid?" Also known as the Pope Lick Monster, this was a siren-like half-man, half-goat creature rumored to live under the Norfolk Southern Railroad trestle across Pope Lick Creek in the Fisherville part of town.

Generations of Louisvillians grew up with the story of how the hairy, hooved being hypnotized trespassers into venturing out onto the narrow trestle, hastening their deaths before an oncoming train. Every couple of years somebody died or sustained serious injuries on the tracks.

I swallowed a bit of bourbon. "No matter how many fences or no-trespassing signs they put up, kids are still going to find a way to get up there. It's a shame."

Kelly closed his laptop and nodded. "So, you found one of the secret S&M clubs? How was it?"

I closed my eyes and moved my head back and forth. "The things I saw."

"I wonder if that was my high school buddy's place. I heard after the basement on Fourth Street, he kept up with the S&M but expanded and moved on to bigger and better digs."

"Well, this place was big alright. The cellar had three rooms that I could see, but to get out, you had to go all the way up a twisting staircase to the top floor and work your way down through three different chambers of horrors." A sigh escaped my lips. "I saw so many things I can't unsee."

"You didn't have any fun at all?

"Fun? I had to crawl through a cage." I shot him an incredulous glare. "Somebody wearing a carved pumpkin on his head touched me. He kept saying, 'Happy Halloweeny, dude!' Someone I teach with was there. Glad he was too busy with the orange traffic cone to notice me," I added under my breath. "There was a news anchorwoman getting spanked on a sawhorse."

"Hey. You didn't see a broad in a cage sitting on a little purple footstool, did you? Wearing nothing but a ball gag and waving at everyone who passed by?"

"Yes, I did! She was in a big bird cage at the exit. Someone said they called her Tweety."

"Well, hot damn!" Kelly clapped his hands together and crowed. "She's still around, god love her."

"But she looked like she had to be at least eighty years old!" I raked my hand through my hair.

"Hubba, hubba. Now you're talking my language." Kelly reverted to his W.C. Fields voice.

I hung my head and sighed again. "I've lost my innocence."

"Aw, it ain't that bad, brother. You just broadened your horizons a bit, that's all."

"That broadened my horizons too much. I thought I was going to get some new information about the murder," I moaned. "It was such a strange place. I don't think it was a normal S&M club."

"Why do you say that, Daddy-O?"

"There was something so bizarre about parts of it, almost absurdist. There were two guys in black turtlenecks and berets just sitting at a café table in the corner, talking and smoking. I'm positive they were Gauloises cigarettes."

"Sounds like a French film to me."

I took another swig of bourbon and chuckled. "That Candy. I'm going to kill her the next time I see her. If it was Candy."

"Candy? Is that the neighborhood cross-dresser?" Kelly added another finger of bourbon to our glasses.

"Well, there are lots of them in Old Louisville, but Candy is the only one I see out after dark. She's kind of like me, loves roaming the streets at odd hours." I lifted my glass in a toast and smiled wanly.

"So what else is bothering you? You seem out of sorts tonight, brother."

I shrugged. "I don't know. This whole case has had me out of sorts. I am so worn out. Some of the people in the neighborhood are mad at me."

"Screw 'em." He chugged his bourbon and slammed the glass down hard.

"Jeffrey and Joey won't talk to me."

"Screw them, too," he said, reaching for the bottle of bourbon. "Broke-dick motherfuckers went to school on the little bus."

"It just seems like I'm ending up at dead ends. Nobody knows what really happened the night Jamie Carroll was killed. So much of it just doesn't make sense. Did the juries really get it right? Every time I go back and watch the trials I come to a different conclusion."

"Life doesn't make sense, brother. Don't sweat it." Kelly palmed out a handful of peanuts from a dish on the bar and pushed it in my direction. "Maybe you just need a little inspiration. A change of scenery. Didn't you say you were planning a trip to Savannah?"

"I was thinking about it. I've never been."

"Yeah, take a trip, Daddy-O. It'll do you good."

"You know, I might as well." I stood and finished my bourbon. "Thanks for the boost. Let's do lunch sometime soon. And work on getting a replacement bottle of the twenty-three-year-old."

"Sounds like a plan." Kelly walked me to a small door that lead into the garage and then outside. I glanced at him and his face seemed somewhat sallow. But I didn't say anything. In the driveway, we stood for a moment in the bracing wind and silently gazed up into the star-speckled sky. I said goodbye and before I turned to go, Kelly hugged me. "Take care of yourself now. You know I love you and the Ramon."

He always called Ramon *the Ramon*. I returned the embrace and hugged him fiercely. "You, too." I waved and clicked the fob to unlock my car.

My breath caught when I neared the road and saw the moon hanging low over the trees in Joe Creason Park. It was enormous—three times as big as a couple of hours before—and there wasn't a cloud in sight.

Against the inky blue background of the paling morning sky, the milkiness of the moon's mottled surface shimmered with hypnotic silver iridescence. I felt the sparkle and glitter as a soft beat pounded in my ear. Another strong breeze stirred, and all around, wind-kissed branches rustled their dry leaves in a comforting, sibilant *sshhhhhhh* that I wished would never end.

# EPILOGUE

RAMON AND I stood in front of the large red-brick house at 1435 South Fourth Street. A semi chugged its way by, low-hanging tree branches scraping along the top of the trailer, and I could hear Debra Richards's curses in my head. Fortunately, though, thoughts other than those of destructive traffic patterns and rehab failures had been occupying her of late. She had joined the efforts to have the world's largest glitter ball installed at the gateway to the Highlands, near the intersection of Baxter and Broadway—near Omega National Products and right in front of the main gate to Cave Hill Cemetery. For the time being, however, the Isle of Wight in England would boast having the world's largest one—at over eleven yards in diameter.

"It would take a lot of work, hobo." Ramon sidled up to me. "Are you up for it?"

"I'd be up for it, sure, but it depends on how much it has deteriorated since the last time we looked at it. And you're the hobo who suggested we look at it—again—so don't start complaining."

He shook his head and laughed. "I won't complain." He peered through a window in the front door and rattled the knob. "I can't believe it's all the way down to a hundred nineteen thousand."

"Insane. That's what happens when you're a stigmatized property. Nobody wants to live somewhere somebody committed a grisly murder. Half the neighborhood thinks it's cursed anyway."

"If we don't, I bet someone buys it before too long. Even if you have to put in half a mil to fix it up, it's a steal for a huge house like this."

Down the block, shouts erupted as two women began screaming. One of them flipped off the other and then jumped into a car and sped away, a string of epithets trailing in the air behind her. The other ran after the car for several yards and threw a Colt 45 can at the wind. It landed in the middle of the road and rolled around, spewing its foamy contents on the asphalt.

"Really classy," I was tempted to yell, but the woman looked tougher than me.

A lockbox still hung on the door, but the code had changed. I dialed the new numbers and took out the key. This time, several *Courier-Journal*s had been pushed through the mail slot and lay on the bare hardwood floor. "I wonder why they still keep delivering the paper when nobody lives here anymore." Ramon used his toe to push a newspaper out of the way.

"Maybe the last person had their subscription paid up years in advance?" I looked down to see a headline about Ethan Melzer, a soldier from Louisville who had leaked sensitive information about his unit to the Order of Nine Angels, a satanic neo-Nazi cult in the U.K., to cause "the deaths of as many of his fellow service members as possible." On a different front page, readers were informed that the parents of a teenager killed on the Pope Lick Trestle would be suing the railroad company. And David Camm, the Indiana state trooper, had been exonerated and released after thirteen years in prison.

A story also ran about national uproar over the arrest of Joseph Bennett, a Louisville bystander livestreaming a traffic stop who provoked physical violence from officers when he refused to produce identification. The reporter pointed out that "pedestrians are not required to provide identification to police officers under Kentucky law and there are no laws on record that prevent citizens from filming police interactions in public."

Another article discussed the recent death of Hamza "Travis" Nagdy, struck by multiple bullets during a suspected carjacking near the University of Louisville campus. The bullhorn-wielding twenty-one-year-old had received national recognition as a leader of the Black Lives Matter protests after the shooting of Breonna Taylor.

Ramon stretched his neck and looked up at the coffered ceiling in the foyer. "Not so sure 2020 is a good year to move house, though."

With the COVID closures and the prolonged protests and riots over the police shooting of Breonna Taylor, who lived near the Pleasure Ridge Park part of Louisville, the city had indeed been reeling—and many argued more so than other struggling cities across the nation. To make things worse, copies of the Ku Klux Klan newspaper, *The Crusader*, began appearing on doorsteps around town. The U.K.'s *Daily Mail* blamed it on white supremacists "trying to capitalize on racial tensions." In the middle of all this, Steve Romines began popping up in the news again, this time representing Taylor's boyfriend in a civil suit against the LMPD. "This is the latest in a cycle of police aggression, deflection of responsibility, and obstruction of the facts," he said repeatedly in official statements.

Ramon had a point, but everyone was struggling.

A car had crashed into the front of Little John's and then the shop was looted, but John Tan was still open for business—and there was talk that he was working out the details for his own reality series. He had also shed the pawnshop persona and advanced to custom-designing his own pieces. The cheesy commercials seemed to peter out for a while, but they had just picked back up again recently. Entitled the "Baddest in the 'Ville," the newest spot featured Little John and his twenty-something son standing in front of an opened set of elaborately carved gold doors in a wall of gold bullion, beckoning one and all to "C-c-come to Little John's to buy, sell, trade." In dark slacks and matching dizzily patterned blazers, the duo proceeded to show off the shop's wares, and after a couple of corny dance moves, Little John signed off by proclaiming: "I'm the most baddest buy-sell-trade jeweler!"

St. Martin of Tours had been in the news as well. Late one night, a drug-crazed individual entered the church and began attacking the altar. Quickly responding police officers and the evening guard managed to subdue the individual, but not before he caused thousands of dollars in damage. He tore down the altar canopy, smashed statues, and desecrated a crucifix. The tombs of Saints Magnus and Bonosa were unharmed; however, locals feared that the church would rescind its policy of staying open around the clock. They didn't close, though, the pastor explaining that "we take great pride in the fact that our church is open twenty-four-seven as a place of peace and prayer in a world that certainly seems to need them more and more."

A fire had destroyed a portion of Whiskey Row and for a time preservationists worried developers would just bulldoze the whole site, but in the end they stepped up and saved everything they could. One of the co-founders of Sun Tan City had just snatched up the last building on Whiskey Row and had already started renovation to turn it into restaurants.

However, as Doug Proffitt of WHAS11 news reported, workers once again made some interesting discoveries the deeper down they went. "That's right. Our city in the 1970s had a dark side that ruled the spaces under what is now historic Whiskey Row." They found "dressing rooms . . . and other rooms believed to be used for sex. Near many of the rooms, there was still a lamp post that would shine a red light when the room was in use." They also found a large keg of beer. "In the 1970s, the building's basement appeared to have had connects to the club Latex," said Proffitt, which was "connected with other Whiskey Row buildings by tunnels that were opened up in the '70s." The system proved much more extensive that previously reported.

Rick Kueber, the new owner of the building, though thrilled to save history, expressed surprise at "just how big Louisville's once thriving underground sex clubs really were." Constructed a century and a half before, the cast-iron-fronted building he now owned served as the original headquarters to Weller and Sons Bourbon, the distillery where a young Pappy Van Winkle got his first job at age eighteen.

I cleared my head. Studying the millwork and wainscotting in the foyer, I tried to imagine myself coming down the grand stairs every morning as the leaded-glass windows diffused slanting shafts of light and scattered bright patches on the hardwood floors. But how long would it take to get everything back in order, and how much would it cost? My eyes drifted to the wood coffered ceiling and I suddenly wondered what it would be like to sleep in the room where somebody had been murdered. Then, I looked at the floor, knowing that the small room where the Rubbermaid container had been entombed lay directly beneath us. A shiver ran down the back of my neck.

The neglected old house where Jamie Carroll met his demise still tugged at my heartstrings, however. I could get over the gruesome past associated with the mansion, but recent events had me reevaluating my priorities. Not only had my brother died, but my mother as well. Death seemed to have a way of putting things in a different perspective.

There had been a lot of death in the handful of intervening years since the murder trials of Jeffrey Mundt and Joseph Banis. So many things had come to an end.

They tore down the Connection, the city's iconic gay bar, and, after thirty-two years, Gavi's stopped serving up borscht and matzo ball soup. When Zina and Ida announced they would retire, local lawyers such as Jason Dattilo bemoaned the loss of the last of the courthouse hangouts.

Mr. Hauck, founder of the Dainty Festival, had just passed away, but not before celebrating his hundredth birthday. His daughters put Hauck's Handy Store on the market, but the 50th Annual World Dainty Championship still went on—with much aplomb, but also with the proper social distancing. Not too long after the *Courier-Journal* reported on the event, they announced that their presses would stop printing after 153 years.

Mr. Hauck wasn't the only one who had died in 2020. Lucie Blodgett had passed away earlier in the year. Andrew Jaycen, the family's spiritual advisor and a good friend and colleague of Margie Cook, helped organize the celebration of the doyenne's life.

And then Margie Cook entered the hospital. People feared the worst when nobody heard from her for months. Just days after Thanksgiving came the news that she had died. I had seen her just the week before she got sick and she gave me another beautiful glitter ball on a chain, which I wore during nightly public readings throughout the worst part of the pandemic. For more than two months straight, viewers from far and wide tuned in every evening at nine as I live-streamed ghost stories and legends, read from my books, and gossiped about Old Louisville. Soon, a community formed and people began calling each other *hobo*.

Then there was Kelly Atkins.

Kelly had remarried in the meantime. One day his wife sent a message that he was gravely ill with liver and kidney disease. A week later he was gone. My friend Wendy and I visited him in the hospital, but he didn't recognize us. Many of the Catholic old guard and former coworkers turned out for his memorial service, at which the eulogist pointed out that Kelly's stories "while true in part . . . were all the work of a true artist." Kelly Atkins stipulated that he wanted to be cremated and his ashes interred at Cave Hill Cemetery.

"Hey, stop daydreaming." Ramon nudged my shoulder. "Let's go back and see what the kitchen is like." He walked across the foyer floor to a long hallway leading to the back of the house.

"Hold your horses. What's the big rush?" I followed, but my thoughts were still in the past. The year 2020 had taken its toll, but the previous years hadn't been all that kind, either. Jim Segrest— "Butchertown's Mainstay," as the *Courier-Journal* had dubbed him— had died and was buried in Cave Hill Cemetery.

As was Muhammad Ali, whose grave now rivaled that of Colonel Sanders for being the most visited tomb in the cemetery. The city turned out in high style to send off its famous son, and soon after his interment, a red Schwinn bicycle appeared over the doorway to the student center at Spalding University, site of the former Columbia Gym. The Champ's boxing career had started there in 1954 when he was twelve years old.

"He left his bike outside and someone stole it and he went inside and said, 'I'm going to whoop somebody,'" said Tori Murden McClure, university president and author of *A Pearl in the Storm*, the story about her successful quest to become the first woman to row solo across the Atlantic. "He ran into a police officer, Joe Martin, who pointed to the ring upstairs and told him he better learn to box if he was going to beat somebody." Joe Martin became his trainer and the rest was history. McClure had the red Schwinn installed to commemorate this event.

Frances Mengel had also died, well into her nineties. I heard the people who moved into her husband's family's old mansion on Million-aires Row also thought of buying 1435 South Fourth Street.

Frances, fortunately, went at a ripe old age but the city was stunned to learn of the premature death of Detective Jon Lesher, who suffered a sudden heart attack at the age of forty-one. Tributes poured in from across the country, many of them appearing on the website for *The First 48*, where he had garnered many loyal fans over the years. The *Courier-Journal* wrote that "Lesher was the lead on many homicide cases in his nearly ten years in the unit, including a high-profile case in 2010 in which he helped dig a body out of the basement of an Old Louisville home." I never had the chance to meet with him to find out what information he had about the CIA.

Perhaps the saddest of all, however, was the passing of Louise Cecil. Her new husband—far from being her Prince Charming—proved to be a jealous and controlling spouse. Just the year before, and while the city was still coming down off the high of the Kentucky Derby, he shot Louise in a fit of rage before killing himself. I had visited her grave in Cave Hill Cemetery the day before.

And for a while, people were sure they had lost Spike the tortoise as well when a motorist accidentally ran over the one hundred thirty-pound creature. The frame slammed into his shell and the car dragged him about ten feet. Nina Mosely, Spike's official owner, received assistance from a dozen police officers in rescuing Spike from under the car and as she raced to the veterinarian one squad car led the way and another followed. Doctors performed surgery, using wire and acrylic paste to put Spike's shell back together, but things looked grim when he showed no interest in eating and dragged himself into the corner.

But then one day, Spike started eating again, chomping down a bag of apple slices, a banana, squash, broccoli, and a taste of home: a large handful of grass from the lawn outside Wayside Christian Mission. He began to improve and donations poured in from around the world.

Support and well wishes also began pouring in from far and wide when word spread that Mark Anthony Mulligan had contracted COVID-19. His condition deteriorated quickly and doctors placed him on a ventilator. The prognosis at first was bleak, but there was hope he would rally and recover.

There had been scandals in the several years since the trials for the murder of Jamie Carroll, too. Papa John Schnatter, Louisville resident and founder of the eponymous pizza chain, was forced to resign after using an insensitive racial term and the University of Louisville removed his name from their stadium.

The University of Louisville had its name sullied again after Coach Rick Pitino—who had already weathered a personal scandal involving a very public extramarital affair—became embroiled in two NCAA scandals, one rooted in a pay-for-play scheme, the other involving strippers and sex workers as brought to light in the book *Breaking Cardinal Rules*. Judge Mitch Perry presided over the resulting civil suit between the publisher and Katina Powell, self-described madam and co-author.

In the same year, a young man claimed to have been sexually abused by officers Kenneth Betts and Brandon Wood when he was a teenager in the Explorer Scouts, a program designed for youths interested in careers in local law enforcement. More victims would surface and more officers would be implicated in improprieties that pointed at the city's shocking role in cover-ups, hiding evidence, and destroying documents—ultimately costing the city millions of dollars.

Wrinkling my nose, I entered the kitchen at the back of the house. A dank, slightly acrid smell permeated the air and it seemed to hang in the miasma of diffuse light behind the raggedy curtains.

"Nice to see the kitchen's still a dump." Ramon walked over to the lone wall with cupboards and he opened a door. A half-full jar of instant coffee sat on one shelf. Nearby, thick plastic wrap sealed the windows, and bits of crumbled plaster lay on the linoleum floor. On a bar countertop rested a crumpled brown paper bag from Ollie's, a beloved hamburger joint in Old Louisville.

"Hey, let's go get burgers after we're done here." Ollie's Trolley was a holdover from the days when the Ollie's Trolley chain had outlets all over the nation—not to mention a dozen throughout Louisville. Besides walk-in stands in the shape of yellow-and-red tram cars, the fast-food relic's shtick included a classified combination of twenty-three herbs and spices—more than double what the Colonel could say of his fried chicken—and a cantankerous proprietor named Ollie, who demanded that his burgers be served rare and with his special sauce only. The Ollie Burger and seasoned fries were legendary.

"Sounds good to me." Ramon pushed a curtain aside and peered out.

I walked to the back door and looked at the yard. "Hey, did they ever find the killer of that woman who used to work at Ollie's, the Fry Lady?" The unsolved death of forty-five-year-old Dorie Epoler still haunted many in Old Louisville. One day in 2009, she left her job as a line cook at the corner of Third and Kentucky and walked to her apartment, just a couple of blocks away. Two days later, a neighbor found her body stuffed in a suitcase in the back alley.

Ramon shook his head. "I don't think so."

I tried to clear my head of unpleasant thoughts as I trailed Ramon up the servants' stairs. Steps creaking, we went all the way to the third floor. We walked from space to space, commenting on the peeling wallpaper and the fissures that had widened in the plaster. In one bedroom, I recognized the fireplace mantel and a triangular bay with windows from an old black-and-white photograph of the Bush-Bandeen Sanatorium. How many people had languished on their deathbeds in this house? In another room, two wooden canes hung from a hook on the back of the door. They looked like the walking sticks I had spied in the cloakroom the first night I had entered and explored on my own.

We descended the main stairs to the second floor and gazed out windows looking down on Fourth Street. Down a small hallway, we found smaller rooms arranged around a parquet landing, one of them the room where Jamie Carroll had been murdered. Suddenly, Ronica Reed's voice echoed in my mind, her terror at what must have been his thoughts during the last seconds of his life. *I'm not going to make it out of this house. I'm not going to make it out of this house.*

This was also where Jeffrey Mundt barricaded himself the night of the infamous 911 call. In that room, we found a box with half a dozen Kizito cookies, still in their wrappers. Elizabeth Kizito, Louisville's beloved "Cookie Lady," grew up on a banana plantation in Uganda, and, with her colorful cotton kitenges and cookie-filled head basket, she rivaled Mark Anthony Mulligan as the most recognized face in the Highlands.

As much as I liked her cookies, I left them untouched and we moved on.

We walked through the living room and paused to examine a crack in the large window in the dining room. In the middle of the parquet floor, Ramon hit his toe on a brass button embedded in the hardwood and he stooped to examine it. "What's this?"

"The bell to call the servants," I said. "The lady of the house tapped it with her foot under the dining table." From what I had read about the Robinsons, the first occupants of the house, Mr. Robinson enjoyed long evening meals with his wife in this room and after she died, he became inconsolable.

"Well, lah-tee-dah," said Ramon. "I guess there were no hobos here." In the next room, an ornately carved mantel gleamed around emerald green tiles. From an old police report, I knew this was the room where Pauline Boren had suffered the brutal attack that landed her in the convalescent home where she never recovered. I ran my hand along the smooth wood of the mantel. I expected it to be dusty, but it was perfectly clean.

The only other place in the house we hadn't explored was the basement.

Without a word, Ramon opened the small door under the grand staircase and followed the gritty steps down. My feet made the same sound as the night I had explored on my own. The same dank smell awaited at the bottom of the stairs, where it accompanied us as we wended through the warren of rooms, feeling for the light switches as we went, and finally emerging into the area with the packed earth floors.

We didn't have to flip on the light in the musty wine cellar, though. The dark little room was already illuminated, brightness beckoning as we entered. A high-wattage bulb shone overhead and two shop lights dangled from the beams. Someone wanted to make sure this area was always flooded with light.

"We'd have to fill that in." Ramon pointed at the gaping pit near a grungy exterior wall.

"I guess so." I forced myself to look away and study the rest of the interior. The shelves for wine bottles still stood against a wall, but everything else had been removed. No sign of glitter balls anywhere. I tried to make out the outline of an altar on the other wall, but the light was too strong to discern much.

I shuddered. I had already woken up in the middle of the night in our current house, wondering what it would be like to wake up in a bedroom at 1435 South Fourth Street, knowing that an empty grave lay below me in the basement. Could I really live here?

Ramon batted cobwebs from a rafter and stuck his head into the next room. "So, did you ever hear anything more from those freaks who used to live here?"

"Mundt and Banis?" I shook my head. "Not much. They're keeping pretty hush-hush about it all."

Ramon grunted and walked into the next space while I stayed put, gazing down into the hole before me. Jeffrey Mundt had unsuccessfully appealed his two convictions. He never responded to any of my attempts at contact so I had no concrete knowledge about his whereabouts or current living situation. I did run into his lawyer, Ted Shouse, one morning at Day's Coffee on Bardstown Road, however. When I asked him if his client was ever going to speak with me, the attorney just shook his head and gave a terse reply. "Jeff's not going to talk to you."

One day Barry Baisden, a former news anchor and reporter, forwarded Joey's new contact information to me; it came from a solicitation for pen pals posted on Joey's Tumblr account.

"I am a lonely gay man who is seeking pen pals and true friends. I am six feet tall, one hundred sixty pounds with several interesting tattoos which comprise a cohesive aesthetic image. I have a swimmers build and I am forty-five years old, although I look at least ten years younger!" The description sat below a picture of him, clad in khakis and a light blue sweater. Farther down appeared more pictures, many from the days when Banis sported his trademark body paint and spiked mohawks.

Joey also explained that his interests varied widely: "I enjoy fine wines, philosophy, theater, electronic dance, music, travel, fashion, and literature. At one point in my life I was a hippie and traveling with the Grateful Dead and then when I became comfortable with my sexuality I evolved into a raver and involved myself in the nightclub and music/event production business." He was "seeking genuine people . . . interested in developing true friendship," explaining "it is lonely in here and I am very different from most other inmates despite what you may think looking at my charges. I am not that type of person. I maintain my innocence and I am appealing my case."

He listed his religion as "agnostic" and his date of birth as February 4, 1972. His earliest possible release date was June 2, 2030. "You may ask anything and I will answer your questions," he said. "If you write or email me via JPay, I will respond. I am a genuine, interesting, intelligent, eclectic, and gentle guy with integrity and I want to make friends outside of prison. You will be surprised if you give me a chance and get to know me."

I emailed Banis at the address provided. Several months went by without a reply, so I emailed again. A half year passed and I gave up. Until one day, I received an email through JPay Services. Joey had finally responded, explaining it had taken so long because he "was in the hole." He seemed eager to talk, optimistically informing me of his upcoming appeal, but he suggested an in-person visit, which was the only way he could ensure his conversations and correspondence weren't being monitored.

I made plans to see him and we corresponded briefly in the meantime. He insisted he never killed Jamie Carroll and seemed taken aback that I was so invested in the details of the case. Even though it was only in writing, there always seemed to be an intensity to his language and he frequently addressed me by name when starting a sentence.

I sent an email asking him about the counterfeiting and CIA connections and he stopped talking to me. I never heard from Joey again.

I confirmed with Darren Wolff that Banis had indeed appealed, most likely exhausting the last of his options with the old chestnut of claims, that of incompetent defense. People I talked to expected the appeal to go nowhere. I spoke with a former corrections officer who had regular contact with Joey and she reported that he had shown himself to be a conscientious worker who was always well-groomed. He meticulously cleaned the bathrooms and enjoyed the company of a younger inmate who doted on him.

Standing under the dusty rafters, I was struck again with a somber realization. Jamie Carroll had lain in the ground at my feet for at least half a year. In this cold, dark room.

In the several years since the trials, I had been able to piece together a more complete portrait of Jamie Carroll. Many of his friends and acquaintances shared their recollections, and though there were those who had negative things to say—most came from the individuals who knew him as a drug dealer—the majority remembered a kind and caring person.

One of these was Barry Baisden, at the time a reporter and weekend anchor in Huntington, West Virginia, where he first met Jamie in the summer of 1998. "Ronica Reed roared off the stage after an electrifying performance. It was more than apparent she ruled at the Stonewall. She struck an imposing presence in her sky-high heels. About twenty minutes after Ronica exited the stage, I was introduced to Jamie Carroll. He emerged from backstage, in what he called his 'boy clothes,'" recalled Baisden. "Standing before me was this slight-framed guy. Without the high heels, he stood nowhere nearly as tall as Ronica Reed. For Ronica's beauty, Jamie was equally handsome. He had toned arms and his casual attire fit him well. To see him, one would never associate him and Ronica as being one and the same."

Jamie's stage persona exhibited vivaciousness. "The few times I saw him perform, he could deliver high energy that had the club's patrons cheering. Or, he could move them to tears with ballads. When he spoke onstage, it was with his signature bluntness, peppered with all-out bawdiness. He was an entertainer and was attuned to what would move an audience." A couple of weeks after his initial meeting with Jamie, Baisden received an invitation to attend a show Jamie was headlining. "When I arrived at the club that night, I was escorted backstage to join him as he made his transformation into Ronica. It was artistry."

Baisden recalled an "extremely modest" individual as well. "While others guys stripped down in the dressing room, putting themselves on full display in anyone's presence, Jamie would turn so not to be frontally exposed, or he would change behind a small curtain, if possible. I never knew if he was simply modest in all cases, or if he was being respectful of me."

Jamie could lighten a mood, and "was what some people might consider earthy. He could be assertive with his thoughts, outspoken, and rarely making any attempt to suppress his feelings. He was usually forthright and spoke candidly." If he faced difficulty or prejudice, said Baisden, he never expressed such. "He just seemed to enjoy his life."

But Jamie's life came to an abrupt end in the very house we had considered buying. As I stood at his temporary gravesite, his friend Barry's words to me came to mind. "Some people have characterized Jamie as a drug dealer, a meth addict, a sex fiend, and any number of negative connotations . . . but that is not at all characteristic of the Jamie Carroll with whom I was associated," said Baisden. "It's not for anyone to judge what he did. Everyone—be they gay or straight—has their likes, dislikes, hang-ups, kinks, fetishes, or whatever. Therefore, no one should be so brazen to be judgmental."

I closed my eyes and breathed in the damp air. But Ramon's gritty footsteps startled me as he came to stand next to me. He put his hands in his pockets. "So, what do you think?"

I shrugged. I didn't know what to think. Was it a good time to move?

The Year of the Pandemic had turned out to be cruel in some regards, but more and more positive national press confirmed that things were looking up for the Derby City—and especially Old Louisville.

And Yolanda Baker was alive and well, still making her mirror balls. She was getting a lot of good press, too, with the blessings of Mayor Greg Fischer, who had hopped on the glitter ball bandwagon. "In Louisville, where people do absurd things because it's fun, a group of friends are trying to build a disco ball sixty-seven feet in diameter, which would obliterate the world record of thirty-three feet," reported Jeffrey Lee Puckett of the *Courier-Journal*. "The project, called The World's Largest Disco Ball, Y'all!, kicks off . . . with a fundraiser . . . normal-sized disco balls will be on hand from Louisville's Omega National Products, the world's largest manufacturer of disco balls."

"Disco balls, you've got to admit, are fun," the mayor said. "This is one of our great local companies and they're going to pursue this world record and we'll rally around it."

"Hey, look at this." Ramon edged into the corner and reached up into the rafters. "I guess I was wrong after all."

I assumed he would bat away more cobwebs, but instead he pulled down something sparkly from a nail pounded into the wood of the beam. "They missed this one." He held out a small glitter ball that dangled from the end of a silver chain. It had the same size as the one Margie had given me and which now sparkled and twirled high up in the branches of the Witches' Tree. And it was like the one Kelly and I had found dangling from the fingers of the marble statue in the Satterwhite monument in Cave Hill Cemetery, the Temple of Love. It was a smaller version of the ones that had hung outside the Connection or were rented out for Derby parties.

Diamonds of light spun around the walls of the room as the little glitter ball slowed its movement. Ramon still looked at me, expectant, then raised his eyebrows as if to repeat his last question.

"Oh, I don't know." I shrugged my shoulders and spoke without looking at him. "Let's sleep on it. We don't have to decide just yet, do we?"

Ramon grunted and kicked a loose pebble into the large rectangular hole in front of us. Then he returned the little glitter ball to its nail and I watched it twirl and throw silvery shadows across several wooden beams.

I reached up to scratch my head but my hand stopped midair and went to my mouth to stifle a yawn instead.

There were many things I did not know, did not understand. What it all meant. Why people did the things they did or said the things they said. What lingered behind the walls of 1435 South Fourth Street and what really happened in the dark basement. What lurked in the dark room found in every human mind.

Or who really killed Jamie Carroll.

Joey? Jeffrey? Both?

But a warm feeling set in then and I could sense my heart beating. I let my eyes close and I relaxed. I breathed in. I breathed out. My lungs tingled. The air seemed fresher all of a sudden. From the ground, a rhythmic pounding surged up and tickled the soles of my feet.

Whatever the case, I would sleep well that night, safe in the knowledge that a bright and shiny orb would keep on spinning in Glitter Ball City.

# ACKNOWLEDGMENTS

SO MANY people helped make this book a reality, but if you appear in *A Dark Room in Glitter Ball City*, I owe you an especially huge debt of gratitude. Carrie Sweet, you've been a great research assistant and friend. You made me appreciate tater tots a lot more. Candy, I hope I did you proud, wherever you are. Thank you both, and all the others, for being a part of my story.

Many didn't appear in these pages but they still played an important part.

I'd like to thank my agent Alice Speilburg for her hard work in finding the right home for *A Dark Room in Glitter Ball City* and for her assistance in bringing it to life. Thanks to Katie McGuire at Pegasus Books for immediately seeing this story's appeal and potential, and thanks to the others at Pegasus who provided help and encouragement along the way: publisher Claiborne Hancock, associate publisher and director of publicity Jessica Case, publicist Jenny Rossberg, production manager Maria Fernandez, and Tori Wenzel, a wonderful editor to work with.

I am also very grateful to the many individuals who reached out and shared their thoughts and firsthand knowledge during the ten years I worked on this book. Many of them were people who knew and loved Jamie Carroll; some knew Jeffrey Mundt or Joey Banis. A handful asked to remain anonymous, but the rest include Keisha Stamper, Vikki Boggs-Crisp, Marc Broering, Jessica Mills, Marie Monroe Doutaz, Linda Krauth, Jessica Sprecher, Kent Baily, Joe Tolnai, James Hoyt, Kathy Lintner, Ruthie Flanery Spears, Kristina Genevieve Goatley, Andy Harpole, Heather C. Watson, Lisa Hornung, Mary Hatfield, Tony Carroll, Marty Carroll, Sue Huffman, Jeanelle Arlene, Jeremy

Butts, Tonya Rose Sample, Ted Palmer, Heidi Owens, Lauren Knopf Montfort, Robert Williamson, Amelia Brooke Huneke, and Susan Atavidis.

And here's a big shout-out to the gang at Chill Bar, where I talked to many people who shared stories and insights about Joey Banis and Jeffrey Mundt or offered their encouragement: Matt Wohlieb, Rick Bancroft, Chad Ballard, Tim Buechele, Richard Thomas, Rich Rankin, Tracey Michelle, Missy Oglesby, Pam Palmquist, Dennis Millay, Joe Gollahon, Daniel Hutchins, Ryan Boshoven, James Oslin, Adam Guthrie Caperton, Roger Tieskoetter, Richard McFarland, Ryan Benningfield, Ryan Phillips, David Green, Tom Mott, Eric Cunningham, Hugo "Pupusa" Salvador, Deborah Ann Massey, Corey Milliman, Kevin Spalding, DeAnna Randall, Tommy Arnold, Jeremy English, Holly Knight, Mike Ice, Travis Myles, Calvin Mitchell Sailing, Holly Knight, Justin Cory Hayes, Rowdy Whitworth, David Graham, and Celeste De Chardonnay.

Writer friends and mentors who provided constant encouragement and support include Cindy Brady, Rosanna Staffa, Rick Brown, Jim Wayne, Kirby Gann, Bonnie Omer Johnson, Kimberly Crum, Kathleen Driskoll, Sena Jeter Naslund, Kelly Creagh, James Markert, Peter Crume, Jerry Rogers, Mary Popham, Rachel Harper, Angela Jackson-Brown, Fred Schloemer, Robin Lippincott, Leslie Daniels, Kenny Cook, Jessica Hildebrandt, Susan Lindsay, Cindy Corpier, Karen Mann, Rose Pressey, Jacob Bennet, Catherine Pond, Alice Jennings, Beverle Graves Myers, Joanne Dobson, Susan Gosselin, Claudia Love Mair, Marti Agan, Nicholas Siegel, Jamie Pearce, and Elizabeth Morris. Thanks to all in the Germantown Writers Group, especially Mary Lou Northern, who was immensely helpful in proofing the final manuscript and fine-tuning the local details. Kelly Hill, Jason Hill, and Julia Blake, thanks for being the first to take a look at *A Dark Room in Glitter Ball City* in its earliest phases.

I'd also like to thank authors and reporters such as Jeremy Priddy, Maria Fleming, Dan Hulbert, Dr. Catherine Fosl, Carlton Jackson, Beverly Kienzle, Andrew Wolfson, Emily Bingham, Ann Braden, John E. Kleber, William Morgen, Samuel W. Thomas, Melville O. Briney, Shawn M. Herron, and Robert Bruce Symon Jr. Their research and knowledge proved invaluable and helped me learn so much more about the city I call home.

Let me give a shout-out to Old Louisvillians or friends of Old Louisville who have been supportive in a variety of ways: Joni Hoke, Carol Galbreath, Carol Kauffman, Caroline Kaufmann, Amity and Krist Thodoropoulos, Nancy Wentzell Walker, Blake Benton de Roucy, T. K. Reed, Rhonda

Williams, Michael Williams, Renee Thompson Ryan, Cindy Thompson Goodrid, Kimberly Thompson, Forest Thompson-Bell, Susan Dallas, Van Breeding and Family, Charlotte Rich, Daniel Borsch, Kelly Dunnagan, Cricket Pepper Fairchild, Aaron Bingham, Amy McGowen, Michael Ellis, Vicky Contreras, Cicely Nevitt, Cheryl Nevitt Benahm, Stefanie McClain Schy, Michele Muir White, Kristin Adams Frarey, Davis Rogers, Trish Patton, Tululah Lane, Vinny Bonny Crastellano, Lyle Janes, Chris Martin, Barbara Winter Martin, Frank Simkonis, Edward Sim, Majestik Henry, Gina Diana, Christopher Porter, Rudy van Meter, Susan Coleman Layman, Jeff Layman, Eric Cooper, Angelique X Stacy, John Paul, Jim and Linda Brooks, Kate Meador, Christopher Kirkland, Jane Harris, Andy Perry, Peggy Cummins, Donna Trickle, Beth and Barb Caldwell, Doug and Madonna Wilson, Derek Inghram, Rob and Margaret Young, Scotty Striegel, Deb Raichel, Martin Yoder, Veronica Walker Earnest, Craig Blakely and Karan Chavas, Mary Warren, John Warren, Kerstin Knopf, Patrick Pössl, Cliff Swearingen, Sherry Wilder, Penny Kommalon Brisson, Lisa Wilder Elble, Heather Gotlib, Gregory Wilson, Timothy L. Endicott-Steele, Amy Pedigo, Camille Christy Roy, Allen Land, Kris Risinger, Brian Buford, Tim Brown, Sharon Combs Martin, David and Leslie Tate, Mitch Rapp, Cindee Quake-Rapp, Jeff Perry, Rollia Knight, Karessa Knight, Mark Bailey and Adrian Boyle, Don Reinhardt, Michael Mawood, Rachel Stump, Ray Avery, Todd Whitesides, Stan Duffy, Adrian Cunningham, Janice Crick, Cricket Bidwell, Robin Garland, Fran Clare, Rachel Platt, Terry Meiners, Isabelle Jonquet, Cathy Cozzens, Peggy Storm Muller, Rita Bancroft, Charles Langnes, Jacky Ray Lundy, Mehdi Poorkay, Susan Scott, Gabriele Bosley, Steven Michael Carr, Kim Eilers, Jason Brett Buttons, Michael Petrig, Kevin Milburn, Wayne Ottaway, Michael Thacker, Derrick Pedolzky, Gwen Wilkinson, Beverly Cebe, Kerry Joss, Josh and Sarah Wade, Michelle I. Moody, Patrizia Barnes-Fasnaugh Charping, Judy Stults, Dollie Johnson O'Connell,Diana Rankin Bauer, Laura Vance Calhoun, Kenneth Dale Calhoun, Terri Houghlin, Terri Frank, Timothy Spaulding, Karen DeSpain, Joni Goodin, Amy McGowan, Colleen Marie Walker, Sue Stacy Atkins, Deborah and David Stewart, and Rachel Resler, my very first official fan.

Thanks to friends and family for the support: Jane Newsom, Wendy Demaree, Elizabeth and Chris Ross, Lori Fields, David McHugh, Timothy Holz, Tad Brooks, Laura and Michael Horan, Laura Wallace, Tim Pardue, Silvia Zañartú, Miguel Zañartú, Olivia Zañartú, Isabel Zañartú,

Ramon Zañartú, Lily Arundel, Mindy Wallace, Luis Miguel Macias, and Hugo Centeno. Also, a big thanks to all my relatives back in Wisconsin.

I owe a huge thank-you as well to my former student and dear friend Sean Stafford for all the encouragement, support, and tech savvy that proved so invaluable during the decade I worked on *A Dark Room in Glitter Ball City*. When I was ready to give up, he stepped in and made things work.

And for all the hobos out there I haven't mentioned yet, thanks for tuning in during the nightly readings and being part of my life. Missy Edwards, Laura Diel Tanner, Chris Knopf, Amanda Rupert, Matt Goldman, Lisa Key, Marcia Andrews, Emily Kay Harp, Amanda and Larry Dyer, Miranda Harrison, Claudia Stafford, Lois Elms, Charles Rains, David Stevens, Sheila Marie Wall, Suzanne Hurst, Maria Barnard, Glenda Hagan, Tingle, Jamie Duncan Kirchner, Thomas and Viji Evers and family, Heather Moore, Jodie Butler, Rebecca Beck Stackhouse and Big Al, Beth Gritty, Kaye Christy, Becky Everhart, Jill Richardson, Saphire Bowman, Nate Kauffman, Jacque Coyer Kauffman, Ashley Oberst, Elaine Duncan Mulvaney, Barbara Heath Reece, Dorothy Heath Miller, Reece Bann, Holly Rudolph, Jim Ghrist, Mitzi Fields Root, Barb Ann, Kathy Greene Gosser, Donnie Porter, Gina Miller, James Polk, Maria Barnard, Jacob Drake, David and Bonnie Domine, Susan Buss, Dana Harrison, Jo Ann Klein, Devin Klein, Kathy Schmitt, Margareta Kessler, Pam Fischer, Katherine Murphy, Sue Gale, Jennifer Schlossberg, Gabriel Trie-Pfefer, Jamie Trie-Pfefer, Mike Kernen, Sandi Knapp, Sue Stacy Atkins, Renee Beck Mote, Bob Markwell, Steve De, Cindy Rutledge, Cynthia Lundgren Anderson, Donetta Hamilton Wolfe, Becky Ritchie, Susan Sams Priest, Jackie Lieble, Marty Huelsmann Jr., Lisa Thompson, Patricia Ayme, Mike Kernen, Odina Lienenluecke, Justin Davis, Patty Domine, Travis Domine, Joe Keith, Greer Fischer, Grace Fischer, John Fischer, Tracy Schott Fischer, Matt Sweeney, Amber Shaw Woods, Dawn Geiger, Marcie Domine, Alex Domine, Cathy Hats, Steve Spratt, Brian Musch, Eva Zinsmeister, Jackie Lieble, Cathy Palmquist Abbot, Abigail Smith Stocker, Diane Dunwell-Hoffman, Matt Wallace and family, Dominic Savio Howard, Shawna Hemming, Antoinette Johnson, Dawn Anderson, Jesse Hendrix-Inman, Sammy Sills, Sara Silva, Claudia Peralta-Mudd, Cathe Crab, Gina Schmidt Priddy, Kim Eilers, Maureen Bacon, Geneva Vair, the Morizur Family, Patricial Kroell, and Taya Hotob.

And for John Berendt: many thanks for the inspiration.

If I overlooked anyone, I'm sorry. Let me know and I'll take you out for a Pappy on the rocks. I can't guarantee it'll be the twenty-three-year-old, though.